Adaptive REUSE

Liliane Wong

Adaptive REUSE

Extending the Lives of Buildings
Revised and Expanded Edition

Birkhäuser
Basel

Layout, cover design and typesetting:
nalbach typografik, Silke Nalbach, Mannheim
(cover photo: construction hoarding at the Berliner Dom)

Production: Anja Haering, Berlin

Paper: 120 g/m² Magno Natural
Printing: Beltz Grafische Betriebe GmbH, Bad Langensalza

Editor for the Publisher: Andreas Müller, Berlin

Library of Congress Control Number: 2024944569

Bibliographic information published by the German National Library
The German National Library lists this publication in the Deutsche Nationalbibliografie; detailed bibliographic data are available on the Internet at http://dnb.dnb.de.

ISBN 978-3-0356-2926-2
e-ISBN (PDF) 978-3-0356-2927-9

Im Westfeld 8
4055 Basel, Switzerland
Part of Walter de Gruyter GmbH, Berlin/Boston

www.birkhauser.com
Questions about General Product Safety Regulation
productsafety@degruyterbrill.com

MIX
Papier | Fördert gute Waldnutzung
FSC® C089473

9 8 7 6 5 4 3 2

Contents

Preface

"Adaptive reuse has existed since time immemorial." These opening words from the first edition of *Adaptive Reuse: Extending the Lives of Buildings* remain relevant nearly a decade after they were penned. Then as now they serve to place the millennial resurgence of an age-old practice within an ancient context. The reuse of caves as domiciles, an early instance of man's resourcefulness, is a parallel from thousands of years ago for the resourcefulness in today's built environment where structures that can no longer accommodate their original program of use are given new life through reuse.

Such projects of reuse, born of common sense and economy, were once the unsung staple of architectural practice. Serviceable and respectable, they provided for the quotidian spatial needs of society. Over time, a variant of reuse emerged as one of poetic and artistic design intervention in heritage sites, exemplified by projects such as Carlo Scarpa's timeless, adaptive reuse of the Castelvecchio in Verona, Italy, as a museum of Romanesque sculpture. Until the second half of the 20th century, adaptive reuse projects fell primarily into the former, quotidian, category. The latter type were venerated as rare and not-to-be replicated works of art. However, the increasingly intense focus on climate change in the first decades of the new millennium has brought about a shift in this bifurcation of adaptive reuse projects. With rising global interest in the conservation of resources, there are now, more than ever, concerted efforts to evaluate the potential of existing and outdated structures for reuse rather than to demolish and build anew. These efforts pertain to design interventions on structures with heritage value but also to those with less historical or architectural significance. This profound embrace of altering architecture for new use as an equally fulfilling and exciting endeavor to building anew has brought about a paradigm shift in which even the most celebrated members of the design profession engage in adaptive reuse. Today there is a wealth of rich and varied reuse projects that extend the lives of structures, creating a new phase in this age-old practice.

This book was first conceived with the intention of illuminating a neglected subject in its own light. At a time with few if any resources available on adaptive reuse, the intent was to present this practice in all of its richness—as heritage, as iconoclastic legacy, as its own typology, as design interventions, as innovative strategy, as new life in the built environment. As such, adaptive reuse was examined through its place in history; its relationship to adjacent fields of study; its position within shifting norms of art, culture, and society; and its typological differences—but also through professional practice and the regulations that governed the interventions of reuse. Completed, I hoped that it would serve as an overview of an ancient practice and its many facets of development over time.

Explored from various viewpoints, these developments conclude in the last third of the book in ideas wholly ensconced in the 21st century, from novel design strategies on existing buildings to virtual interventions made possible by nascent technology. Today, with the hindsight of almost a decade since its publication, it can be argued that these developments, in fact, could be viewed under the vast umbrella of climate change. What allowed for the exuberant embrace of reuse in the first years of the millennium could well be summarized in nine words: "the greenest building is one that is already built."[1] The words (and title of an article) were those of American Institute of Architects (AIA) President Carl Elefante. They were made at a time when the impact of the built environment was officially linked to global carbon emissions.[2] The statement was quantified four years later by the Preservation Green Lab, a research arm of the National Trust for Historic Preservation, which reported the finding that "it takes 10 to 80 years for a new building that is 30 percent more efficient than an average-performing existing building to overcome, through efficient operations, the negative climate change impacts related to the construction process."[3] With a practice in historic preservation, Elefante connected historic structures, reuse, and sustainability.

The completion of *Adaptive Reuse: Extending the Lives of Buildings* late in 2016 coincided with the enforcement of the Paris Agreement that had been adopted the previous year. This simultaneity was a prescient indication of the path forward for adaptive reuse. Much of the architectural profession would henceforth view architecture in relation to carbon. In that sense, the explorations within this book capture a moment in the development of adaptive reuse at a time when sustainability equated to the use of the existing building stock, a time to relish the design potential of existing structures and the many permutations of interventions they permitted. The severity of climate events during the summer of 2023—excessive heat, wildfires, smoke, storms—dictated a new role for architecture. The vanguard of the architectural world would now equate sustainability with climate-change action. By the end of the first quarter of the 21st century, almost a decade after the publication of this book, innovative projects of adaptive reuse would extend beyond interventions to existing structures. In climate-crisis mode, reuse would not be limited to spatial endeavors within the built environment but would also include physical ones in which existing buildings would be reconsidered as construction materials.

In that sense, Chapter 00: "Babel," a glossary of terms, offers a snapshot of this brief moment in adaptive reuse, a time reflecting architecture's shifting relationship with sustainability and climate. The terms used there included refurbishment, renovation, rehabilitation, and remodeling, nestled among the historical terms of conservation and restoration. Phrases such as "net-zero" or "design for deconstruction" would not have yet been in use. Most notably, the term "repair" in Chapter 00 references John Ruskin and the 19th-century debate on maintenance, fueled by the work of Eugène Emmanuel Viollet-le-Duc. At the 2016 publication date, that term had not catapulted into its present cult status. Chapter 00: "Babel," then, serves as a gauge of time passing.

Terms grow old or older, as do the many students and student assistants who were invaluable in the making of this book—especially Jenna Balute, Clara Halston, and Yue Zhang. In addition, the many graduate students from around the world, whose discussions in class are woven into these chapters, now explore adaptive reuse and sustainability themselves as professionals in the world of architecture and design. They will always be a special part of this book. While published in 2016, the concepts underlying the book began at the turn of the millennium, when the term adaptive reuse was not familiar or commonplace. These ideas of reuse had their roots in the Department of Interior Architecture at the Rhode Island School of Design, where, under the far-sighted leadership of Brian Kernaghan, a scrappy young department redefined the scope of interior architecture and broadened its scope to encompass the reuse of structures—great and small—in the built environment. The many ideas herein have their genesis in the collegial conversations within that faculty. This book would not be what it is without Silke Nalbach, whose graphic-design vision gave my words a visual life of their own. I will always be grateful to my editor, Andreas Müller, who believed in this book from the start. Most of all I am profoundly grateful that a whole new generation of students and readers will have access to this phase of adaptive reuse through this 2nd edition.

Providence, RI
January 2025

1 Carl Elefante, "The Greenest Building is One That is Already Built," Forum Journal 21, no. 4 (Summer 2007): 26–38. 2 Architecture 2030 states that the built environment is responsible for more than 40% of global carbon emissions in "Why the Built Environment?," Architecture 2030, accessed July 2, 2024, https://www.architecture2030.org/why-the-built-environment. 3 The Preservation Green Lab, The Greenest Building: Quantifying the Environmental Value of Building Reuse: National Trust for Historic Preservation, 2011).

> The Arts never die. Their principles remain true for all time, because humanity is always the same. However its customs and institutions may be modified, its intellectual constitution is unchanged: its faculty of reasoning, its instincts and sensations proceed from the same source now as they did twenty centuries ago. It is moved by the same desires and the same passions, while the various languages it employs do but enable it to express in every age the same ideas, and to call for the satisfaction of the same wants.
>
> EUGÈNE VIOLLET-LE-DUC[1]

The story of adaptive reuse is interwoven with the history of ancient monuments and the development of policy for the preservation of heritage. The telling of this tale necessarily comprises terminology already embedded in this history—from conservation to restoration and from preservation to maintenance. These terms exist in multiplicity, with nuanced and, at times, disparate definitions (and opinionated viewpoints) for the same word. Characterized by what Italian conservationist/architect Giovanni Carbonara calls "the historical fickleness of the very concept of conservation,"[2] these terms, in and of themselves, convey a history not just of the many changes within the field but one that illuminates and explicates the roots of an emerging adaptive reuse practice.

The regard for and the desire to protect heritage has recorded instances in the Ancient Far East, Classical Greece, the Roman Empire and medieval Europe, but a common terminology related to modern preservation, restoration and conservation emerged primarily from the early 19th-century efforts to preserve and restore key monuments damaged in the French Revolution. Without formal precedent, the notions of preservation and restoration were shaped by a series of events centered upon an unsuspecting Viollet-le-Duc and an advocacy for stylistic restoration. The firestorm unleashed by opponents of such practice in an anti-Restoration rhetoric eventually formed the foundation of the modern conservation movement. As such, these terms—restoration, conservation and maintenance—each reference an original intent.

Since the late 19th century, art and architectural historians, curators, architects, archaeologists, conservationists and art critics have reflected upon, dissected, reinterpreted, redefined and expanded upon these terms. In his seminal 1903 essay *Der moderne Denkmalkultus: Sein Wesen und seine*

Babel 00

FIG.0: *Turris Babel*, Athanasius Kircher, Amsterdam, 1679. (manipulated detail)

Entstehung (The Modern Cult of Monuments: Its Essence and Its Development) Alois Riegl refers to "the modern cult of monuments or historic preservation," inferring an equivalence between a 20th-century approach to heritage and historic preservation while offering differentiated values that define the modern monument. With a proliferation of viewpoints, events in history and developments in methodology, in conjunction with an ever-changing set of mores, these terms continued to evolve. The ensuing endless cycle of shifts was aptly described by Marguerite Yourcenar: "The great lovers of antiquities restored out of piety. Out of piety, we undo what they did."[3]

In his concept of *Kunstwollen*, Riegl proposes that "[m]an is not only a passive sensorily recipient being, but also a desiring, active being who wishes to interpret the world in such a way (varying from one people, region or epoch to another) that it most clearly and obligingly meets his desires."[4] This human condition accounts for much of the changing nature of the terminology around conservation and preservation practices. In the years since the aftermath of the French Revolution, there was an expansion of what we preserve and how preservation takes place—changes reflective of man interpreting the evolving world around him.

In the early 20th century, the expansion of this field began to overlap with art conservation, in which semi-ruined sculpture and built heritage evoked similar strategies of recovery. In the international collaboration of post-World War II, the definition of heritage extended from built monuments to groups of buildings and sites, urban landscapes, landscapes, cultural landscapes, modern built heritage of the 20th century, vernacular heritage and, most recently, intangible cultural heritage. Each expansion of scope has been accompanied by a change in related terminology to reflect such development. As a result, many identical terms have accumulated augmented definitions with the passing of time.

Many of the terms referred to in this book have more than one definition. As in the mythical Tower of Babel from the biblical Book of Genesis, this variation of language leads to confusion in the use of these terms. For example, the 1995, 2006 and 2016 definitions of "preservation" by the U.S. Department of the Interior differ one from the other, reflecting the particular context in which the term was defined. As this book focuses on adaptive reuse (rather than conservation or preservation), the significance of these terms is not conditioned upon a single understanding defined at a single moment in time. Rather, it is these very shifts in the understanding of conservation and preservation that give rise to and provide the basis of adaptive reuse practice. Conservation as addressed in the Venice Charter of 1964 can, in fact, be viewed as a foundation of adaptive reuse while subsequent definitions broaden its scope.[5]

Within the alphabetical order of this babylonian list, the various definitions, interpretations, opinions and uses of each term are organized chronologically.

While by no means comprehensive, they include perspectives, wherever possible, from different viewpoints: earliest definitions, official adopted language of international organizations such as ICOMOS, international building regulations (United Kingdom and USA), building science and historic commissions. Notably, the oldest terms are "restoration" and "maintenance," terms from the 19th century that attest to the origin of conservation practice. Conversely, the newest terms are definitions of only the past decade or so, often driven by building engineering. Some terms include many different viewpoints while others are defined only through a particular lens. While it is the intent of this book to embrace this less-than-cohesive language reflecting the many efforts made in the quest of a similar goal, the term "preservation" used throughout implies a broad interpretation such as that of Paul Philippot's 1972 definition of "being equivalent ... to conservation or restoration—[and] can be considered, from this point of view, as expressing the modern way of maintaining living contact with cultural works of the past."[6] As the story unfolds, it is hoped that the reader will refer to these changing definitions and, in doing so, understand their development between "the emphasis on either practical craftsmanship or subtle theoretical interpretation of principle ..."[7]

1 Eugène Viollet-le-Duc, *On Restorations* (London: Sampson Low, Marston, Low and Searle, 1875), p. 9. 2 Giovanni Carbonara, "The Integration of the Image: Problems in the Restoration of Monuments," in Nicholas Price, M. Kirby Talley, Jr., and Alessandra Melucco Vacarro, eds., *Historical and Philosophical Issues in the Conservation of Cultural Heritage* (Los Angeles: The Getty Conservation Institute, 1996), p. 236. 3 Marguerite Yourcenar, "That Mighty Sculptor, Time," in Price, Talley, Jr., and Melucco Vacarro, eds., p. 214. 4 Alois Riegl, "The Main Characteristics of the Late Roman Kunstwollen" (1901), in Christopher S. Brown, ed., *The Vienna School Reader, Politics and Art Historical Methods in the 1930s* (New York, NY: Zone Books, 2000), p. 95. 5 *International Charter for the Conservation and Restoration of Monuments and Sites (The Venice Charter 1964)*, Article 5, ICOMOS The International Council of Monuments and Sites. 6 Paul Philippot, "Historic Preservation: Philosophy, Criteria, Guidelines, I," in Price, Talley and Vacarro, eds., p. 268. 7 Carbonara, p. 236.

Adaptation

Any work to a building over and above maintenance to change its capacity, function or performance.[1]

JAMES DOUGLAS, 2006

Adaptation means the process(es) of modifying a place for a compatible use while retaining its cultural heritage value. Adaptation processes include alteration and addition.[2]

ICOMOS NEW ZEALAND, 2010

Adaptation means changing a *place* to suit the existing *use* or a proposed use.[3]

THE BURRA CHARTER, ICOMOS AUSTRALIA, 2013

Addition

Additions cannot be allowed except in so far as they do not detract from the interesting parts of the building, its traditional setting, the balance of its composition and its relation with its surroundings.[4]

THE VENICE CHARTER, 1964

Alteration

Action to secure the survival or preservation of buildings, cultural artefacts, natural resources, energy or any other thing of acknowledged value for the future.[5]

BS7913:1998, BRITISH STANDARDS INSTITUTION

Modifying the appearance, layout, or structure of a building to meet new requirements (Watt, 1999). It often forms part of many adaptation schemes rather than being done on its own.[6]

JAMES DOUGLAS, 2006

A change in formation, that is removal of partition walls to enlarge a space within the fabric of a building, or conversely the introduction of partition walls to subdivide a space into smaller units.[7]

PAUL WATSON, 2008

Work intended to change the function or appearance of a place.[8]

HISTORIC ENGLAND, PREVIOUSLY A PART OF ENGLAND'S HISTORIC BUILDINGS AND MONUMENTS COMMISSION, 2008

Conservation

The conservation of monuments is always facilitated by making use of them for some socially useful purpose.[9]

THE VENICE CHARTER, 1964

Action to secure the survival or preservation of buildings, cultural artefacts, natural resources, energy or any other thing of acknowledged value for the future.[10]

BS7913:1998, BRITISH STANDARDS INSTITUTION

Conservation is the ensemble of means that, in carrying out an intervention on an object or its environment, seek to prolong its existence as long as possible.[11]

MARIE BERDUCOU, 1990 (ARCHAEOLOGY)

[A]ll efforts designed to understand cultural heritage, know its history and meaning, ensure its material safeguard and, as required, its presentation, restoration and enhancement. (Cultural heritage is understood to include monuments, groups of buildings and sites of cultural value as defined in article one of the World Heritage Convention).[12]

ICOMOS, NARA DOCUMENT ON AUTHENTICITY, 1994

Modern conservation is principally characterized by the fundamental change of values in contemporary society, a paradigm based on relativity and the new concept of historicity.[13]

JUKKA JOKILEHTO, 1999

The use of the term Conservation in the title of this series refers to the whole subject of the care and treatment of valuable artefacts, both movable and immovable, but within the discipline conservation has a meaning which is distinct from restoration. Conservation used in this specialized sense has two aspects: first, the control of the environment to minimize the decay of artefacts and materials; and, second, their treatment to arrest decay and to stabilize them where possible against further deterioration.[14]

SERIES EDITORS, ELSEVIER/BUTTERWORTH-HEINEMANN, 1999

Preserving a building purposefully by accommodating a degree of beneficial change.[15]

JAMES DOUGLAS, 2006

The process of managing change to a significant place in its setting in ways that will best sustain its heritage values, while recognising opportunities to reveal or reinforce those values for present and future generations.[16]
HISTORIC ENGLAND, PREVIOUSLY A PART OF ENGLAND'S HISTORIC BUILDINGS AND MONUMENTS COMMISSION, 2008

Preservation of the existing building and its fabric and fittings, in their current state, for the future. Restoration implies a degree of repair to bring fabric, components or fittings back to an acceptable standard.[17]
PAUL WATSON, PROFESSOR OF BUILDING ENGINEERING, 2008

The process of caring for a place so as to safeguard its cultural heritage value.[18]
JOHN H. STUBBS, 2009

The purpose of conservation is to care for places of cultural heritage value. Conservation means all the processes of understanding and caring for a place so as to safeguard its cultural heritage value. Conservation is based on respect for the existing fabric, associations, meanings, and use of the place. It requires a cautious approach of doing as much work as necessary but as little as possible, and retaining authenticity and integrity, to ensure that the place and its values are passed on to future generations.[19]
ICOMOS NEW ZEALAND CHARTER, 2010

Conservation means all the processes of looking after a *place* so as to retain its *cultural significance.*[20]
CLAUSE 1.4, *THE BURRA CHARTER*, ICOMOS AUSTRALIA, 2013

The objective of conservation is to maintain the significance of the architectural heritage or site. Significance is constituted in both the tangible and intangible forms.[21]
INTACH (INDIAN NATIONAL TRUST FOR ART AND CULTURAL HERITAGE) CHARTER, 2016

Conversion

Making a building more suitable for a similar use or for another type of occupancy, either mixed or single use.[22]
JAMES DOUGLAS, 2006

[w]ork including a change in function or change in use, such as converting an office block and making it suitable for residential use ...[23]
PAUL WATSON, 2008

Conversions always affect the structure of a building. They extend the concept of refurbishment to interventions in the loadbearing members and/or the interior layout.[24]
GEORG GIEBELER, 2009

Extension

Expanding the capacity or volume of a building, whether vertically by increasing the height/depth or laterally by expanding the plan area.[25]
JAMES DOUGLAS, 2006

[W]ork that includes an increase in size, which can be horizontal or vertical expansion ...[26]
PAUL WATSON, 2008

Any extension is a new structure that is directly connected with the use of the existing building.[27]
GEORG GIEBELER, 2009

Maintenance

Take proper care of your monuments, and you will not need to restore them. A few sheets of lead put in time upon a roof, a few dead leaves and sticks swept in time out of a water-course, will save both roof and walls from ruin. Watch an old building with an anxious care; guard it as best you may, and at any cost, from every influence of dilapidation. Count its stones as you would jewels of a crown; set watches about it as if at the gates of a besieged city; bind it together with iron where it loosens; stay it with timber where it declines; do not care about the unsightliness of the aid; better a crutch than a lost limb; and do this tenderly, and reverently, and continually, and many a generation will still be born and pass away beneath its shadow. Its evil day must come at last; but let it come declaredly and openly, and let no dishonouring and false substitute deprive it of the funeral offices of memory.[28]
JOHN RUSKIN, 1880

It is for all these buildings, therefore, of all times and styles, that we plead, and call upon those who have to deal with them, to put Protection in the place of Restoration, to stave off decay by daily care, to prop a perilous wall or mend a leaky roof by such means as are obviously meant for support or covering, and show no pretence of other art, and otherwise to resist all tampering with either the fabric or ornament of the building as it stands; if it has become inconvenient for its present use, to raise anoth-

er building rather than alter or enlarge the old one; *in fine* to treat our ancient buildings as monuments of a bygone art, created by bygone manners, that modern art cannot meddle with without destroying.[29]
WILLIAM MORRIS, 1887

[C]ontinual activity to ensure the longevity of the resource without irreversible or damaging intervention.[30]
ICOMOS APPLETON CHARTER, 1989

Actions which "retain an item in, or restore it to, a state in which it can perform its required function."[31]
BS3811:1993 BRITISH STANDARDS INSTITUTION

A "combination of all technical and administrative actions, including supervision actions, intended to retain an item in, or restore it to, a state in which it can perform a required function" (BS 3811:1993). Maintenance involves routine work necessary to keep the fabric of a building, the moving parts of machinery, etc, in good order (BS 7913:1992). In other words, it consists of regular ongoing work to ensure that the fabric and engineering services are retained to minimum standards (Ashworth, 1997).[32]
JAMES DOUGLAS, 2006

Routine work regularly necessary to keep the fabric of a place in good order.[33]
HISTORIC ENGLAND, PREVIOUSLY A PART OF ENGLAND'S HISTORIC BUILDINGS AND MONUMENTS COMMISSION, 2008

Repair and/or replacement work to keep or restore any/every part of a building, to current standard(s).[34]
PAUL WATSON, 2008

Maintenance means regular and on-going protective care of a place to prevent deterioration and to retain its cultural heritage value.[35]
ICOMOS NEW ZEALAND, 2010

Maintenance means the continuous protective care of a place, and its *setting*.[36]
THE BURRA CHARTER, ICOMOS AUSTRALIA, 2013

Modernization

Bringing a building up to current standards as prescribed by occupiers, society and/or statutory requirements.[37]

JAMES DOUGLAS, 2006

Preservation

When we speak of the modern cult of monuments or historic preservation, we rarely have "deliberate" monuments.[38]

ALOIS RIEGL, 1903

The word *preservation*—in the broadest sense, being equivalent in some cultures to *conservation or restoration*—can be considered, from this point of view, as expressing the modern way of maintaining living contact with cultural works of the past.[39]

PAUL PHILIPPOT, 1972

Implies the maintenance of the artifact in the same physical condition as when it was received by the curatorial agency. Nothing is added to or subtracted from the aesthetic corpus of the artifact.[40]

JAMES MARSTON FITCH, 1990

Standards for Preservation: 1. A property will be used as it was historically, or be given a new use that maximizes the retention of distinctive materials, features, spaces, and spatial relationships.[41]

U.S. SECRETARY OF THE INTERIOR, 1995

Preservation is defined as the act or process of applying measures necessary to sustain the existing form, integrity, and materials of an historic property. Work, including preliminary measures to protect and stabilize the property, generally focuses upon the ongoing maintenance and repair of historic materials and features rather than extensive replacement and new construction. New exterior additions are not within the scope of this treatment; however, the limited and sensitive upgrading of mechanical, electrical, and plumbing systems and other code-required work to make properties functional is appropriate within a preservation project.[42]

U.S. SECRETARY OF THE INTERIOR, 1995.

[P]reservation is no longer a retroactive activity but becomes a prospective activity.[43]

REM KOOLHAAS, 2004

Preservation is defined as the act or process of applying measures to sustain the existing form, integrity, and material of a building or structure, and existing form and vegetative cover of a site. It may include initial stabilization work, where necessary, as well as ongoing maintenance of the historic building materials.[44]

U.S. SECRETARY OF THE INTERIOR, 2006

Arresting or retarding the deterioration of a building or monument by using sensitive and sympathetic repair techniques. Preservation means "the state of survival of a building or artifact, whether by historical accident or through a combination of protection and active conservation" (BS 7913:1998). It also can be defined as "the act or process of applying measures necessary to sustain the existing form, integrity and materials of an historic property" (Weeks and Grimmer, 1995). Preservation focuses on the maintenance and repair of existing historic materials and retention of a property's form as it has evolved over time. It includes protection and stabilization measures.[45]

JAMES DOUGLAS, 2006

Preservation means to maintain a place with as little change as possible.[46]

ICOMOS NEW ZEALAND, 2010

Preservation means maintaining a place in its existing state and retarding deterioration.[47]

THE BURRA CHARTER, ICOMOS AUSTRALIA, 2013

Preservation focuses on the maintenance and repair of existing historic materials and retention of a property's form as it has evolved over time.[48]

U.S. DEPARTMENT OF THE INTERIOR, 2016

Reconstruction

Re-establishment of the design of a building or artifact, or of what existed or occurred in the past, on the basis of documentary or physical evidence.[49]

BS 7913:1999 BRITISH STANDARDS INSTITUTION

Reconstruction is defined as the act or process of depicting, by means of new construction, the form, features, and detailing of a non-surviving site, landscape, building, structure, or object for the purpose of replicating its appearance at a specific period of time and in its historic location.[50]

U.S. SECRETARY OF THE INTERIOR, 1995

The re-establishment of what occurred or what existed in the past, on the basis of documentary or physical evidence (BS 7913:1999). Reconstruction, in other words, re-creates vanished or non-surviving portions of a property for interpretative purposes (Weeks and Grimmer, 1995).[51]
JAMES DOUGLAS, 2006

Reconstruction is defined as the act or process of reproducing by new construction the exact form and detail of a vanished building, structure, or object, or a part thereof, as it appeared at a specific period of time.[52]
U.S. SECRETARY OF THE INTERIOR, 2006

Reconstruction is the rebuilding of a structure that no longer exists, i.e. strictly speaking it is new building work.[53]
GEORG GIEBELER, 2009

Reconstruction is distinguished from restoration by the introduction of new material to replace material that has been lost. Reconstruction means to build again as closely as possible to a documented earlier form, using new materials.[54]
ICOMOS NEW ZEALAND, 2010

Reconstruction means returning a *place* to a known earlier state and is distinguished from *restoration* by the introduction of new material.[55]
THE BURRA CHARTER, ICOMOS AUSTRALIA, 2013

Reconstruction re-creates vanished or non-surviving portions of a property for interpretive purposes.[56]
U.S. DEPARTMENT OF THE INTERIOR, 2016

Reconstruction based on minimal physical evidence is appropriate where it is supported by the knowledge of local craftspeople, including folklore, beliefs, myths and legends, rituals, customs, oral traditions, etc. The objective of this practice must be to interpret the original meanings of the resource in the contemporary context and reinforce its bond with society.[57]
INTACH (INDIAN NATIONAL TRUST FOR ART AND CULTURAL HERITAGE) CHARTER, 2016

Refurbishment

Modernizing or overhauling a building and bringing it up to current acceptable functional conditions (Watt, 1999). It is usually restricted to major improvements primarily of a non-structural nature to commercial or public buildings. However, some refurbishment schemes may involve an extension.[58]

JAMES DOUGLAS, 2006

[W]ork that is related to a change in performance.[59]

PAUL WATSON, 2008

The refurbishment of a building always means adapting it to meet current standards, too, whether because of change in users' demands or new technical regulations.[60]

GEORG GIEBELER AND PETRA KAHLFELDT, 2009

The difference between refurbishment and conversion, however, is that refurbishment does not involve any major changes to the loadbearing structure or interior layout. It therefore lies exactly between maintenance and conversion, but the extent of refurbishment works can vary enormously.[61]

GEORG GIEBELER, 2009

Rehabilitation

[M]odification of a resource to contemporary functional standards which may involve adaptation for new use.[62]

ICOMOS APPLETON CHARTER, 1989

Rehabilitation is defined as the act or process of making possible a compatible use for a property through repair, alteration, and additions while preserving those portions or features which convey its historical cultural or architectural values.[63]

U.S. SECRETARY OF THE INTERIOR, 1995

Work beyond the scope of planned maintenance, to extend the life of a building, which is socially desirable and economically viable (Watt, 1999). It is a term that strictly speaking is normally confined to housing. Rehabilitation can also be defined as "the act or process of making possible a compatible use for a property through repair, alteration and additions while preserving those portions or features which convey its historical, cultural or architectural values" (Weeks and Grimmer, 1995). It acknowledges the need to alter or add to a historical property to meet

continuing or changing uses while retaining the property's historic character.[64]
JAMES DOUGLAS, 2006

An upgrade in an element or elements of a building. A suitable example here would be the installation of a new central heating system with appropriate controls and zoning, to an older property.[65]
PAUL WATSON, 2008

Rehabilitation acknowledges the need to alter or add to a historic property to meet continuing or changing uses while retaining the property's historic character.[66]
U.S. DEPARTMENT OF THE INTERIOR, 2016

Relocation

Relocation and dismantling of an existing resource should be employed only as a last resort, if protection cannot be achieved by any other means.[67]
ICOMOS APPLETON CHARTER, 1983

Dismantling and re-erecting a building at a different site. It can also mean moving a complete building to a different location nearby.[68]
JAMES DOUGLAS, 2006

Remodeling

This is a North American term analogous to adaptation. It essentially means to make new or restore to former or other state or use.[69]
JAMES DOUGLAS, 2006

Renewal

Substantial repairs and improvements in a facility or subsystem that returns its performance to levels approaching or exceeding those of a recently constructed facility.[70]
JAMES DOUGLAS, 2006

Comprehensive dismantling and replacement of an element of a place, in the case of structures normally reincorporating sound units.[71]
HISTORIC ENGLAND, PREVIOUSLY A PART OF ENGLAND'S HISTORIC BUILDINGS AND MONUMENTS COMMISSION, 2008

Renovation

Upgrading and repairing an old building to an acceptable condition, which may include works of conversion.[72]

JAMES DOUGLAS, 2006

Renovation does not add anything new to the building stock, nor does it replace old with new. Instead it maintains the value and the function of the existing building through competent "upkeep."[73]

GEORG GIEBELER, 2009

Repair

Take proper care of your monuments, and you will not need to restore them.[74]

JOHN RUSKIN,1889

Work beyond the scope of regular maintenance ... to return a building or artifact to good order without alteration or restoration.[75]

BS 7913:1998 BRITISH STANDARDS INSTITUTION

This is the "restoration of an item to an acceptable condition by the renewal, replacement or mending of worn, damaged or decayed parts" (BS 8210:1993). It is associated with the rectification of building components that have failed or become damaged through use and misuse (Ashworth, 1997).[76]

JAMES DOUGLAS, 2006

Work beyond the scope of maintenance, to remedy defects caused by decay, damage or use, including minor adaptation to achieve a sustainable outcome, but not involving restoration or alteration.[77]

HISTORIC ENGLAND, PREVIOUSLY A PART OF ENGLAND'S HISTORIC BUILDINGS AND MONUMENTS COMMISSION, 2008

Repair means to make good decayed or damaged fabric using identical, closely similar, or otherwise appropriate material.[78]

ICOMOS NEW ZEALAND, 2010

Replicate

In consonance with traditional ideals, replication can be accepted as an appropriate strategy not only to conserve unprotected historic buildings, but especially if such replication encourages historic ways of building.[79]

INTACH (INDIAN NATIONAL TRUST FOR ART AND CULTURAL HERITAGE) CHARTER, 2016

Restoration

The proper meaning of the word Restoration is the re-establishment of parts of a building more or less damaged that one up-grades to its working order. In architecture, Restoration is said to be less mechanically natural than the work that the artist undertakes based on the remains or descriptions of a monument, its entirety and the comprehensive measurements, proportions and details. Very often it suffices for one to know some traces of columns, entablature and capitals of columns of a Greek architecture to rediscover the order of a temple.[80]

QUATREMÈRE DE QUINCY, 1832

The term Restoration and the thing itself are both modern. To restore a building is not to preserve it, to repair, or rebuild it; it is to re-instate it in a condition of completeness which could never have existed at any given time. It is only since the first quarter of the present century that the idea of restoring buildings of another age has been entertained; and we are not aware that a clear definition of architectural restoration has as yet been given. Perhaps it may be as well to endeavour at the outset to gain an exact notion of what we understand, or ought to understand, by a restoration ...[81]

EUGÈNE VIOLLET-LE-DUC, 1875

[A] strange and most fateful idea, which by its very name implies that it is possible to strip from a building this, that, and the other part of its history — of its life that is — and then to stay the hand at some arbitrary point, and leave it still historical, living, and even as it once was.[82]

WILLIAM MORRIS, 1877

It means the most total destruction which a building can suffer: a destruction out of which no remnants can be gathered: a destruction accompanied with false description of the thing destroyed. Do not let us deceive ourselves in this important matter; it is impossible, as impossible as to raise the dead, to restore anything that has ever been great or beautiful in architecture.[83]

JOHN RUSKIN, 1889

Restoration is generally understood as any kind of intervention that permits a product of human activity to recover its function ... Restoration is the methodological moment in which the work of art is appreciated in its material form and in its historical and aesthetic duality, with a view to transmitting it to the future.[84]

CESARE BRANDI, 1963

Its aim is to preserve and reveal the aesthetic and historic value of the monument and is based on respect for original material and authentic documents.[85]

THE VENICE CHARTER, 1964

Restoration is defined as the act or process of accurately depicting the form, features, and character of a property as it appeared at a particular period of time by means of the removal of features from other periods in its history and reconstruction of missing features from the restoration period. The limited and sensitive upgrading of mechanical electrical and plumbing systems and other code-required work to make properties functional is appropriate within a restoration project.[86]

U.S. SECRETARY OF THE INTERIOR, 1995

Restoration is the continuation of [conservation], when conservation treatment is thought to be insufficient, to the extent of reinstating an object, without falsification, to a condition in which it can be exhibited.[87]

SERIES EDITORS, ELSEVIER/BUTTERWORTH-HEINEMANN, 1999

To bring back an item to its original appearance or state (BS 3811). It is often undertaken to depict a property at a particular period of time in history, while removing evidence from other eras. This usually involves reinstating the physical and/or decorative condition [of] an old building to that of a particular date or event. It includes any reinstatement works to a building of architectural or historic importance following a disaster such as extensive fire damage.[88]

JAMES DOUGLAS, 2006

Restoration is defined as the act or process of accurately recovering the form and details of a property and its setting as it appeared at a particular period of time by means of the removal of later work or by the replacement of missing earlier work.[89]

U.S. SECRETARY OF THE INTERIOR, 2006

To return a place to a known earlier state, on the basis of compelling evidence, without conjecture.[90]

HISTORIC ENGLAND, PREVIOUSLY A PART OF ENGLAND'S HISTORIC BUILDINGS AND MONUMENTS COMMISSION, 2008

The return of something to a former, original, normal, or unimpaired condition.[91]

JOHN H. STUBBS, 2009

Restoration means finishing an incomplete structure.[92]
GEORG GIEBELER, 2009

The process of restoration typically involves reassembly and reinstatement, and may involve the removal of accretions that detract from the cultural heritage value of a place. Restoration means to return a place to a known earlier form, by reassembly and reinstatement, and/or by removal of elements that detract from its cultural heritage value.[93]
ICOMOS NEW ZEALAND CHARTER, 2010

Restoration means returning a *place* to a known earlier state by removing accretions or by reassembling existing elements without the introduction of new material.[94]
CLAUSE 1.7, *THE BURRA CHARTER*, ICOMOS AUSTRALIA, 2013

Alteration of the fabric of a building ... or artifact ... to make it conform again to its design or appearance at a previous date.[95]
JAMES SIMPSON, 2016

Restoration depicts a property at a particular period of time in its history, while removing evidence of other periods.[96]
U.S DEPARTMENT OF THE INTERIOR, 2016

Restoration is an appropriate conservation strategy to reinstate the integrity or complete the fractured "whole" of the architectural heritage/site. It must aim to convey the meaning of the heritage in the most effective manner. It may include reassembling of displaced and dismembered components of the structure and conjectural building or replacement of missing or severely deteriorated parts of the fabric. Invariably, restoration work must be preceded and followed by comprehensive documentation in order to base interventions on informed understanding of the resource and its context, and in conformity with contemporary practices of local craftspeople.[97]
INTACH (INDIAN NATIONAL TRUST FOR ART AND CULTURAL HERITAGE) CHARTER, 2016

Retrofitting

The redesign and reconstruction of an existing facility or subsystem to incorporate new technology, to meet new requirements or to otherwise provide performance not foreseen in the original design (Iselin and Lemer, 1993). In other words, retrofitting is the replacement of building components with new components that were not available at the time of the original construction (Ashworth, 1997).[98]

JAMES DOUGLAS, 2006

1 James Douglas, *Building Adaptation* (Chennai: Elsevier, 2006). 2 "ICOMOS New Zealand Charter for the Conservation of Places of Cultural Heritage Value, Revised 2010," p. 9. http://www.icomos.org.nz/nzcharters.html (accessed July 2, 2016). 3 "Australia ICOMOS Charter for Places of Cultural Significance, The Burra Charter, 2013," Australia ICOMOS Incorporated International Council on Monuments and Sites, p. 2. 4 *International Charter for the Conservation and Restoration of Monuments and Sites (The Venice Charter 1964)*, Article 13, ICOMOS The International Council of Monuments and Sites. 5 Tony Burke, "Principles of Building Adaptation and Conservation," *Open Resources for Built Environment Education*, http://creativecommons.org/licenses/by-nc-sa/2.5/ (accessed March 5, 2016). 6 Douglas, p. 583. 7 Paul Watson, "The Key Issues When Choosing Adaptation of an Existing Building over New Build," in *Journal of Building Appraisal* (Palgrave MacMillan), Vol. 4, No. 3, p. 218. 8 Paul Drury and Anna McPherson, *Conservation Principles Policies and Guidance* (London: English Heritage, 2008), p. 71. https://content.historicengland.org.uk/images-books/publications/conservation-principles-sustainable-management-historic-environment/conservationprinciplespoliciesguidanceapr08web.pdf/ (accessed March 7, 2016). 9 *International Charter for the Conservation and Restoration of Monuments and Sites (The Venice Charter 1964)*, Article 5, ICOMOS The International Council of Monuments and Sites. 10 This British Standard has since been withdrawn and replaced by BS7913:2013. 11 Marie Berducou, "Introduction to Archaeological Conservation," in Price, Talley, Jr., and Melucco Vacarro, eds., p. 248. 12 *The Nara Document on Authenticity*, ICOMOS International Council on Monuments and Sites, 1994. 13 Jukka Jokilehto, *A History of Architectural Conservation* (Oxford: Butterworth-Heinemann, 1999), p. 295. 14 Andrew Oddy and Derek Lindstrom (series eds.), "Series Editors' Preface," in Jokilehto. 15 Douglas, p. 584. 16 Drury and McPherson, p. 71. 17 Watson, p. 218. 18 John H. Stubbs, *Time Honored: A Global View of Architectural Conservation* (Hoboken, NJ: Wiley & Sons, 2009), p. 23. 19 ICOMOS New Zealand, p. 1. 20 ICOMOS Australia, p. 2. 21 http://www.intach.org/about-charter-principles.php#b3 (accessed March 7, 2016). 22 Douglas, p. 584. 23 Watson, p. 218. 24 Georg Giebeler, Rainer Fisch, Harald Krause, Florian Musso, Karl-Heinz Petzinka and Alexander Rudolphi, *Refurbishment Manual. Maintenance Conversions Extensions* (Basel: Birkhäuser), p. 14. 25 Douglas, p. 585. 26 Watson, p. 218. 27 Giebeler, Fisch, Krause, Musso, Petzinka and Rudolphi, p. 15. 28 John Ruskin, *The Seven Lamps of Architecture*, 6th ed., (Kent: George Allen, 1889), p. 196–197. 29 William Morris, "The Manifesto" (SPAB Society for the Protection of Ancient Buildings, 1887), https://www.spab.org.uk/what-is-spab-/the-manifesto/ (accessed March 13, 2016). 30 "Appleton Charter for the Protection and Enhancement of the Built Environment," ICOMOS Canada, 1983, p. 3. 31 Burke, Section 2. 32 Douglas, p. 586. 33 Drury and McPherson, p. 71. 34 Watson, p. 218. 35 ICOMOS New Zealand, p. 6. 36 ICOMOS Australia, p. 4. 37 Douglas, p. 587. 38 Riegl, p. 69. 39 Paul Philippot, "Historic Preservation: Philosophy, Criteria, Guidelines, I," in Price, Talley and Vacarro, eds., p. 268. 40 James Marston Fitch, *Historic Preservation: Curatorial Management of the Built World* (Charlottesville: University of Virginia Press, 1990), p. 46. 41 Kay Weeks and Anne Grimmer, *The Secretary of the Interior's Standards for the Treatment of Historic Properties with Guidelines for Preserving, Rehabilitating, Restoring and Reconstructing Historic Building* (Washington, DC: US Dept of the Interior, 1995), p. 26. 42 Weeks and Grimmer, p. 17. 43 Rem Koolhaas, "Preservation Is Overtaking Us," in *Future Anterior*, Vol. I, Winter 2004, p. 2. 44 William J. Murtagh, *Telling Time, The History and Theory of Preservation in America* (Hoboken, NJ: John Wiley & Sons, 3rd ed. 2006), p. 5. 45 Douglas, p. 588. 46 ICOMOS New Zealand, p. 10. 47 ICOMOS Australia, p. 2. 48 http://www.nps.gov/tps/standards/four-treatments.htm (accessed March 6, 2016). 49 James Simpson, "The Anatomy of Theory," www.buildingconservation.com (accessed March 5, 2016). 50 Weeks and Grimmer, p. 165. 51 Douglas, p. 588. 52 Murtagh, p. 5.

53 Giebeler, Fisch, Krause, Musso, Petzinka and Rudolphi, p. 11. 54 ICOMOS New Zealand, p. 7. 55 ICOMOS Australia, p. 4. 56 http://www.nps.gov/tps/standards/four-treatments.htm (accessed March 6, 2016). 57 http://www.intach.org/about-charter.php (accessed July 2, 2016). 58 Douglas, p. 589. 59 Watson, p. 218. 60 Giebeler, Fisch, Krause, Musso, Petzinka and Rudolphi, p. 16. 61 Ibid., p. 13. 62 ICOMOS Canada, p. 3. 63 Weeks and Grimmer, p. 61. 64 Douglas, p. 589. 65 Watson, p. 218. 66 http://www.nps.gov/tps/standards/four-treatments.htm (accessed March 6, 2016). 67 ICOMOS Canada, p. 5. 68 Douglas, p. 589. 69 Ibid. 70 Ibid. 71 Drury and McPherson, p. 72. 72 Douglas, p. 589. 73 Giebeler, Fisch, Krause, Musso, Petzinka and Rudolphi, p. 11. 74 Ruskin, p. 196. 75 James Simpson, "The Anatomy of Theory," http://www. buildingconservation.com (accessed March 5, 2016). 76 Douglas, p. 589. 77 Drury and McPherson, p. 72. 78 ICOMOS New Zealand, p. 10. 79 http://www.intach.org/about-charter.php (accessed July 2, 2016). 80 "Restauration. C'est, dans le sens propre du mot, le rétablissement qu'on fait des parties d'un bâtiment plus ou moins dégradé pour le remettre en bon état. Restauration se dit, en architecture, dans un sens moins matériellement mécanique, du travail que l'artiste entreprend, et qui consiste à retrouver, d'après les restes, le débris ou les descriptions d'un monument, son ancien ensemble, et le complément de ses mesures, de ses proportions et de ses détails. On sait qu'il suffit très-souvent de quelques fragmens de colonnes, d'entablemens et de chapiteaux d'une architecture grecque, pour retrouver du moins l'ensemble d'une ordonnance de temple." Quatremère de Quincy, *Dictionnaire Historique d'Architecture* (Paris: Librarie d'Adrien Le Clere, 1832), English translation by Veronica Dewey. 81 Viollet-le-Duc, p. 9. 82 Morris. 83 Ruskin, p. 194. 84 Brandi, pp. 230–231. 85 *International Charter for the Conservation and Restoration of Monuments and Sites (The Venice Charter 1964)*, Article 9, ICOMOS The International Council of Monuments and Sites. 86 Weeks and Grimmer, p. 117. 87 Oddy and Lindstrom. 88 Douglas, p. 590. 89 Murtagh, p. 5. 90 Drury and McPherson, p. 72. 91 Stubbs, p. 23. 92 Giebeler, Fisch, Krause, Musso, Petzinka and Rudolphi, p. 11. 93 ICOMOS New Zealand, p. 7. 94 ICOMOS Australia, p. 4. 95 James Simpson, "The Anatomy of Theory," in http://www.buildingconservation.com (accessed March 5, 2016). 96 http://www.nps.gov/tps/standards/four-treatments.htm (accessed March 6, 2016). 97 http://www.intach.org/about-charter.php (accessed July 2, 2016). 98 Douglas, p. 590.

FIGS. 1a–b: Can all structures be reused and for any purpose?

Could the Lincoln Memorial in Washington, DC, commemorating the 16th president of the USA, be used as a residence? Conversely, could a large suburban mansion be adapted to memorialize the president who abolished slavery? (figs. 1a–b)

These are rhetorical questions that probe the design foundations of adaptive reuse, a practice that is broadly defined as the "reuse of pre-existing structures for new purposes."[1] While the first recorded use of this term is recent, the practice has its roots in ancient history, where reuse was often necessitated by a scarcity of resources. The first noted use of the term in 1973[2] curiously coincided with the global oil crisis, which triggered an awareness of natural resources. Until recently the reuse of existing structures was most often associated with renovation and refurbishment, previously considered as a bread-and-butter staple of architectural practice not meriting design recognition. With a global focus in the last decades on the effects of climate change, and the acknowledgment that "buildings are the major source of global demand for energy and materials that produce by-product greenhouse gases,"[3] the practice of adaptive reuse has come into its own.

Within today's context of climate change, the term "adaptive reuse" is redefined, and in a significant manner. One of three destinies for existing structures, adaptive reuse, in contrast to demolition and preservation, perpetuates a continuum of growth and change. Routinely referred to as "transforming an unused or underused building into one that serves a new use, the practice of adaptive reuse is rich and varied and its importance includes not only the reuse of existing structures but also the reuse of materials, transformative interventions, continuation of cultural phenomena through built infrastructure, connections across the fabric of time and space and

New Order: The Frankenstein Syndrome

01

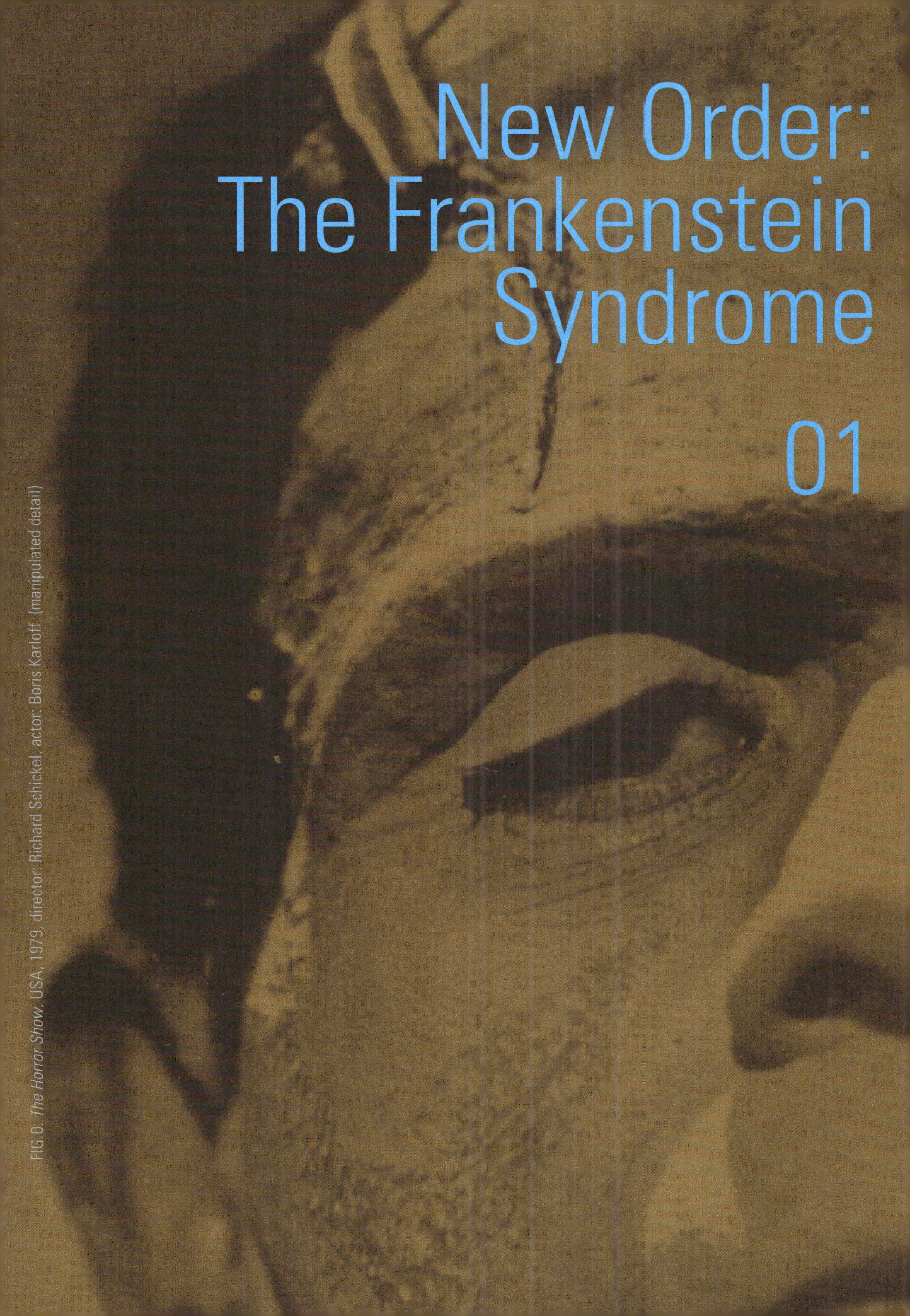

FIG.0: *The Horror Show*, USA, 1979, director: Richard Schickel, actor: Boris Karloff. (manipulated detail)

FIG.2: The Mezquita de Córdoba, Spain.

FIG.3: The Gare d'Orsay in Paris converted to the Musée d'Orsay by Gae Aulenti.

FIG.4: *Splitting*, Gordon Matta-Clark, 1974.

preservation of memory—all of which result in densely woven narratives of the built environment with adaptive reuse as their tool."[4]

A Christian church in southern Spain, the Mezquita de Córdoba, was converted in the 7th century AD to an Islamic mosque and from the 13th century was reconverted to a Christian church. The Zollverein coal mine and coking plant in Essen, Germany, was declared a UNESCO World Heritage Site in 2001 and converted to an exhibition center. The first electrified urban rail terminal in the world, the Gare d'Orsay in Paris, France, was converted in 1986 to a museum for Impressionist art. An abandoned house on Humphrey Street in Englewood, New Jersey, USA, was "split in two" in 1974 by artist/architect Gordon Matta-Clark. Each of these projects exemplifies one aspect of the breadth of adaptive reuse practice. What distinguishes each of these types of reuse from the other? (figs. 2, 3, 4, 5)

In Córdoba, religious supremacy led conquering Islamists to use the existing Christian church as the site of their mosque, as had done the Christians before them when they had erected their church on the ruins of a Roman temple dedicated to Janus. At Essen, the legacy of coal mining in the history of industry led to the site's status as World Heritage and its subsequent

FIG.5: Elements of the Zollverein coal mine in Essen are part of a new exhibition center designed by OMA.

transformation for the education of visitors. In Paris, the new use as a museum saved a noted turn-of-the-century train station from demolition. In New Jersey, a reflection on the temporality of the built environment elevated to art an unremarkable derelict home. Each of these interventions to existing structures consciously engages with and alters the interpretation of the past. Some are acts of overwriting with the purpose of expunging history, while others extend that history with a new and different chapter through reuse and reinterpretation. What constitutes a "successful" engagement of the past? And what are the principles of such engagement that differentiate these acts as a distinct practice?

Examples of adaptive reuse exist all around us. A few are highly celebrated conversions of notable heritage buildings. The majority, however, are simply part of a contemporary practice often driven by economics; schools converted to condominiums, jails to hotels, factories to artist studios, churches to restaurants. Which of these many conversions are successful? How is that success calibrated? Is it through the merits of the new use? Or is it through a meaningful dialogue with the existing structure? What is the role of economics? What of the conservation of materials and energy?

While much has been written over the centuries on the principles of architecture, there is silence on the principles of designing *within* pre-existing architectural principles. Should the existing principles prevail? How could new ones be introduced? Adding to, subtracing from, enveloping, extending, inserting, weaving amongst, co-existing with—these are all possible operations on and within an existing structure. Herein, this rich and overlooked architectural practice will be explored in all of its iterations; as historic precedence, through typological classification, through analysis, as enabled by technology and new means.

The Frankenstein Syndrome

Mary Shelley's 1818 novel *Frankenstein or The Modern Prometheus* is the tale of a scientist who created a living creature as an experiment. Thematically complex, it is a contemplation upon, among many themes, nature, existence and creation. Our present-day understanding of the novel, however, is derived more from James Whale's 1931 film *Frankenstein* than from a familiarity with Victorian themes. As a society steeped in visual culture, the mention of Shelley's famed novel evokes Boris Karloff's now iconic portrayal of the "Monster." Appropriated by pop culture, the "Monster" is a thing of horror, dramatically different from Shelley's ill-conceived and tortured (poetry-loving) creature.

Our association with *Frankenstein* is that of a creature, assembled from fragments of various deceased persons, coming to life on a table raised to an undefined life-giving source of energy. Shelley alludes to a creation process, but it is Hollywood that supplies the details of body parts retrieved through grave robbing and other nefarious means. In the film, we glimpse seams—on wrists, neck—by which the different parts are attached to resemble the whole. Dr. Frankenstein created in the likeness and order of what he knew: man, a being uniquely defined by a singular and consistent DNA. The "Monster" resembles a man in form as its creator assumed a familiar and pre-existing order; a living structure of bilateral symmetry. The "Monster" was, instead, created from multiple body parts, comprised of the uniquely different DNA of uniquely different men. By doing so, Dr. Frankenstein introduced a new order into the known structure of man. Bypassing Shelley's multilayered themes, Hollywood credits the ultimate failure of the creature to the defect of one particular body part—an "abnormal" brain of felonious DNA. In the framework of Hollywood's work of science fiction, the implication is that the substitution of dissimilar DNA subverted a structure developed for its own original DNA. The failure of this new creature, therefore, lies in the introduction of a new and incompatible order within an existing one. This incompatibility is the Frankenstein Syndrome.

New Order

"Order Is."[5] Louis Kahn's brief declarative sentence speaks of order as a demanding and perhaps willful master. "In the nature of space is the spirit and the will to exist a certain way," Kahn tells us, and "design must closely follow that will."[6] Acknowledging the volition of order and applying it to the practice of adaptive reuse, any change to or within an existing structure necessitates a reckoning of that order.

Order is all around us. We negotiate cities in grids; rectilinear in the case of Manhattan and radial in the case of Rome or Washington, DC. Order is audible; from bird calls that are species-specific to the two-note siren of an ambulance, sounds are recognizable by their structure. This order of sounds is visible when transcribed as music through time signature, a notational structure assigning an order of beats and measure to sound. The fabric of the clothing we wear and ultimately feel is ordered, woven in a grid system of warp and weft. The spaces we occupy are ordered by the structure of supports and planes that we can touch. (figs. 6a–b, 7, 9)

Successful interventions to any type of existing order, be it a city plan, music or textiles, constitute a change to an already established order. Present-day

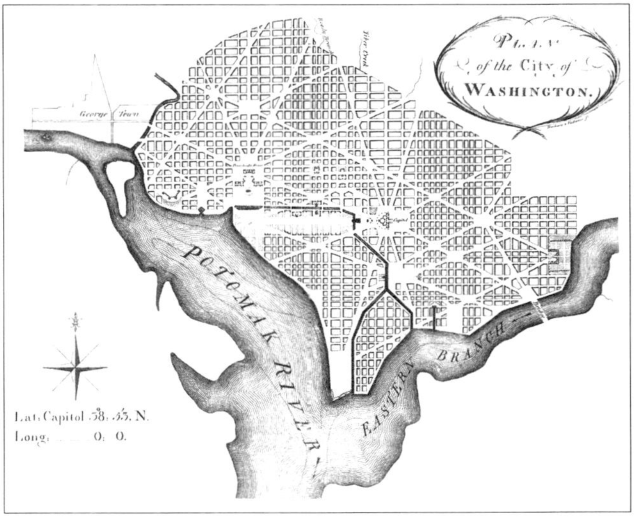

FIGS. 6a–b: Cities such as New York and Washington, DC are characterized by their own particular order.

FIGS.7, 8: Order is audible in music as rhythm. The order of Bach's *English Suite No. 2* differs dramatically from the order of Bartók's *Mikrokosmos V, Nr. 131*.

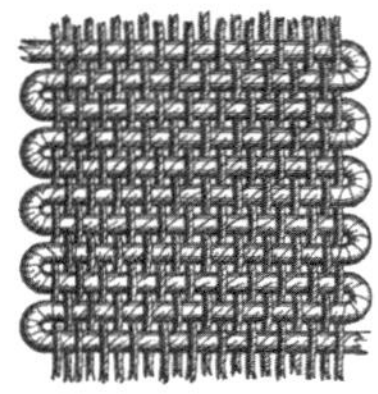

FIG.9: Traditional textiles are ordered by warp and weft.

Istanbul, for example, is a city on a triangular piece of land, evolved from the ancient city of Constantinople. It is planned around 6th-century landmarks such as the Hagia Sophia and the Baths of Zeuxippus that are still in existence today. While no regular grid is visible, there is a perceptible order and set of connections in the vast city between and in-between the monuments. In a proposed masterplan for Kartal Pendik, the industrial outskirts of Istanbul, a new order is introduced within the existing order of the city. Within this order a new dimension rises in the z direction, or vertical direction, through the use of topographic devices, made possible by digital technology. A new urban space of responsive structures is created as a new order within the framework of the old. (figs. 10a–c)

A similar parallel can be made in music for the work of Hungarian composer Béla Bartók, composing in the early 20th century. His work in ethnomusicology fuses essential elements of folk music with classical music. Within the structure of classical music are embedded, a few measures at a time, new

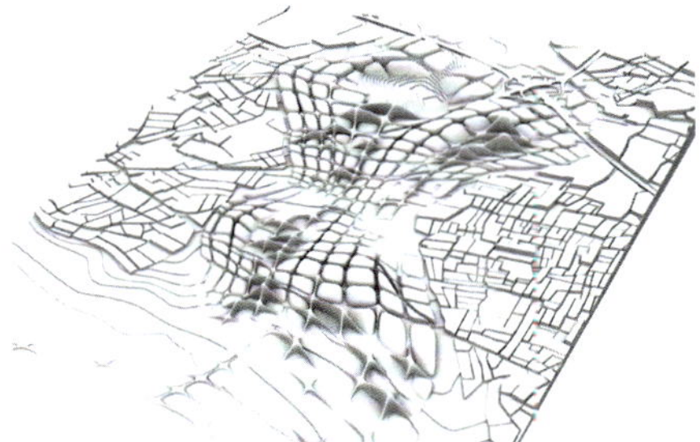

FIGS.10a–c: The historic center of Istanbul is characterized by its own order. At Kartal Pendik, Zaha Hadid Architects' proposal introduces a new order in the z-direction.

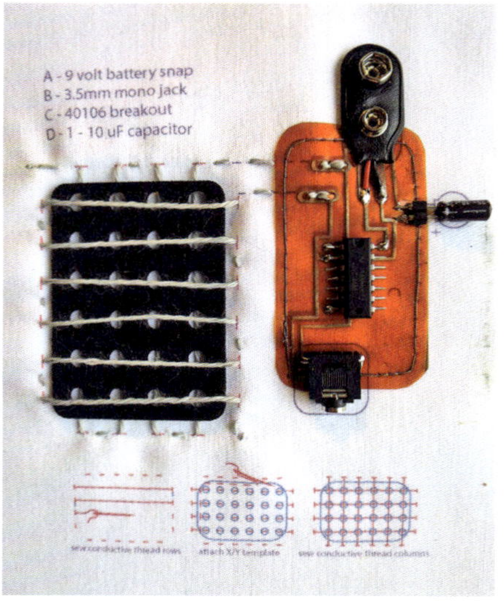

FIGS.11a–b: E-textiles introduce a new order of electronic elements within a fabric's own order.

time signatures (and subsequently new order) to arrive at a composition at times dissonant and syncopated. (fig. 8)

In the field of textiles, e-textiles, a type of technical textile, incorporate electronic devices and digital components into the age-old warp-and-weft structure of woven cloth. The seamless integration of such devices into cloth requires an understanding and acceptance of the existing structure, so as to create a new one within it. One variant is achieved through directly embedding devices such as sensors and microcontrollers into fabric with stitches that surround these new elements, isolating them and interrupting the fabric's flow of linear rows. Alternately, cloth can be woven with conductive metal wire as a substitute for thread. The introduction of a new type of thread within the old order of warp and weft simply and dramatically transforms a piece of fabric into an electronic element. (figs. 11a–b)

Interventions to existing buildings and structures, too, begin with an understanding of order. With the "Monster" as an analogy to an adapted host building, Dr. Frankenstein's premise for creation provides insight into assumptions for adaptive reuse. To copy in the likeness and structure of oneself is an intervention of duplication. The substitution of different body parts within this structure, however, is a deviation, a subversion of the structure. Both types of interventions—duplication and subversion—have parallels in architectural history.

FIG.12: Neoclassicism's replication of classical elements is an act of duplication: Kedleston Hall by Robert Adam.

DUPLICATION

FIGS.13a–b: The ideal image of the temple is translated onto the facade of the U.S.Supreme Court.

Deliberate architectural duplication has its roots in the late 18th century, with the emergence of archaeology as a science. The enthusiasm in the Western world for classical antiquity had for centuries resulted in travelers in search of Greco-Roman monuments and a subsequent interest in the replication of the structures of the ancient past and its classical elements. The works of Palladio, Schinkel, Chambers, Adams are exemplary of this return to classical forms. The act of duplication in Neoclassical architecture is a replication of a perceived, pure ideal. The use of the Greek temple front as the facade of a government building, such as the U.S. Supreme Court in Washington, DC, is a transfer of ideals through architecture. Duplication has its parallel in adaptive reuse, in which a historic structure, or its remnants, is returned to its original state through restoration. The duplication of a given, pre-existing order as a new one is in itself an intervention. It is an act that denies change and preserves for posterity through the refusal to recognize time and space. (figs. 12, 13a–b)

The subversion of an existing order, too, has its parallel in the history of architecture. Deconstructivism in architecture is a strategy premised upon an intentional dislocation of order. Inspired by Jacques Derrida, Peter Eisenman's 1989 Wexner Center for the Arts at Ohio State University, USA, with its juxtaposition of divergent grids, has become an icon of this concept. In adaptive reuse there are many instances of the blatant alteration of order,

FIG.14: Deconstructivism's intentional dislocation of order in Peter Eisenman's Wexner Center for the Arts.

often subconscious, that juxtapose the old and the new, with the practice of facadism at one extreme. Daniel Libeskind's Military History Museum in Dresden, Germany, is a conversion of a Neoclassical armory through a conscious dislocation of order. The introduction of a shard-like glass volume that pierces the Neoclassical structure both in plan and elevation exemplifies such subversive intent in adaptive reuse. (figs. 14, 15)

The reuse as housing of an unused school versus an underused church offers examples of a different type of subversion in adaptive reuse. The typologies of school and housing are ones that share the characteristic of an order created by double loaded corridors. The order of a church, on the other hand, is premised upon a religious ritual expressed as a linear procession through a single space of grand scale. The introduction of housing into the school is a natural one, but such an intervention into the church necessitates a subversion of its existing order. In adaptive reuse, as opposed to deconstructivism, this same dislocation can often be a subconscious one. It is a product of economics that

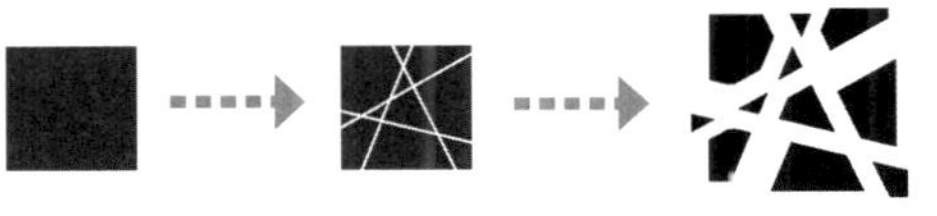

FIG.15: Subversion.

does not necessarily account for architectural principles and can easily fall prey to an incompatibility betwen the existing and the new.

In adaptive reuse practice we find a fascinating story between duplication and subversion. This tale will unfold in the following chapters as we examine the distance between these two poles of intervention. Through a close scrutiny of events and viewpoints, past and present, we will ultimately determine methods by which one can approach an existing structure so as to devise adaptive interventions that do not fall prey to the Frankenstein Syncrome. It is a tale of power and greed, of mathematics and ego, of evolution and revolution, of retribution and redemption, of profit and poetry.

1 Merriam-Webster Dictionary, http://www.merriam-webster.com (accessed January 7, 2016). 2 Ibid. Merriam-Webster notes that the term "adaptive reuse" was first used in 1973. 3 http://www.architecture2030.org (accessed December 7, 2015). 4 Markus Berger, Heinrich Hermann and Liliane Wong, Editorial, *The Int|AR Journal*, Vol. 01, 2009. 5 Louis I. Kahn, "Order and Form," *Perspecta*, Vol. 3, (Cambridge, MA: The MIT Press, 1955), p. 46–63. 6 Ibid.

Adaptive reuse is born of violence.

Its history parallels the unfolding of civilization and the development of man from hunter-gatherers. The familiar time lines of history depicting the development of civilizations also represent a map of destruction. The evolution of civilization from one cultural society to another is the product of factors that include trade, colonization, religious conversion, social dominance, natural disaster and invasion. Most often one, or a combination, of these factors resulted in the elimination of one civilized group by another. This pattern of conquest is ubiquitous through history from the Fertile Crescent to the Ancient Near East, from the Aegean to Africa and the Pre-Columbian Americas. Each of these conquests was naturally accompanied by victory and its resultant spoils of war. These spoils of looted goods, prisoners and existing infrastructure form the basis of early adaptive reuse.

Andrea Mantegna's *Triumphs of Caesar* is a nine-canvas series portraying the return of Julius Caesar from a military campaign. With details based on Plutarch, the canvases convey the magnitude of these spoils of war. From these canvases emerges a list of war booty that includes looted paintings, statuary, sections of architectural woodwork, metal in the form of armor, coats of arms, shields, helmets, trophies, precious metals in the form of silver and gold, vases and goblets of all sizes, animals such as oxen and elephants, vast quantities of coin and precious stones and captives, both young and old. This war booty was a commodity and utilized in a number of tangible ways. The art was appropriated for Caesar's collection, the animals for sacrifice or games, the profitable items from metal to precious stones for sale and the prisoners for the slave trade. The profit from these objects replenished depleted coffers and even subsidized large-scale civic projects.

Plunder: Erasure & Redemption

02

FIG.0: "Grande Ludovisi" Sarcophagus, c.252 CE, Palazzo Altemps (manipulated detail).

A hidden inscription on a stone in the Roman Colosseum confirms that by order of the Emperor Caesar Vespasian Augustus the new amphitheater was erected with the spoils of war, in this case the AD 70 Siege of Jerusalem.[1] (figs. 1a–i)

Not all physical plunder, however, was converted to coin. Some occupied places of honor in their new destinations as a commemoration of victory. In present-day Rome, eight of the many obelisks in the city were looted from Heliopolis in 30 BC, upon Augustus' defeat of Cleopatra. Re-erected as symbols of victory in public piazzas, many of these hieroglyph-covered obelisks were subsequently felled by the Goths with the fall of Rome, then rediscovered in the 16th century by Pope Sixtus V, repaired and reused as part of an urban plan that is still in existence. Other pieces of booty, such as sculpture or art, are today coveted parts of museum collections around the world. (fig. 2)

Plunder of a different nature is found within the vanquished cities. Occupied by victors, the remnants of the cities became sites for adaptive reuse. New styles of habitation, the hallmark of a foreign culture, were introduced into the remaining structures and infrastructure—structures whose purpose and importance in one society are made obsolete by the customs of another.

FIGS.1a–i: *The Triumphs of Caesar*, Andrea Mantegna, c. 1484–1492, Hampton Court Palace.

Adapted for new use, the existing structures are overwritten as a slow occupation that embeds itself over time. Accommodating mundane, quotidian needs, domestic structures are knit into and in-between grand structures of old, creating a patchwork in the fabric of the city. Driven by the needs of the new culture, these small interventions are made without consideration of

FIG.2: Egyptian obelisks found in different *piazze* in Rome.

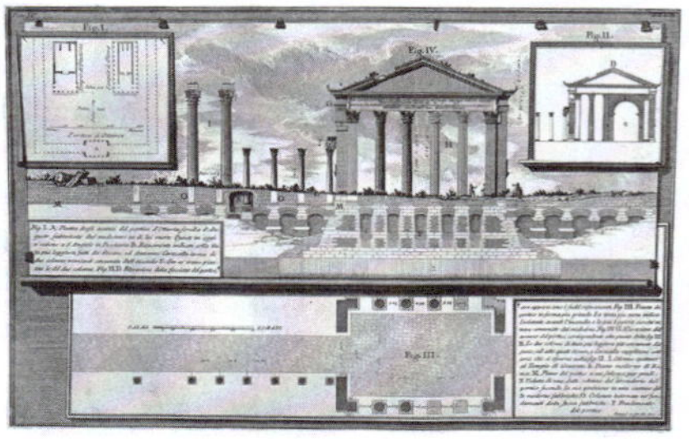

FIGS.3a–b: Centuries of inhabitation are visible today on the remains of the Porticus Octaviae, Rome.

the purpose or organization of the existing architecture itself. The host buildings become simply an economy of means.

Evidence of this type of intervention is visible in many ancient cities today. As an act of overwriting, it occurs at different scales. At the scale of a single structure, the interventions of different societies/civilizations are superimposed upon each other as architectural layers. The layers reflect functions and styles specific to that society and culture that in sum resemble a visible patchwork narration—the physical manifestation of changing use over time. Augustus' Porticus Octaviae, a colonnaded civic enclosure from the 1st-century BC in Rome, Italy, is one such example in which the history of a single structure is displayed as a living collage. Part of today's Roman Jewish Ghetto, the Porticus' temple front and two of the original Corinthian columns

FIGS.4a–b: The amphitheater of Arles, originally a place of Roman games, as medieval city and today's tourist site, Arènes d'Arles.

remain. A brick arch has replaced the other columns, casualties of a devastating earthquake. Remnants of a Christian structure stand in the place of the original courtyard. Visible patches of varying building materials are scars on the facade that attest to a slow transformation that occurs over time. (figs. 3a–b)

A difference in customs often precludes the victors' reuse of another society's structures, resulting in the obsolescence of entire parts of a city. Such impact on the urban fabric is not readily discernible, as it occurs very slowly over time. A comparison of city maps over centuries is akin to a quasi time lapse photography that records the displacement resulting from the introduction of new societal norms. Such comparisons offer us a picture of change in the contraction and expansion of a city, or parts of a city, over time. The history of the amphitheater of Arles, France, is exemplary of this type of change. In its heyday, it accommodated a population of 20,000 Romans accustomed to a tradition of spectacle. With the fall of the Roman Empire and the wane of this ritual of games, the amphitheater lost its relevance. The greatly reduced populace, living in constant fear of raids by the Saracens and later the Visigoths, was instead in need of defense. The amphitheater was reevaluated for its structure of 120 arches to serve as the substrate of a walled city of 200 homes. This reuse of the amphitheater as fortification reduced the once vibrant city to the limits of the structure itself. The full extent of the city was only restored with the amphitheater's designation as a monument in the 19th century. (figs. 4a–b)

The fall to obscurity of another amphitheater, the Colosseum in Rome, Italy, further illustrates urban consequences of reuse. Its position, depicted on

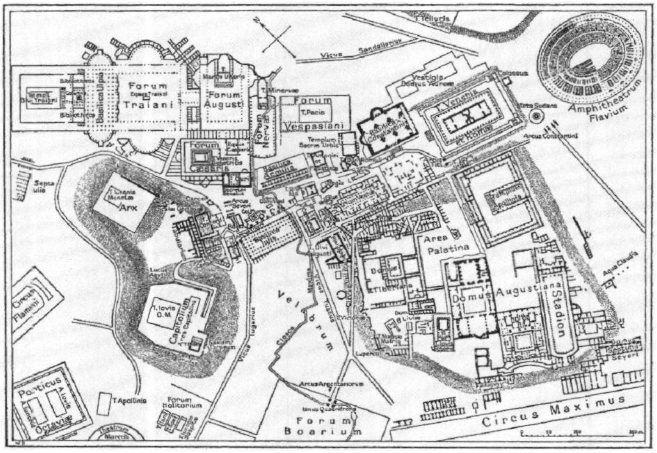

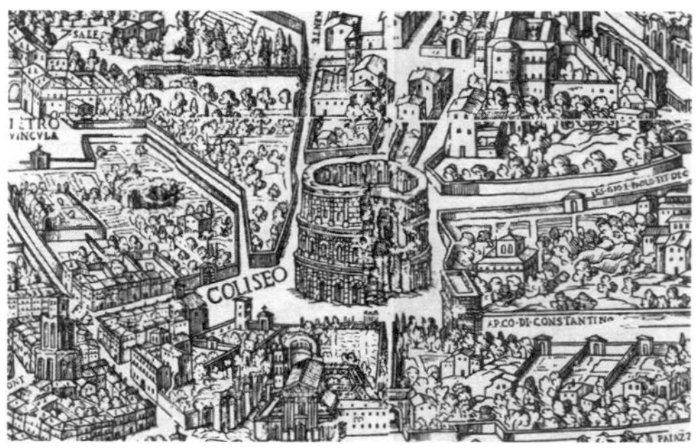

FIGS.5a–b: Maps of Rome during and after the Roman Empire demonstrate the changing role of the Colosseum in the city.

maps of Rome from different eras, demonstrates its changing role in the fortunes of the city. At the height of the Empire, the Colosseum occupied a prominent location in the city, evidenced by its placement just east of the Roman Forum. As a place of civic celebration, its location off a main thoroughfare attests to accessibility for the masses. On a map depicting the city after the fall of Rome, the Colosseum, abandoned and relegated to use as a garbage dump, is sited in isolation, in an area of walled precincts without connections to and relevance in the introspective life of the city in the Middle Ages. (figs. 5a–b)

FIG.6: Military History Museum, Dresden, adapted from an armory by Daniel Libeskind.

Contrary to the gradual adaptive reuse that occurs over time is the deliberate and intentional overwriting of structures as an assertion of supremacy. Undertaken on behalf of religious convictions or for the expansion of empire, this assertion of supremacy was often the primary justification for the reuse of structures, especially religious ones. The Military History Museum in Dresden, Germany, demonstrates this idea as architectural concept with the new, aggressive, geometric form piercing the existing structure, epitomizing the actions of many military endeavors over time. From the Egyptian New Kingdom of 1400 BC to the 8th-century AD reign of Umayyad prince Abd al-Rahman in Córdoba, Spain, there are examples of religious and civic structures superimposed directly upon those of the vanquished civilization. This type of intervention can be seen in multiple acts of overwriting on the Temple of Luxor in Egypt of the New Kingdom, a linear complex designed in a manner consistent with the sacred processions of important religious festivals. Within the remains today are seen the remnants of a large 3rd-century Roman

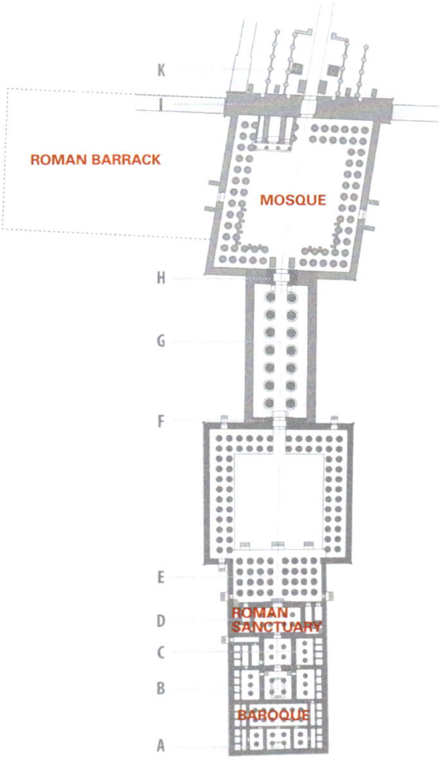

FIG.7: The many types of occupation over time at the Luxor Temple, Egypt.

military fort, superimposed upon the entry courtyards, a 4th-century Christian chapel and a startlingly white 14th-century mosque, rising out of the sandstone. Each conqueror chose to build on the same site, in a territorial act that de-sanctified the structure of the previous victor, attesting to the desire of Egypt's many conquerors to demonstrate their might in the region of the Nile. This type of intervention, of which there are many examples, leaves us with a historic typology of adaptive reuse as erasure. (figs. 6, 7)

Is there relevance today for interventions motivated by conquests? How have we evolved as a civilization in the 21st century? What do we battle over? What are the consequences? Are there triumphs? What types of plunder do we take? (figs. 8a–b)

Millennia separate the conquests of ancient civilizations and our present-day hostilities. Yet there are salient similarities. Religious differences remain at the heart of many modern conflicts. The desire to expand exists although acquisitive encroachment occurs in a less overt fashion. There are new causes for engaging in warfare, some more honorable than others, but diplomacy

FIGS.8a–b: Plunder, then and now: Sack of Rome, 410 AD by the Visigoths; Baghdad, 2003.

and global agreements serve as built-in deterrents of explicit aggression. Yet we still take prisoners. We still loot.

The advancement of technology accounts for the many differences in warfare. Weapons with the capability to inflict global destruction remotely and with little combat engagement have changed the face of war. Controlled from a distance, the resultant destruction has an air of detachment that redefines the nature of plunder. Physical objects are looted much as they were in centuries past but not by victors. Taking advantage of the conditions of war, lawless individuals use it as an opportunity to steal. Stolen art and archaeological finds from Afghanistan and Syria are today's Elgin Marbles. Sold on a black market, this type of plunder converts to coin in the tradition of Caesar's triumphs. Plunder in the form of re-appropriated structures as an expression of supremacy has little relevance today due to this changed concept of warfare, in which there are no opportunities for inhabiting such a structure. These same developments in weaponry and technology have, however, extended the potential of plunder. Looting through the annihilation of

FIGS.9a–b: Modern weapons have changed the nature of plunder: Japan, 1945, and Syria, 2015.

architectural heritage as in the ancient city of Palmyra is a new form of plunder. This act of erasure is not a consequence of conquest but a tactic in an ongoing game of war. The glory associated with monumental battlefield confrontations of ideals has given way to the fear and cynicism of localized terrorist aggressions without a defined sense of place. Modern war monuments, such as the Vietnam War Memorial, attest to these altered sentiments. (figs. 9a–b)

The reuse of war-related structures in the modern era is not one of commemoration; rather, they serve as a vehicle for expressing the toll of war and bearing witness to its atrocities for future generations. Many of the surviving structures of war are inconvertible due to the ineradicable nature of events that occurred. Instead, they become memorials and/or museums with the sole purpose of remembering and educating. The Memorial and Museum Auschwitz-Birkenau reuses the concentration camps as a memorial to its 1,100,000 victims. Its buildings and objects, largely kept *in situ*, are used as evidence for future generations. With the identical objective, S-21, formerly the Chao Ponhea Yat High School, a primary school in Phnom Penh, Cambodia, used as a prison and torture site during the reign of the Khmer Rouge, now

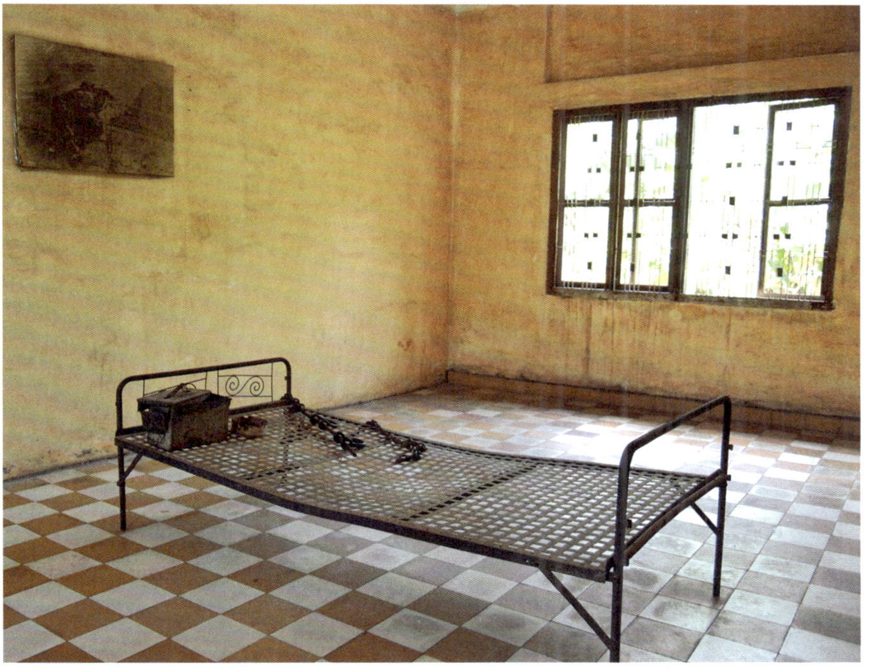

FIG.10: A classroom of the Chao Ponhea Yat High School, transformed to a torture cell at S-21, is now the Tuol Sleng Genocide Museum in Phnom Penh.

serves as a memorial and museum. As silent witnesses, these structures cannot be demolished. Difficult pasts and our present-day conscience render them impervious to adaptation. In their reuse as living memorials and museums their history is forever preserved. (fig. 10)
War structures with less difficult associations, however, are opportunities for architectural intervention. The Nazi Party Rally Grounds in Nuremberg, Germany, an 11-square-kilometer site utilized for the display of power, is one such example. The north wing of the Congress Hall was converted to an archive and exhibition center through an architectural intervention similar to that at the Military History Museum of Dresden. A deconstructivist glass-and-steel shaft piercing the structure and exiting the brick-and-stone facade is a modern act of erasure—one of de-consecration inspired not by religious supremacy but by redemption. Architecture is employed in this instance as a commentary on war, a departure from the triumphs of victory. This design intervention is an overt act of adaptive reuse as exorcism. (fig. 11)
In instances of total destruction, interventions employ referential strategies to recall what had been. For example, at the site of the 1840 Dresden Synagogue, which was razed on Crystal Night 1938, a new synagogue was

FIG.11: Günther Domenig's Documentation Center pierces the existing Nazi Congress Hall in Nuremberg as an act of exorcism.

consecrated in 2002. The placement of the original building was preserved in a courtyard and the new building erected on one edge of this footprint. A cube that torques upwards from a ground-level geometry of its own, the New Synagogue twists almost imperceptibly to align at the upper level with the geometry of the destroyed synagogue. A relationship is created between the new and the old by an intangible but ever-present intervention of memory. Similarly, at Ground Zero in New York City, the 2002 installation *Tribute in Light* used 88 searchlights to form two ghostly towers with gigantic beams of light, emitted from and recalling the site of the destroyed World Trade Center. In the intervention of memory lies the hope of redemption. (figs. 12a–b, 13)

In exploring the roots of adaptive reuse in this way, two distinct types of reuse emerge that have developed from the original archetype of the plunder of military conquests: a gradual overwriting of existing structures and a deliberate intervention of erasure. These two types, overwriting and erasure, continue to evolve over time, incorporating ongoing developing technologies

FIGS.12a–b: The Dresden New Synagogue by Wandel Lorch Architekten torques to pay homage to Gottfried Semper's razed Dresden Synagogue.

FIG.13: *Tribute in Light* by Julian LaVerdiere and Paul Myoda recalls the twin towers of the World Trade Center, destroyed on September 11, 2001.

FIG.14a: Interior of accessory building, Dachau Concentration Camp Memorial Site.

FIG.14b: Dachau Concentration Camp, 1945.

FIG.14c: Syrian refugees, September 2015.

and a greater global accountability. Erasure as a concept has a limited modern relevance and today we find in its place a reuse of memorial and redemption.

For Consideration

The reuse of an accessory structure at the former Dachau concentration camp as refugee housing.

The 2015 exodus of some four million refugees of the Syrian Civil War has created a new challenge to adaptive reuse related to structures of war, memory and trauma. As part of a solution to alleviate the housing crisis created by record numbers of refugees entering Europe, 50 refugees in Dachau, Germany, were offered shelter in the former accessory building of the herb garden at what was once the Dachau concentration camp. These structures previously served as "a school of racially motivated alternative medicine."[2] What are the pros and cons of this action in the context of the different types of adaptive reuse occurring as a result of military conquests? (figs. 14a–c)

1 Bruce Johnston, "Colosseum built with loot from sack of Jerusalem temple," *The Guardian*, June 15, 2001. As the construction of the Colosseum dates to 72 AD, there is no doubt that it refers to the spoils from Sack of Jerusalem in the Roman Jewish War of 70 AD. 2 Sophie Hardach, "The Refugees housed at Dachau: 'Where else should I live?'" *The Guardian*, September 19, 2015.

Faces of Immortality

The quest for immortality is the stuff of legends. From the Spanish explorer Juan Ponce de León to Harry Potter's headmaster Albus Dumbledore, the fascination with the elusive "fountain of youth" is one that transcends time. Buildings, like humans, also experience a finite life span. At its conclusion, they, like us, face an end: demolition. Through the practice of adaptive reuse, however, this end, for some buildings, can be denied and perhaps even postponed indefinitely in an immortalization of sorts. (fig. 1)

The desire to evade death is universal. We find numerous and varying promises of life after death in religions of all denominations, from Christianity to Hinduism. With a common objective to posit life as an unending cycle, the various religions offer nuanced views of extending life. The immortality enabled by the practice of adaptive reuse, like that in religion, is similarly nuanced by different intervention strategies. An examination of these concepts in major religions offers us a point of departure for such concepts in adaptive reuse.

The Christian concept of afterlife is premised upon the resurrection of Jesus Christ, who died and was raised from the dead after three days. This resurrection, implied by the evidence of an empty tomb, was additionally corroborated by Jesus' appearance after death to his disciples on the road to Emmaus. In resurrected form, Jesus resembled himself from the moment of death. Caravaggio's *Doubting Thomas* depicts this resurrected Jesus who, as proof of his existence, displays the wounds inflicted by crucifixion to his disbelieving disciple. Jesus stayed on earth for only a short period of time before he ascended to heaven. Our knowledge of him remains at age 33, an age that is instrumental to our understanding of his role in history.

The Quest for Immortality 03

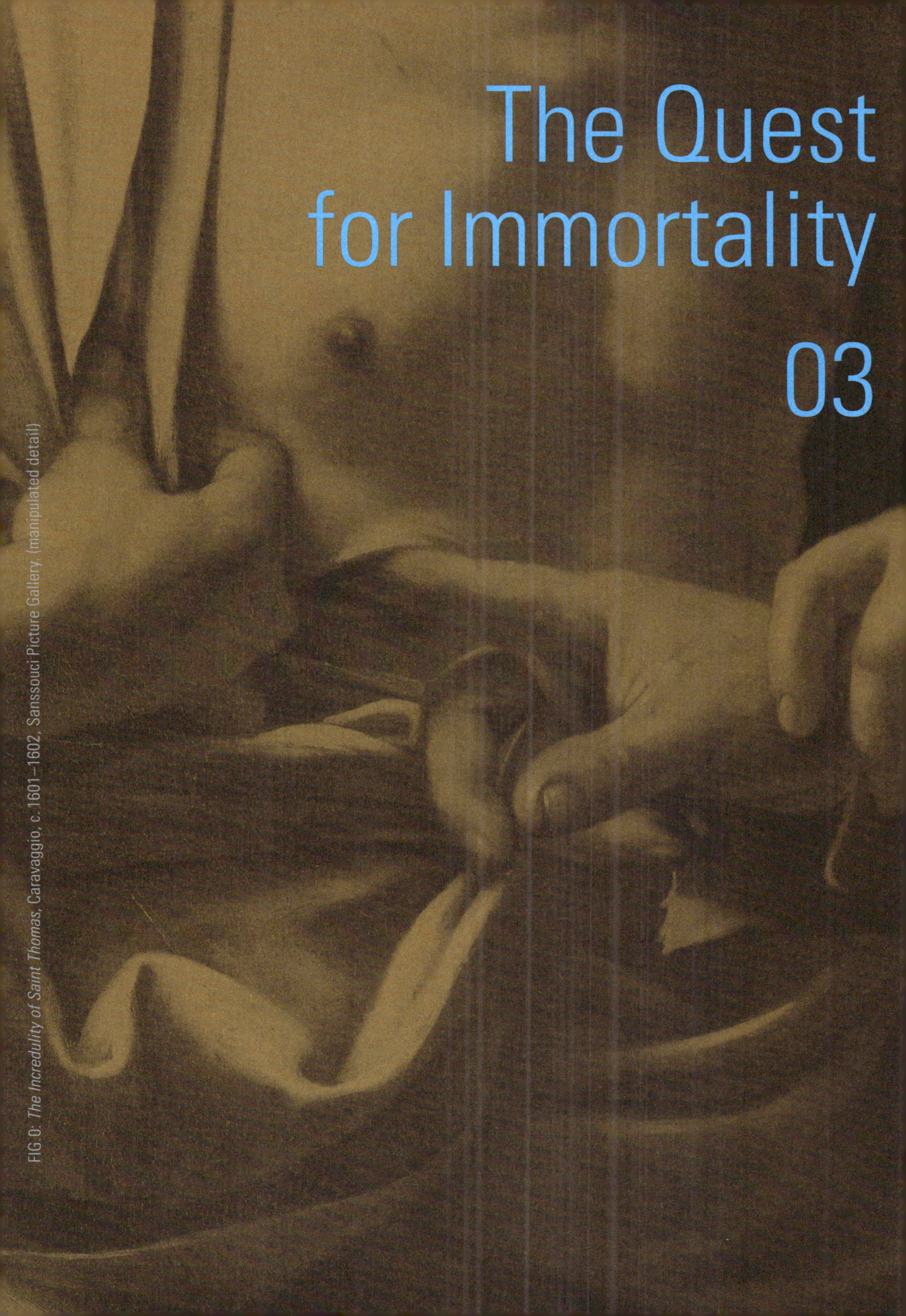

FIG.0: *The Incredulity of Saint Thomas*, Caravaggio, c. 1601–1602, Sanssouci Picture Gallery (manipulated detail)

FIGS.1–2: Plimoth Plantation and Greenfield Village are resurrected to the respective historic moments of 1620 and 1908.

Structures that have lost their relevance in time are sometimes resurrected from obscurity for posterity. Small communities of buildings such as colonial Plymouth or the village of young Henry Ford are examples of such structures that are no longer pertinent as living cities. Their significance lies in the recall of a moment in history. Their preservation as living museums maintains these specific moments in time: Plimoth Plantation in Plymouth, Massachusetts, USA, as the original 17th-century settlement of English colonists in the New World and Greenfield Village in Detroit, Michigan, USA, as the late 19th-century community in which Henry Ford invented the Model T. Populated by actors, these interactive museums recreate life of that particular period.

FIG.3: *The Raising of Lazarus*, Duccio di Buoninsegna, c. 1310–11, Kimbell Art Museum.

Like Jesus Christ, these structures are brought back to life, restored to a time that is most representative of their role in history and suspended forever in that moment. (figs. 1, 2)

In Christianity we find a second type of resurrection in the account of young Lazarus whom Jesus, in performing his miracles, restored to life four days after an untimely death. Lazarus returned to life in real time, resumed the cycle of living and eventually died a second, natural death. Lazarus' resurrection is differentiated from Jesus' by his ability to age with time. Lazarus' resurrection is a temporary immortality and a brief reprieve from death. The Hedmark Museum in Hamar, Norway, also a living museum, is differentiated from Plimoth Plantation or Greenfield Village through such shades of temporality. An active archaeological site with various remains of Norwegian civilization dating from the 13th century, the site and the building remnants were kept *in situ* as a "cold" museum. While the architectural interventions of Sverre Fehn bring these archaeological remains to life as a museum, they make no attempt to restore the structures. Instead, elements such as ramps or a shed roof, created to provide the visitor with a detached view of the ruins, are simply attached to the fragments. "There has been no attempt to repair or to restore a specific period in the barn's history. It gives no signal of time in suspension; the buildings and objects openly continue a process of disintegration, but the temporal aspect is slower."[1] (figs. 3, 4a–b)

In contrast to both types of resurrected structures, Plimoth Plantation and the Hedmark Museum, the reconstruction of Old Town Market Place in Warsaw, Poland, resembles a concept of afterlife akin to the Egyptian idea

FIGS.4a–b: Sverre Fehn's interventions at the Hedmark Museum (the Storhamar Barn), Hamar.

of *ka*. Part of a complex symbolism, the *ka* refers, in instances of afterlife, to a spiritual double of man that lives on after death. The *ka* survives on condition that it has the ability to return to a body each night, accounting for the elaborate ritual of embalmment in ancient Egyptian culture. Originating from the 13th century, the bustling Market Place in the heart of old Warsaw was once the meeting place of guilds and merchants, with signature late-Baroque pastel-colored buildings occupied by a wealthy merchant class. During the invasion of Poland in the Second World War, the Old Town market square suffered severe damage from bombing that destroyed many of the buildings and left the square a skeletal structure. In the early 1950s, the

FIGS.5a–c: Old Town Market Square, Warsaw, before and after the Bombing of Warsaw, 1945.

war-ravaged square was restored with new modern buildings behind a re-creation of the 17th century facades. The replicated 17th-century shell is skin deep, as the facades are disengaged from the modern functions of the buildings behind them and the roles of their occupants. In this restored state the market became anew the heart of Old Town, filled with outdoor cafés, musicians and vendors. While the square is once again infused with a bustling spirit, it is a spirit made possible by the restoration of the facades. The reconstructed facades serve as the embalmed double of the 17th-century Old Town Market Place, to which the spirit of touristic commerce returns each day. (figs. 5a–c)

An Eastern approach to afterlife, reincarnation is rebirth as another form of being. Complex variations exist between different beliefs—Hinduism, Buddhism, Sikhism, etc.—with an accord, however, in the belief of the immutability of the soul within a changing body. This analogy is applicable in adaptive reuse for a majority of existing structures that gain a second life, serving a new and unrelated function. From church to apartment building, from jail to hotel, factory to museum, change of use is a common phenomenon for old

FIGS.6a–b: Remains of the Gothic St. Kolumba Church knit into Peter Zumthor's Kolumba Museum, Cologne.

buildings. While frequently attempted, many such conversion projects fail due to a lack of recognition and even denial of the essence of the existing structure. The Kolumba Museum in Cologne, Germany, and the Selexyz Bookstore in Maastricht, Netherlands, are, by contrast, examples in which the reuse of an ecclesiastical structure is premised on the essence of the original one. Severely damaged in the bombing of Cologne, only parts of the exterior wall and tower and a statue of the Mother of God atop a pillar remained of the Gothic Saint Kolumba church. These relics of the old structure are knit physically into the facade as part of the collection in the new diocesan museum. Their original placement and significance are points of departure of the conversion. As highlights of the museum, the ruins provide not only an enhanced experience of history that inspires the language of the new architecture but a continuity of the building's original intent. (figs. 6a–b)

In the Selexyz Bookstore, where the existing church was entirely intact, the intervention instead referenced the rituals inherent in the church typology. Program functions such as the wine bar are placed in the altar and apse, alluding to the transubstantiation of Christ at the altar. Such juxtapositions through building program connect, albeit with wit, the old and new uses. The presence of the soul, the essence of the host building—physical or referential—distinguishes a project of adaptive reuse from that of a simple change of function. In the proviso for the endurance of the soul may lie a principle for a meaningful practice of reuse. The lack of this condition can be seen in Frankenstein's failed creature. (fig. 7)

An entirely different immortality emerges in the 21st century for a society in which the role of religion has diminished. In its place is a newfound reverence for technology and the opportunities it portends. New construction means, for example, enabled the translocation of the 1888 Harriet Rees House in Chicago, Illinois, USA, one of three surviving Romanesque Revival houses in the city. Over time, urban development had slowly changed the

FIG.7: The new life of the 13th-century Dominican church as the Selexyz Dominicanen Bookstore, Maastricht.

context of the house from residential to commercial. To accommodate the development of a new mega entertainment complex, the house was moved to a residential neighborhood. With enormous efforts and at incredible expense, the Harriet Rees House is once again in an appropriate context although not its original one. These extraordinary means allow for a fragile immortality that is not possible or available for the many existing structures facing a similar plight. The U.S. Embassy in Karachi, Pakistan, designed by Richard Neutra, though symbolic of architecture at a uniquely expansive political moment, could not be resuscitated and saved in the age of terrorism. It now faces demolition or a new life as a shopping mall.

With previously unimaginable means that allow for virtual realities, even immortality is not necessarily dependent on the experience of an original work and its iterations through time. From the Eiffel Tower to the UNESCO-listed Austrian village of Hallstatt, duplicated in China, architectural heritage

FIGS.8a–b: The UNESCO town of Hallstatt and its duplicated self in China.

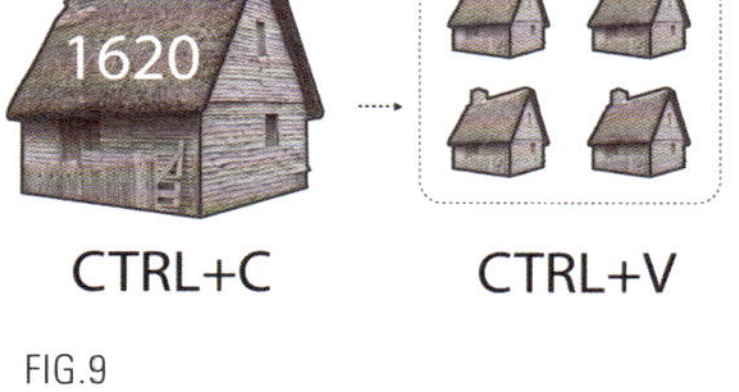

FIG.9

has experienced a new immortality in cloning. Reflecting the copy-paste function inherent in the digital world, this act of replication leads us to new questions of afterlife and our means for achieving it. (figs. 8a–b, 9)

The Road to Immortality

With the reuse of spoils as a starting point, the road from plunder to immortality is a long one. Looting in its many forms continued through to the 17th century, with rare glimpses of a growing awareness of heritage value. In the Christianization of the late Roman Empire, earlier pagan structures became the subject of plunder. Building materials were removed and reused for new construction projects, to the extent that this behavior inadvertently resulted in the making of policy. A regulation of November 30, 382 AD from the Codex Theodosianus, a transcription of laws issued in the late Roman Empire, decreed that the pagan temple "in which images are reported to have been placed must be measured by the value of their art rather than by their divinity."[2] This 4th-century law is prescient in its recognition of heritage value, despite its roots in the objectives of the Christian Roman emperors and their abhorrence of pagan practice.

Curiosity about antiquity did not resurface again until the Renaissance and the ancient monuments, both Christian and pagan, succumbed to further plunder and reuse. Medieval interest in ancient texts, methods and monuments had remained primarily with the clergy. The age of Humanism in the 14th and 15th centuries brought about a revived interest in antiquities and their restoration. In Rome, papal support included the efforts of Martin V and Pius II, who issued papal bulls extending protection and maintenance over ancient monuments. In the 16th century, protectors of the classical monuments included artists such as Raphael, whom Leo X appointed as supervisor of Roman excavations.[3] With their deaths and Holy Roman Emperor Charles V's Sack of Rome in 1527, the Renaissance of the popes officially came to a close. The ascension of Paul III to the papacy during the Reformation led to the establishment of the first Commissioner of Antiquities, Latino Giovenale Manetti, who was instructed "to ensure that the monuments ... are well maintained as possible, and will be freed of scrub and ivy; no new buildings will be attached to these and nothing will be demolished, burnt in a limekiln, or be removed from the city."[4] Despite the clear intention of this charge, subsequent popes were less overt in their adherence to a preservation of heritage.

Pope Pius IV, who ascended to the papacy in the Counter Reformation, instead advanced the practice of adaptive reuse. In 1561, he commissioned Michelangelo to build the Catholic Church of Santa Maria degli Angeli e degli Martiri within the ruins of the pagan Thermae of Diocletian. The *thermae*

FIG.10: Pope Pius IV. Painting by Bartolomeo Passarotti.

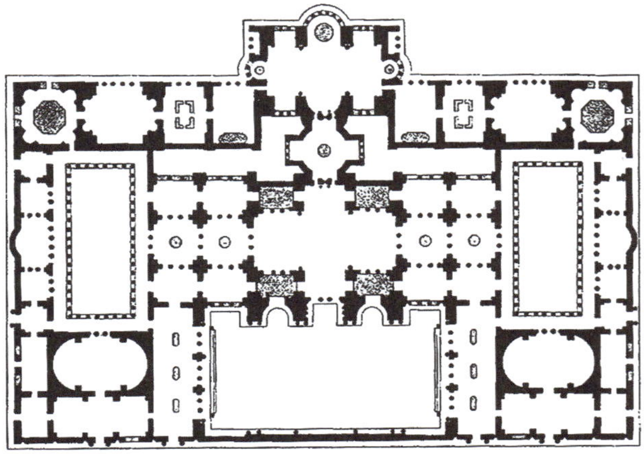

FIG.11a: The floor plan of the Baths of Diocletian with the frigidarium at its center.

FIG.11b: The vaulted remains of the Baths of Diocletian, 1575, Étienne Du Pérac.

were the largest baths of ancient Rome and accommodated over 3,000 visitors at one time. Its remains, as depicted in artists' renderings from Étienne du Pérac to Piranesi, attest to a colossal scale with monumental architectural features. As an abandoned structure, its potential lay in these characteristics, which Pope Pius IV viewed as architectural features common to both the pagan baths and the Christian church. Michelangelo's church was built with minimal new exterior construction, inside the frigidarium and within the existing cross vaults, some still standing. Adapting the remains of three vaulted rooms, Michelangelo created a Greek cross with a monumental transept of more than 90 meters, derived from the colossal forms of the existing baths. While in retrospect, this project was a deviation from the spirit of preservation, it was groundbreaking as an architectural intervention into an existing structure. (fig. 10)

Surprisingly, there is no formal entrance to this impressive basilica. It is accessed instead through the remains of a coved apse of the *thermae*, left in

FIG.11c: Santa Maria degli Angeli e dei Martiri converted from the Baths of Diocletian by Michelangelo Buonarroti, 1563–1564.

its original, ruined form. The relationship of intervention to existing structure and the decision to retain the ruins as a temporal reference are far-thinking. The discussion of these relationships as key issues of conservation is not broached for another 400 years. (figs. 11a–c)

Following upon the example of the Church of Santa Maria degli Angeli, other proposals for the reuse of existing monuments such as those pertaining to the Colosseum illustrate an evolving mind-set in the 16th and 17th centuries. Surviving a late-15th-century plan for demolition, the Colosseum was the subject of proposals for new use that included an outdoor theater, a wool factory with workshops and housing for the wool guild, a Bernini proposal for a memorial dedicated to Christian martyrdom and a Fontana proposal for transformation to a basilica. None of these grand schemes of transformation materialized; it was instead used as a cattle pasture and a manure deposit until an edict of 1744 by Pope Benedict XIV that "rigorously prohibited profanation of this spot."[5]

FIG.12: Designation for national heritage sites in France.

THE·ANTIQVITIES·OF
ATHENS·

MEASVRED · AND · DELINEATED
BY · JAMES · STVART · F.R.S. AND · F.S.A.
AND · NICHOLAS · REVETT·
PAINTERS · AND · ARCHITECTS·

VOLVME · THE · FIRST·

LONDON
PRINTED · BY · JOHN · HABERKORN · MDCCLXII.

FIG.13: Stuart and Revett's *The Antiquities of Athens*, 1755.

In other parts of Europe, the Reformation and Counter Reformation exacted a toll on ecclesiastical property, from the dissolution of religious houses in Zurich, Switzerland, to their destruction by Oliver Cromwell in England. Changes in service requirements resulted in adapted church structures. But these changes were undertaken as the product of a new sensibility from England to Scandinavia. A 17th-century proclamation in Sweden, sponsored by King Karl XI, is exemplary of this spirit. It "provided protection for antiquities and monuments, however insignificant, if they contributed to the memory of an historic event ..."[6] This provision is prescient in its expansion of the role of preservation/conservation. Its application still defines much of preservation and conservation today, where the recall of time and events past constitutes a significant part of its framework of purpose. By the late 18th century there was growing acknowledgment of the historic value of structures, with ensuing attempts at limiting and regulating plunder, which culminated in a new sensibility to heritage.

While the interest in the value of historic structures was gradual, catalysts in bringing about this awareness can be attributed to several concurrent developments. First, the French Revolution of the late 1780s inflicted a violent toll that included the destruction of many significant structures representative of the monarchy and the clergy, from royal tombs to sacred buildings. The French government's recognition of such architectural devastation resulted in the appointment of a commission to safeguard the nation's architectural heritage. This eventually led to the formation of the French Commission for Historic Monuments (Commission des monuments historiques) and the publication in 1840 of a first list of 934 historic monuments. Today heritage buildings and sites in France still carry the designation of MH, Monument Historique. (fig. 12)

The second development is less event-specific and results from a revived interest in the 18th century for antiquity and archaeology. Inigo Jones' travel in the 17th century and his interest in Classicism inspired *grand tours* in the 18th century. An 18th-century full English translation of Vitruvius' *De Architectura* and the 1755 publication by Stuart & Revett of *The Antiquities of Athens and Other Monuments of Greece,* with its illustrations of buildings and details from antiquity, brought about an awareness and subsequent fascination with the subject. Interest in archaeology led to discoveries of important sites with found objects and structures, structures that required some form of preservation, conservation and/or restoration. There were naturally differing opinions on these issues of preservation. From the 19th century these voices were heard in a battle over immortality. (fig. 13)

1 Per Olaf Fjeld, *Sverre Fehn. The Pattern of Thoughts* (New York, NY: The Monacelli Press, 2009), p. 116. 2 Transl. Clyde Pharr in collaboration with Theresa Sherrer Davidson, Mary Brown Pharr, *The Theodosian Code and Novels, and the Sirmondian Constitutions* (New Jersey: The Lawbook Exchange, Ltd., 2008), p. 472. 3 Alois Riegl, *The Origins of Baroque Art in Rome* (Los Angeles: Getty Research Institute, 2010), p. 163. 4 Jukka Jokilehto, *A History of Architectural Conservation*, (Oxford: Butterworth-Heinemann, 1999), p. 34. 5 Charles Isidore Hemans, *Catholic Italy, Its Institutions and Sanctuaries Pt 2*, (Florence: M. Cellini and Co., 1862), p. 13. (Digitized by Oxford University.) 6 John H. Stubbs, *Time Honored: A Global View of Architectural Conservation* (Hoboken, N.J.: John Wiley & Sons, 2009), p. 195.

The 18th century's fascination for antiquities, whet by grand tours and seminal publications, was increasingly sharpened by the archaeological discoveries at Ostia, Pompeii and Herculaneum. The unearthing of entire buried cities with statuary, houses, shops and amphitheaters prompted inquiry into many different issues, from excavation procedures to the export of objects to collections outside of Italy. At the close of the century and the start of the next, the interests in these discoveries and the concerns for a systematic approach to these excavations posited Italy, specifically Rome and its environs, with France as significant centers crucial to the development of conservation principles for architectural heritage.
With legislation for the protection of ancient monuments supported by the Papal See, efforts for the restoration of antiquities in Rome attracted many scholars to the city. The Napoleonic Wars and the annexation of Rome further intertwined the restoration efforts in Rome with those principles developed in France addressing the destruction caused by the French Revolution. The foremost scholar of classical antiquities of his time, Johann Joachim Winckelmann, a classicist from Dresden, Germany, was nominated the Chief Commissioner of Antiquities in Rome in 1763. His experience with the burgeoning but unregulated archaeological excavations at Herculaneum led to the formation of a critical theory: the need to preserve ancient art in its original form. With a reliance on scientific evidence, Winckelmann's theory differentiated between the original work and later additions and subtractions, a seminal differentiation that was a precursor to later conservationist ideas for built structures. The views on antiquity of Neoclassical sculptor Antonio Canova, Ispettore delle Belle Arti in 1802, responsible for policy and quality control in the inspection and evaluation of antiquities and works of art,[1] paralleled Winckelmann's as evidenced by his refusal to restore the Elgin Marbles from

Battle of the Immortals

04

FIG.0: Clockwise from top left: William Morris, Abbé Henri Grégoire, Rem Koolhaas, Alois Riegl.

the Parthenon. The Abbé Henri Grégoire, a prelate and part of a commission responsible for the protection of monuments, coined the term "vandalism" with respect to the destruction of French property. By the use of this word, he noted that "[P]ublic monuments should remind [the people] of its courage, its triumphs, its rights, its dignity; they should speak a language intelligible to everyone, that should be the vehicle of patriotism and virtue, qualities which should penetrate the citizens through all the senses."[2] His viewpoint established the role of architectural heritage as documentary evidence in the understanding of history. Quatremère de Quincy, in his role as secretary of the Académie des Beaux-Arts and the Intendant général des arts et monuments publiques, defined "restoration"[3] in his 1832 *Dictionnaire Historique d'Architecture* first and foremost as the repair of an ancient monument. Acquainted with Winckelmann's ideas and a friend of Canova's, Quatremère advocated the return of museum objects to their rightful owners. In doing so he established the importance of cultural context in the discussion of heritage value. Relating directly to artifacts and monuments, these voices provided a backdrop for the contentious opinions that emerged in the mid- to late 19th century regarding the proper treatment of those same artifacts and monuments as heritage.

With the restoration of the Bourbons in the July Revolution of 1830, the position of Inspector General for the Historic Monuments of France was established to oversee the inventory of damaged historic monuments and to begin the process of restoring them. By 1849, the 934 monuments enumerated in the first inventory of buildings in dire need of repairs of 1840 had grown to 3,000 monuments. The Abbey of La Madeleine at Vézelay was one project meriting immediate priority. Its restoration by Eugène Emmanuel Viollet-le-Duc led to commissions of similar projects at Notre-Dame de Paris and Carcassonne, projects that were pivotal in the discussion of the restoration of heritage.

Of great significance in the development of the Gothic style in the 12th century, the Romanesque nave of La Madeleine of Vézelay, by the 19th century, lay in a ruinous state, pervious to water infiltration and growth. Viollet-le-Duc's project to repair the collapsed nave exemplifies some early dilemmas of restoration. It focused on the compromised structure of buttresses, transverse arches and roof, built in the Romanesque style and rebuilt after a collapse in a later Gothic style. The reconstruction of these stylistically diverse areas enabled Viollet-le-Duc to form a theory of restoration. He chose to rebuild the Gothic vaults to an earlier Romanesque style to provide, in his view, an aesthetic coherence to the whole.

The further evolution of this approach is evident in his project at the Cathedral of Notre-Dame de Paris. Begun in the 12th century, the church had been modified over six centuries with changes to both the interior and the exterior. While the proposed restoration of Viollet-le-Duc (and his partner Jean-Baptiste Lassus) was based on the principle of restoring each part to its own style, scant architectural information in fact resulted in work that was based on an idea of what he believed may have existed rather than on evidence. At Notre-Dame, critics maintained that when he completed his restoration "all signs of previous alterations by royalty and clergy, of destruction by mobs, revolutions and former misguided repairs and restorations, as well as the decay of six centuries, had been removed."[4]

Viollet-le-Duc's approach became solidified as theory in the restoration of the city of Carcassonne. A Roman fortification modified in the 13th century, the military fort had lost its function by the 19th century. Resulting reuse over time of its material caused the loss of a great part of the structure, especially at the upper levels of the various edifices. Commissioned in 1846 to study the restoration of the entire fortification, Viollet-le-Duc brought the entire city to a hypothetical Gothic vision, ignoring its earlier roots. Having consolidated his definition of restoration by this time, he felt that "[b]oth the word and the thing are modern. To restore an edifice means neither to maintain it, nor to repair it, nor to rebuild it; it means to reestablish it in a finished state, which may in fact never have actually existed at any given time."[5] (figs. 1a–b)

Behind these now renown and notorious words lay the dilemma of the restoration of structures that were completed over a lengthy period of time and in several styles. While this definition of restoration met approval in France and was accepted by many institutions in Europe and the USA, it unleashed a furious debate on the principles of restoration and the extent of such efforts. Proponents of Viollet-le-Duc's interpretation of history in reconstruction advocated *stylistic restorations*. They felt strongly that restoration of this nature perpetuated the monuments' function in society, differentiating between "dead" and "living" monuments. This type of restoration was referred to as "in the style of" its restorer.

Critics of Viollet-le-Duc and stylistic restoration formed an anti-restoration contingency that eventually became the basis of the modern conservation movement. This movement was based primarily in England with John Ruskin as one of its earliest advocates. In *The Seven Lamps of Architecture*, Ruskin is unequivocal that restoration "means the most total destruction which a building can suffer: a destruction out of which no remnants can be gathered; a destruction accompanied with false description of the thing destroyed ..."[6] He argued that "[w]e have no right whatsoever to touch them."[7] Instead he proposed "... neither [to] have repairs nor things ruined ... Let them take the greatest possible care of all they have got, and when care will preserve it no longer, let it perish inch by inch."[8] With these strong words, Ruskin established the concept of maintenance.

Fellow critics of restoration agreed for the most part with Ruskin's stance. Their differences in shades of interpretation ultimately encouraged maintenance and repair of ancient structures as the alternative to restoration. In

FIG.1a: Carcassonne before ...

1862, Sir George Gilbert Scott presented a paper to the RIBA proposing a classification system of ancient architecture for the application of conservation practices. This led to the 1865 publication of a set of practical rules entitled *Conservation of Ancient Monuments and Remains*. Twelve years later, in 1877, William Morris founded the Society for the Protection of Ancient Monuments (SPAB). The principles of this society were delineated in what is now known as the Manifesto, a condemnation of restoration and a call "to put Protection in the place of Restoration, to stave off decay by daily care, to prop a perilous wall or mend a leaky roof by such means as are obviously meant for support or covering, and show no pretence of other art, and otherwise to resist all tampering with either the fabric or ornament of the building as it stands."[9] In Morris' eyes, a work of heritage included additions and alterations that, undisturbed, represented an authenticity of material. The manifesto established authenticity as a value and extended this authenticity to a wide range of structures. The notion of authenticity applied to "anything which can be looked on as artistic, picturesque, historical, antique, or substantial: any work in short, over which educated, artistic people would think it worthwhile to argue at all."[10]

The voices of Ruskin and Morris reverberated beyond England with its anti-restoration sentiments, dividing opinion on the immortality of monuments.

FIG.1b: ... and after restoration by Viollet-le-Duc.

Supporters of both groups included architects as well as artists and writers from many parts of Europe: France, Germany, Italy, Austria. They included Anatole France, Gottfried Semper, Hermann Muthesius, Camillo Boito. This polarization defined the discussion of heritage and its reuse in the latter part of the 19th century. There were equal demonstrations of both camps: protest against the restoration of the Frauenkirche in Munich, Germany, versus the full reconstruction of Knossos, Crete, by Sir Arthur Evans. It was not until the beginning of the 20th century that the conservation movement gained momentum, influencing the direction of the afterlives of structures.

Viollet-le-Duc, John Ruskin, William Morris—these were prophets proselytizing to a 19th-century audience yet unformed in their views of heritage. The fervent and often confrontational language between the two groups found a subtler, more nuanced expression in the early 20th century. With the maturing of conservationist ideas, there was a realization that neither of these views was absolute. In fact, there was recognition that past restoration efforts, style aside, contributed to the salvation of monuments that would otherwise have been lost. In the early 20th century, theories emerged that acknowledged the problems of stylistic restoration while tempering the extreme anti-restoration rhetoric. With the realization that conservation would, by necessity, need to extend beyond maintenance and repair for a *continued existence*, these theories address many basic issues that remain at the forefront of conservation/preservation today. How do we define heritage? What do we conserve? How do we determine its value? What is its relationship with history? With art? And its inverse: what do we not conserve? And what does this mean for the afterlife of a structure?

The varied responses to these questions clarified positions for the practices of conservation and preservation, leading eventually to formalized regulations. Over time, however, an unpredented number of structures came to be protected as heritage under these guidelines. Within this framework, the 19th-century question of "continued existence" for heritage sites would take on new signficance directly relating to the purpose of such structures. From the small intersection of the polarized interests of restorationists and conservationists in the question of a possible continued existence would ultimately emerge consideration of sites both with and without cultural significance. At the turn of the century, Austrian art historian Alois Riegl led this effort through his attempt to define a value system by which to differentiate between monuments in his 1903 essay, "The Modern Cult of Monuments: Its Essence and Its Development." These debates continued but were brought to new significance with the losses wreaked by the First and then the Second World Wars. The destruction brought about an international effort to put in place regulations for the conservation of monuments. (fig. 2)

1 Jukka Jokilehto, *A History of Architectural Conservation*, (Oxford: Butterworth-Heinemann, 1992), p. 75. 2 Anthony Vidler, "The Paradoxes of Vandalism," in Jeremy D. Popkin and R. H. Popkin, eds., *The Abbé Grégoire and His World,* (Dordecht:Springer, 2000), p. 136. 3 Quatremère de Quincy, *Dictionnaire Historique d'Architecture*, (Paris: Librarie D'Adrien Le Clere, 1832), p. 375. 4 Daniel D. Rieff, "Viollet Le Duc and Historic Restoration: The West Portals of Notre Dame," *Journal of the Society of Architectural Historians*, Vol. 30, No. 1, March 1971, p. 17. 5 Eugène Emmanuel Viollet-le-Duc, "Restoration," in *The Foundations of Architecture: Selections from the Dictionnaire Raisonné*, trans. Kenneth D. Whitehead (New York, NY: George Braziller, Inc, 1990), p. 195. 6 John Ruskin, *The Seven Lamps of Architecture* (London: George Allen, 1889), p. 195. 7 Ibid., p. 197. 8 John Ruskin, "Letter to His Father 1845", in *The Works of John Ruskin*, (London: G. Allen, 1901), p. 49. 9 William Morris, "Manifesto of the Society for the Protection of Ancient Buildings," from "The Principles of the Society [for the Protection of Ancient Buildings] As Set Forth Upon Its Foundation," *Builder* 35 (August 25, 1877). 10 Ibid. 11 Cesare Brandi, "Theory of Restoration, I," in Nicholas Price, M. Kirby Talley, Jr., and Alessandra Melucco Vacarro, eds., *Historical and Philosophical Issues in the Conservation of Cultural Heritage* (Los Angeles: The Getty Conservation Institute, 1996), p. 230.

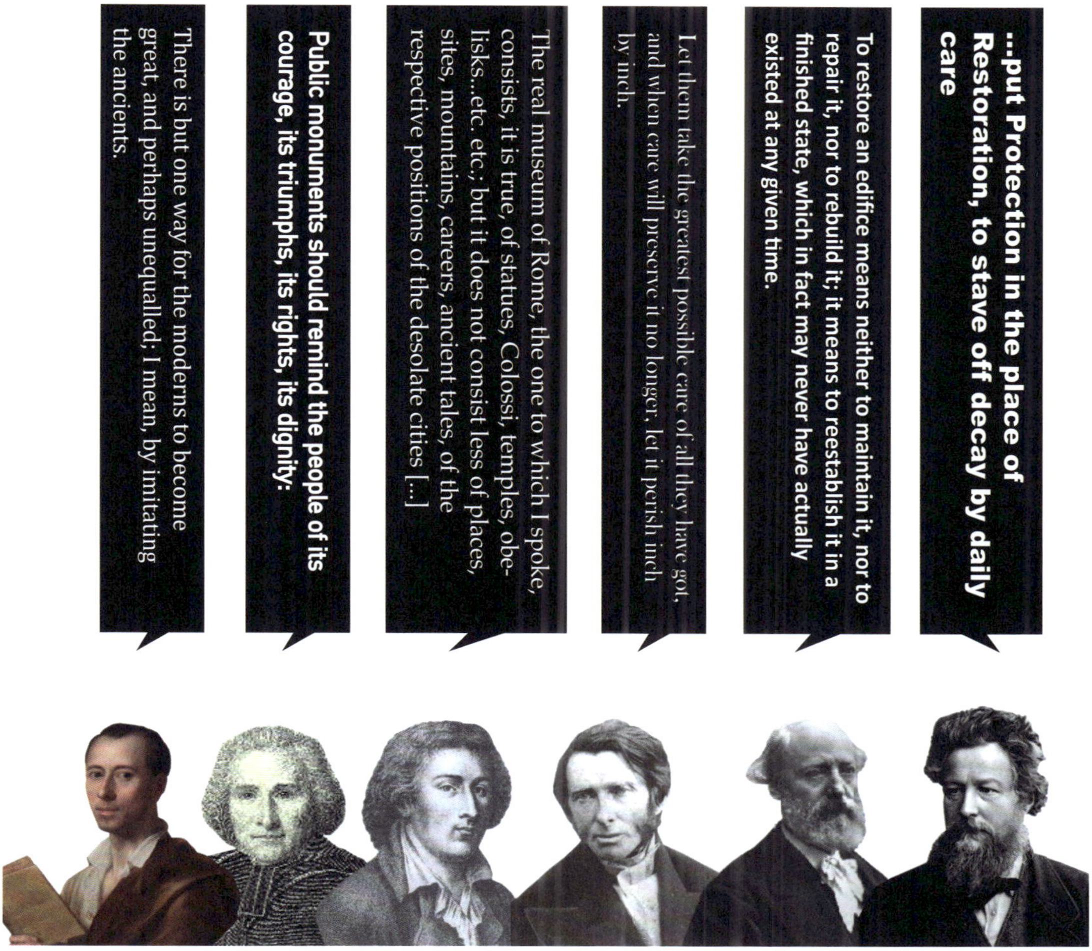
...put Protection in the place of Restoration, to stave off decay by daily care
To restore an edifice means neither to maintain it, nor to repair it, nor to rebuild it; it means to reestablish it in a finished state, which in fact may never have actually existed at any given time.
Let them take the greatest possible care of all they have got, and when care will preserve it no longer, let it perish inch by inch.
The real museum of Rome, the one to which I spoke, consists, it is true, of statues, Colossi, temples, obelisks...etc. etc.; but it does not consist less of places, sites, mountains, careers, ancient tales, of the respective positions of the desolate cities [...]
Public monuments should remind the people of its courage, its triumphs, its rights, its dignity:
There is but one way for the moderns to become great, and perhaps unequalled; I mean, by imitating the ancients.

FIG.2

The contentious dialogue of the mid- to late 19th century between the respective proponents of restoration and conservation may be understood as a part of a larger conversation—one elicited by shifting attitudes towards life and God. The act to "restore," in the meaning of Viollet-le-Duc, to a state "which may in fact never have actually existed"[1] is, in a sense, a belief in a resurrection to a place unknown and unimaginable, a place beyond space and time. The hope of immortality implicit in this concept of restoration, rooted in a feudal mind-set of a spiritual culture, was one that by the 19th century had widely outlived its pertinence. The mid- to late 19th century of Ruskin and Morris was a place dramatically altered by the realities of the dawn of industrialism and a sea change of ideas. Blind faith as a corollary of a primarily agrarian society had slowly been replaced by the uncertainties inherent in a society ensconced in the new industrial capitalism. These doubts in the divine eternity culminated in the late 19th century with Friedrich Nietzsche's declaration: "The most important of more recent events—that 'God is dead'; that the belief in the Christian God has become unworthy of belief—already begins to cast its first shadows over Europe."[2] (fig. 1)

Such doubts had already begun to seep into the fabric of society prior to the advent of the Industrial Revolution. German philosopher Georg Wilhelm Hegel, whose life paralleled the First Industrial Revolution, voiced them with regard to art in his lectures on *Aesthetics* at the University of Heidelberg in the 1820s. "The conditions of our present time are not favourable to art. It is not, as might be supposed, merely that the practising artist himself is infected by the loud voice of reflection all around him and by the opinions and judgements on art that have become customary everywhere ... the point is that our whole spiritual culture is of such a kind that he himself stands within the world of reflection and its relations, and could not by any act of

Immortality Redefined

05

FIG.0: *Wanderer Above the Sea of Fog*, Caspar David Friedrich, Hamburger Kunsthalle. (manipulated detail)

FIG.1: Georg Wilhelm Friedrich Hegel (1770–1831).

FIG.2: Friedrich Wilhelm Nietzsche (1844–1900).

will and decision abstract himself of it ..."[3] Speaking of a world that "no longer affords that satisfaction of spiritual needs which earlier ages and nations sought ..."[4] marks a paradigm shift from the familial parameters of farm and God to that of worker in a capitalistic society. Nietzsche refers to the new spirit as "... something invulnerable, unburiable ... within me, something that breaks rocks: it is called my will."[5] Relying on oneself to negotiate the challenges of a changed world, American Transcendentalist Ralph Waldo Emerson called for "Self-Reliance" in an essay that speaks also to a diminished dependence on government and religion. In this light, the stances of the conservationists can be viewed as a need to focus on the potential of the "here and now" rather than on the lure of afterlife. In an analogy to human mortality, Ruskin offered, in place of immortality, the embrace of aging and a natural death. Morris, with his advocacy of maintenance and care, promoted a slightly less passive program akin to regular doctor's visits with eventual hospice care. In the developing history of conservation/preservation, these were the viable alternatives to restoration. (figs. 1, 2)

The effect of Ruskin's writings and William Morris' anti-restoration Society for the Protection of Ancient Buildings (SPAB) Manifesto reverberated through many parts of Europe, influencing the early development of conser-

conservation, not restoration

FIG.3: Georg Gottfried Julius Dehio (1850–1932).

vation practice. The many individual contributions from late 19th century Western Europe further broadened this practice. While this history is not the focus of this book, some key individual concepts resulting from this time are crucial to the understanding, formation and development of adaptive reuse practice. In France, where "... the state had refused to take part in the maintenance of historic monuments, ... the attitude of the central government gradually changed, and priority was given to the repair of buildings ..."[6] In Germany, the sentiments against restoration grew and instances such as the restoration of the Frauenkirche in Munich provoked "the first public German Debate about restoration and its effects on the integrity of an historic building."[7] Architects like Hermann Muthesius advocated maintenance rather than restoration or reconstruction. While establishing this concept within society, these accompanying conversations extended the discussion of conservation beyond individual monuments. In turn-of-the-century Austria, Georg Dehio, sometimes referred to as the "founder of German architectural conservation,"[8] is credited with the commandment, "conservation, not restoration,"[9] and the statement: "We conserve a monument not because we consider it beautiful but because it is a piece of our national life."[10] Championing the cause of conservation, he extended its motivation beyond aesthetics and history to the realm of political importance.[11] In the same period, Austrian architect Adolf Loos, in an article of 1907, stated that "heritage was conceived as extending from monument to historic areas, and from significant natural features to whole landscapes ..."[12] In Italy, civil engineer, academic and art and urban studies scholar Gustavo Giovannoni "expanded the use of [Boito's] *restauro scientifico* (scientific restoration) approach (also called archaeological restoration) for all historic buildings, not just classical monuments ... He particularly emphasized the formerly discounted value of

FIG.4: Adolf Franz Karl Viktor Maria Loos (1870–1933).

the 'minor architecture' of historic urban centers and towns, which makes an important contribution to the overall historic environment."[13] Introducing the concept of "*diradamento*, or 'thinning out' the urban fabric"[14] in the modernization of Rome, he proposed the principle of 'selective restoration' in which historic centers could be represented by buildings of a key period that characterizes a district."[15] As an alternative approach to an indiscriminate demolition of historic areas, buildings of lesser significance could be demolished to make way for modern amenities, such as open spaces and circulation. (fig. 3)

Despite these defining and progressive early-20th-century ideas, the "roots of preservation lay in a conservative impulse to guard against revolutionary historicide."[16] Its accepted aim remained that of safeguarding; the idea of reusing monuments for a different function had not yet arrived. While extending the breadth of the notion and practice of conservation on the one hand, Adolf Loos, in 1910, corroborated the conservative view, on the other hand, in an analogy between monuments and art, positing them together as opposites to functional architecture. "The work of art is a private matter for the artist. The house is not. The work of art is brought into the world without a direct need for it. The house satisfies a requirement. The work of art is responsible to none; the house is responsible to everyone."[17] Focusing on the artistic aspect of a monument, this comparison conveyed the contemporary sentiment that "monuments are divorced from any contemporary use."[18] (fig. 4)

In this respect, and in an interesting parallel to restoration, the aim of preservation until the early 20th century remained somewhat aligned with Christian resurrection, akin to Jesus' resurrection from death in perpetuity at age 33. The fallacy of this aim for conservation was its reliance on the ability to maintain an object, a monument, at its original state while doing so at a different time. Some claim that this type of conservation is simply a denial of time, time being an ever-changing element. After all, even Jesus changed with resurrection: eight days after his death the resurrected Jesus walked through locked doors to appear to his disciples,[19] an ability never mentioned prior to his death. Forty days after crucifixion, he ascended to heaven and was never seen again on earth, his new existence entirely alien to that prior to his death. Resurrection is in itself a transformative act that involves change. "Change is far more radical than we are at first inclined to suppose,"[20] wrote Nobel laureate Henri Bergson in *Creative Evolution*, an anti-Darwinian theory of evolution published in 1907. Applying this thought to the idea of restoration/conservation, it can be said that "[p]reservation begins with the act of recognizing the diverse transformations monuments have undergone in time. This recognition is also an insight into the understanding of preservation as another transformation."[21]

A unique recognition of this understanding is the example of the Ise Jingu in Mie Prefecture of Ise, Japan. The Ise Jingu is a Shinto shrine complex dedicated to the goddess Amaterasu Omikami dating to the Heian Period. In keeping with Shinto beliefs, the two shrine buildings are torn down and rebuilt every 20 years. This tradition exemplifies "all that is authentic by acknowledging three simple realities: nothing lasts, nothing is finished and nothing is perfect."[22] The process of renewing through rebuilding is intended "to preserve the original architect's design against the otherwise eroding effects of time."[23] This action both recognizes and accepts the change that is inherent in time. It rejects preservation of the existing physical object. Rather, in replicating the original design explicitly, it perpetuates and transmits artisan skill, tradition and culture to the next generation. As a singular intervention that denies time and, in doing so, authenticity, this tradition is uniquely antithetical to the concept of adaptive reuse, a practice premised upon transformative change over time. (fig. 5)

Other forms of preservation in the wider sense since the late 19th century, however—from Viollet-le-Duc's restoration of Carcassonne and Arthur Evan's re-creation of Knossos to the restoration of the Parthenon and the excavation/restoration of Pompeii and Herculaneum—have striven to preserve structures from change. Today, such preserved sites are museums, and contrary to Loos' classification they serve a function other than their original

one. If preservation is indeed a transformation, then with hindsight this act, which since the late 19th century has changed many monuments, can be perceived as the introduction of a new and contemporary function to the existing monument. Acceptance of such an idea would require a confluence of minds at a later time. In the meantime, with a general consensus on the breadth of conservation, investigations progressed towards the development of a systematized understanding of heritage. (figs. 6, 7)
Austrian art historian Alois Riegl made such an attempt at systematization in his 1903 essay, "The Modern Cult of Monuments: Its Essence and Its Development." In this seminal piece, he introduced a value system that in sum allowed for the evaluation and differentiation of monuments or works of art. His definition of historic preservation as the "modern cult of monuments" led to the differentiation of "artistic and historical monuments" and "deliberate monuments." In making such a distinction, Riegl, like Hegel, acknowledged the effect of shifting contemporary ideas on the concept of artistic value. Establishing that "everything that once was can never be again, and that everything that once was forms an irreplaceable and inextricable link in a

FIG.6: UNESCO World Heritage site Carcassonne, restored by Viollet-le-Duc.

FIG.5: The shrines at the Ise Grand Shrine complex in Japan are rebuilt every 20 years.

FIG.7: The Cretan Palace of Knossos restored by Sir Arthur Evans.

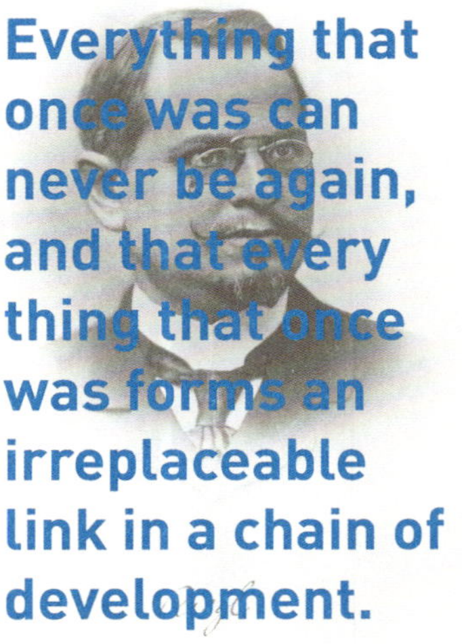

FIG.8: Alois Riegl (1858–1905).

FIG.9: Riegl's values for the evaluation of monuments.

chain of development,"[24] he concluded that the artistic monument and the historical monument must in fact be, in some ways, merged. (fig. 8)
In this classification, historical monuments are unintentional as opposed to "deliberate monuments"; both, however, have commemorative values that can be categorized. In establishing age value, historical value and deliberate commemorative value as related determinants for viewing a work, Riegl raised issues of intention, emotional appeal, objectivity, aesthetics and perpetuity. He also considered the "present day" values of use and newness as additional determinants. Together these values form a quasi-rubric that allows us to evaluate complex relationships when judging and assessing monuments and their continued existence. (fig. 9)
A different type of classification was proposed by one of the "founding figures of modern Italian conservation," Camillo Boito. In his 1893 *Questioni pratiche di belle arti, restauri, concorsi, legislazione, professione insegnamento*, a theory in the form of a Socratic dialogue, he suggested "to divide

the art of restoration" into corresponding historic periods: Antiquity for the first quality, Middle Ages for the second and Renaissance for the third.[25] By such classification Boito intentionally acknowledged the existence of additions to monuments over time and the subjectivity with which these additions are viewed. He proposed an eight-point system as a set of guidelines to distinguish between the original and subsequent interventions These points underscore the need to differentiate between the new and the old through stylistic construction and material differences as well as more overt documentation of each phase of new work. Boito's proposal lays the foundation for the differentiation of interventions in later preservation documents of the 20th century.

The theories of Riegl, Boito and others expand on the evaluation of heritage, case by case, criteria by criteria. These methods each allude to differences, great and slight, in types of heritage that require appropriate courses of action. In this context, early-20th-century individuals contributed to the developing methods of conservation (and subsequently reuse) focused on recognizing and preserving heritage. It is a period in which systems were developed that would pave the way for universal guidelines that still serve as the basis of international conservation regulations today. In this development, with its expansions beyond immortality, lie the roots of adaptive reuse practice.

1 Eugène Viollet-le-Duc, *On Restoration* (London: Sampson Low, Marston, Low and Searle, 1875), p. 9. 2 Friedrich Nietzsche (ed. Bernard Williams, transl. Josefine Nauckhoff), *The Gay Science* (Cambridge, UK: Cambridge University Press, 2001), p. 199. 3 G. W. F. Hegel, *Hegel's Aesthetics: Lectures on Fine Art*, transl. T. M. Knox (Oxford: Clarendon Press, 1975), p. 11. 4 Ibid., p. 10. 5 Friedrich Nietzsche (transl. Thomas Common), *Thus Spake Zarathustra. A Book for All and None* (Project Gutenberg EBook #1998, release date 2008), Verse XXXIII, "The Grave Song." 6 Jukka Jokilehto, *A History of Architectural Conservation* (Oxford: Butterworth-Heinemann, 1992), p. 187. 7 John H. Stubbs, *Time Honored: A Global View of Architectural Conservation*, (Hoboken, NJ: Wiley & Sons, 2009), p. 231. 8 Ibid., p. 232. 9 "Georg Dehio, [Gottfried Julius]," Dictionary of Art Historians, https://dictionaryofarthistorians.org/index.htm (accessed December 7, 2015). 10 Rudy Koshar, *Germany's Transient Pasts: Preservation and National Memory in the 20th Century* (Chapel Hill: University of North Carolina Press, 1998), p. 32. 11 Jokilehto, p. 217. 12 Jokilehto, p. 201. 13 Stubbs, p. 16. 14 Guido Zucconi, "Gustavo Giovannoni: A Theory and a Practice of Urban Conservation," *Change Over Time*, Vol. 4, No. 1, Spring 2014, p. 76–91. 15 Zucconi, p. 80. 16 Koshar, p. 34. 17 Adolf Loos, "Architektur" (1910), translation from *The Architecture of Adolf Loos: An Arts Council Exhibition* (London: the Arts Council, 1985), p. 104. 18 Manuel Martín-Hernández, "Time and Authenticity," *Future Anterior*, Vol. 11, No. 2, Winter 2014, p. 42. 19 *The Bible*, New King James Version (Thomas Nelson, Inc., 1982), John 20:24. 20 Henri Bergson, *Creative Evolution* (New York, NY: Palgrave Macmillan, 2007), p. 1. 21 Martín-Hernández, p. 43. 22 Richard R. Powel, *Wabi Sabi Simple* (Avon, MA: Adams Media, 2004), p. 19. 23 Rachel Nuwer, "This Japanese Shrine Has Been Torn Down & Rebuilt Every 20 Years for the Past Millennium," Smithsonian.com (accessed October 4, 2013). 24 Alois Riegl, "The Modern Cult of Monuments: Its Essence and Its Development," in Nicholas Price, M. Kirby Talley, Jr., and Alessandra Melucco Vacarro, eds., *Historical and Philosophical Issues in the Conservation of Cultural Heritage* (Los Angeles: The Getty Conservation Institute, 1996), p. 70. 25 Camillo Boito, "Questioni pratiche di belle art: restauri, concorsi, legislazione, professione insegnamento," transl. Cesare Birignani as "Restoration in Architecture: First Dialogue" in *Future Anterior*, University of Minnesota Press, Vol. 6, No. 1, 2009, p. 69.

National policies on the conservation of architectural heritage were emerging by the early 20th century within many countries of Western Europe as well as in parts of the USA, Asia and some Islamic states, but there was no formalized agreement or policy between them. There was indeed a need for such a policy, its urgency mandated by late-19th-century issues of repatriation of art and architecture, such as the paintings looted by Napoleon, the Elgin Marbles looted by the British or the Altar of Pergamon looted by the Germans. While the concept of a universal heritage was not unfamiliar to 17th- and 18th-century philosophers such as Locke, de Vattel and Kant, the formal acknowledgment of common values among man would not emerge until the mid-20th century with the 1954 introduction of the modern term "Common Heritage of Mankind" at the Hague Convention for the Protection of Cultural Property in the Event of Armed Conflict. (fig. 1)
Inextricably intertwined with the evolution of international law, the development of such policy finds its roots in the 1874 International Declaration Concerning the Laws and Customs of War, adopted at the Conference of Brussels, which established that the occupier of a state could only be considered as usufructuary of the properties. In particular, "... [e]very seizure, destruction of, or wilful damage to, such establishments, historical monuments, or works of art ... should be prosecuted by the competent authorities."[1] Aspects of this document led to the codification of the protection of cultural property under the broad term of "public buildings and property" at both Hague Conventions of 1899 and 1907.[2] Without the exigencies of actual warfare, however, these precautionary provisos lacked specificity and purpose. It was only in the wake of the First World War, with its devastation of monuments in Europe, that tangible efforts were made for cooperation between nations on issues of heritage.

Immortality Codified

06

FIG.0: U.S. Generals inspect stolen art treasures hidden in a salt mine in Germany, April 1945.

The Athens Charter 1931

The peace negotiated after the First World War led to the establishment of organizations for creating international cooperation on conservation. The International Museums Office was established in 1926 through the League of Nations to organize "international conferences on matters of importance for the international museum community."[3] In 1931, a meeting was organized in Athens at the First International Congress of Architects and Technicians of Historic Monuments to discuss the conservation of architectural monuments. Attended by representatives of 23 countries, the meeting concluded in a document now known as the Athens Charter of 1931, the first international policy on modern conservation. The Athens Charter comprised seven main resolutions addressing the need for cooperation through national and international advisory legislative groups for knowledgeable restoration and historic preservation, the protection of historic sites and surrounding areas and the use of modern techniques and materials for restoration.

Several key points discussed in the general conclusions of the Athens Charter 1931, important for the establishment of new ideas towards modern conservation, impacted the development of adaptive reuse practice:

> The Conference recommends that the occupation of buildings, which ensures the continuity of their life, should be maintained but that they should be used for a purpose which respects their historic or artistic character. (From Section I. DOCTRINES. GENERAL PRINCIPLES)

> The experts heard various communications concerning the use of modern materials for the consolidation of ancient monuments. They approved the judicious use of all the resources at the disposal of modern technique and more especially of reinforced concrete. They specified that this work of consolidation should whenever possible be concealed in order that the aspect and character of the restored monument be preserved. (From Section III. AESTHETIC ENHANCEMENT OF ANCIENT MONUMENTS)

> In the case of ruins, scrupulous conservation is necessary, and steps should be taken to reinstate any original fragments that may be recovered (anastylosis), whenever this is possible; the new materials used for this purpose should in all cases be recognisable. (From Section VI. THE TECHNIQUE OF CONSERVATION)

The impact of these points in the Athens Charter of 1931 on the emergence of adaptive reuse practice cannot be overstated. With the acknowledgment

FIG.1

of the reuse of a historic building as one based in continuity and with purpose, the Doctrines' section established the concept of adaptive reuse. With the implication that a new and different intervention must introduce modern materials where *anastylosis* is not possible, these concepts paved the way for the design intervention, a salient principle of adaptive reuse practice.

The Athens Charter 1933

The IV International Congress of Modern Architecture (CIAM) also met in Athens two years later. Their meeting resulted in a document named "Charter of Athens (1933)." The focus of this meeting was not the conservation of monuments but "the functional city" in urban planning and development. Le Corbusier, a key member of the Congress, published *La Charte d'Athènes 1933,* elaborating upon the points made in the group document. While the majority of the points were directly related to city planning, the recommendations regarding historic cities provided interesting insight on adaptive reuse in the urban fabric.

Under the category "Historic Heritage of Cities," points 65 to 70 addressed "architectural assets [that] must be protected, whether found in isolated buildings or in urban aggregations. They will be protected if they are the expression of a former culture ...,"[4] with the proviso, however, that such protection should not entail the perpetuation of slum conditions around monuments, which are recognized as "... regrettable but inevitable."[5] The final point speaks to the "harmful consequences [of] the practice of using styles of the past on aesthetic pretexts for new structures erected in historic areas ... Never has a

FIG.2: The devastation of Cologne, 1945.

FIG.3: *Ruins of St. Mark's Campanile 14 July 1902.*

return to the past been recorded, never has man retraced his own steps ... The mingling of the 'false' with the 'genuine,' far from attaining an impression of unity and from giving a sense of purity of style, merely results in artificial reconstruction capable only of discrediting the authentic testimonies that we were most moved to preserve."[6] Both Athens Charters—1931 and 1933—advanced the boundaries of conserving and of adding to existing monuments, especially with evolving references to style and authenticity.

The immense devastation of the Second World War with the total destruction of entire cities questioned and tested these positions. The plight of historic cities obliterated by war was instrumental to the discussion on authenticity. While restoration as reconstruction was no longer truly viable with the advancement of conservation policies in the 20th century, the idea was never-

FIGS.4a–c: Market Square, Warsaw, c. 1900, c. 1945, c. 2012.

theless considered anew in these particular circumstances. With unique precedents of restoration/reconstruction, such as the reconstruction of Venice's Campanile after its 1902 collapse or the rebuilding of Athens' Acropolis after Greece's War of Independence, the case for complete and total restoration/reconstruction was deemed acceptable in "those cases in which natural disasters or human events caused catastrophic damage. In such cases it was seen as acceptable to reproduce a monument exactly as it once was."[7] The total restoration/reconstruction of Warsaw to its prewar state—at least on the exterior—was one such case. The modernized interior of the structures, however, disconnected from the facades, differentiated this instance of restoration as an afterlife akin to the resurrection of Lazarus rather than that of Christ. The rebuilding of Rotterdam, equally demolished in the war,

FIG.5: United Nations Educational, Scientific and Cultural Organization, created 1945.

as a totally modern city provided a polar viewpoint and an opposite strategy of reincarnation. (figs. 2, 3, 4a–c)

The aftermath of the Second World War also led to renewed efforts in international cooperation for the conservation of monuments and heritage: the League of Nations, founded after the First World War, became the Organization of United Nations in 1945; the International Committee of Intellectual Cooperation, an advisory of the League of Nations, became part of the United Nations Educational, Scientific and Cultural Organization (UNESCO) in 1945 and the International Museums Office became the International Council of Museums (ICOM) in 1946. In 1956, the International Centre for the Study of the Preservation and Restoration of Cultural Property (ICCROM) was created at a UNESCO session as "an intergovernmental centre for the study and improvement of methods of restoration."[8] And the International Council on Monuments and Sites (ICOMOS), an advisory body of the World Heritage Committee for the Implementation of the World Heritage Convention of UNESCO, was created in 1965 "to promote the conservation, protection, use and enhancement of monuments, building complexes and sites."[9] More than half a century later, these organizations remain relevant. They not only maintain the founding principles of the conservation of heritage but expand upon them beyond buildings and monuments to fostering abstract ideals such as peace, education, freedom of expression and sustainability. (fig. 5)

Among the various theories that emerged in the post-war period, the work of Cesare Brandi stands out for its far-reaching ideas that influenced the development of principles in international policy as well as in UNESCO missions. His 1963 *Teoria del restauro* (*Theory of Restoration*)[10] defines restoration as "any kind of intervention that permits a product of human activity to recover its function ...,"[11] with a differentiation between the restoration of industrial products (as common objects) and works of art. In the former, the aim of restoration would "be to reestablish the functional properties of the product"[12] and in the latter, "to reestablish the potential unity of the work of art, as long as this is possible without producing an artistic or historical forgery and without erasing every trace of the passage of time left on the work of art."[13] Such a differentiation in the understanding of "function" between common object and work of art and, more so, between restoration and other possible interventions to a "work of art," serves to clarify the ambiguity of "preservation" itself. For "works of art," adaptive reuse is distinguished by a *change* of function rather than the *recovery* of function. While the reuse of non-heritage structures as "art" would not emerge for some decades, Brandi's definition offers a fascinating point of departure for such consideration. Within the confines of his definition, utilitarian structures such as warehouses or defunct power plants, not considered "works of art," might be considered "common objects." In this light, the re-establishment of their functional properties might be a restoration of resuscitation in which adaptive reuse would play a part.

In addition, the latter part of Brandi's definition applied to monuments establishes the importance of the creative process in the work of art. Jukka Jokilehto, formerly the Assistant to the Director General of ICCROM and actively involved in UNESCO, underscores the importance and far-reaching implication of this point in that "[r]ecognition is a fundamental part of the process, because this is the basis that will guide one's critical judgment of the necessary analysis and treatments that should follow."[14] Within this framework Brandi also addresses the dilemma of the restoration/conservation of additions: "an addition to a work of art is nothing more than new testimony to human activity and, thus, is part of history ... Consequently, the conservation of an addition is the norm, removal the exception."[15] Expanding further, he maintains "that every restoration should not prevent but, rather, facilitate possible future restorations."[16] These critical arguments stand as a backdrop to the development of significant international policy in the following year.

The Venice Charter

The 2nd International Congress of Architects and Technicians of Historic Documents was held in Venice in 1964. Through ICOMOS, the Congress adopted the Venice Charter, a key document that reexamined the basic principles defined in the Athens Charter of 1931, and enhanced its scope, based on new evidence and critical development since. The Venice Charter of 1964 comprises 16 articles that together address six topics: the historic monument, objectives of conservation practice, objectives of restoration practice, care of historic sites, excavations and documentation. It broadened the term "historic monument" with a definition that encompassed not only a single work but also an entire setting with historic significance. The designation of

FIG.6

FIG.7: Oscar Niemeyer's National Congress building in Brasilia, Frank Lloyd Wright's Fallingwater in Bear Run and the Apollo lunar landing site on the moon.

monument was extended to modest works that "acquired cultural significance with the passing of time."[17] Finally it introduced the concept that monuments are conserved and restored "no less as works of art than as historical evidence."[18]

The Venice Charter made a clear distinction between conservation, whose purpose is to maintain, and restoration whose "aim is to preserve and reveal the aesthetic and historic value of the monument."[19] Within this differentiation, it established some basic protective principles of conservation through the prohibition of "construction, demolition or modification" of all or part of the monument while re-enforcing through further clarification of what was already stated in the Athens Charter, namely that conservation is facilitated by "making use of [monuments] for some socially useful purpose."[20] At the same time, it set limits on restoration, requiring a basis in original substance and authentic documents as well as establishing a proviso that restoration must stop "at the point where conjecture begins."[21] The Venice Charter further added that "any extra work which is indispensable must be distinct from the architectural composition and must bear a contemporary stamp."[22] This latter part of the clause has been interpreted broadly and is, in fact, a *raison*

FIG.8

d'être for distinctive modern design interventions and additions. This clause has also been a lightning rod for proponents of historic restorations such as Britain's Prince Charles who claims that "... the Venice Charter—by requiring us to make distinct the breach between past and present, has likewise often caused the spirit to fly from old buildings and places."[23] (fig.6)

The adoption of the Venice Charter, together with the establishment of the many organizations dedicated to global cooperation in the field, marks a major point in the international development and consolidation of conservation policies. Other important developments followed, including the 1981 Burra Charter of ICOMOS Australia that provided guidelines for cultural heritage management, the 1983 Appleton Charter of ICOMOS Canada for the Protection and Enhancement of the Built Environment, the 1994 Nara Document on Authenticity and the 1998 establishment of DOCOMOMO International (International Committee for Documentation and Conservation of Buildings, Sites and Neighborhoods of the Modern Movement). More recently, the role of the international organizations has been instrumental in expanding the scope of heritage; the 1972 UNESCO Convention for the Protection of World Cultural and Natural Heritage, the 1997 Proclamation of Masterpieces of the

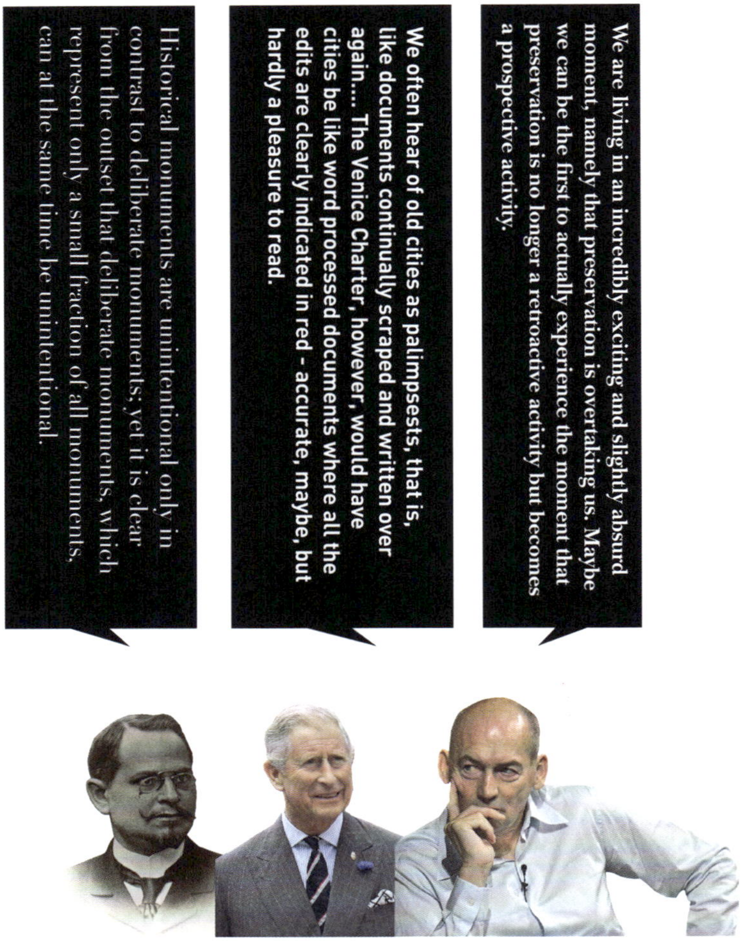

FIG.9

Oral and Intangible Heritage of Humanity, the 2001 UNESCO Universal Declaration on Cultural Diversity and the 2003 UNESCO Convention for the Safeguarding of the Intangible Cultural Heritage.

In the 21st century, what constitutes heritage encompasses much more than the monuments of the past. While a proposal to list the Apollo Lunar Landing on the moon as a UNESCO World Heritage site failed, monuments now include buildings of the 20th century such as those of Niemeyer, Le Corbusier, Wright or Utzon. The designation of OMA's Maison à Bordeaux as *Monument Historique Immeuble classé*, or classified building, as part of France's national heritage three years after its completion in 1998, however, raised the question of what we are preserving. Inspired by a commission of the Beijing government to "investigate and define a form of preservation," this question was raised by Rem Koolhaas himself in his 2004 article, "Preservation is Overtaking Us."[24] He states that the interval between the present and what we preserve is continually shrinking from 2,000 years in the early 19th century to 20 years in the latter half of the 20th century, so that we now "experience the moment in which preservation is no longer a retroactive activity but becomes a prospective activity."[25] For the preservation of historic Beijing OMA proposed a scheme of arbitrary preservation zones in the form of a barcode-like pattern of stripes: buildings falling within one stripe are preserved, and within the next demolished. While Koolhaas is a skillful provocateur, his thoughts beg the consideration of what must or must not, should or should not be preserved. (figs. 7, 8)

Through Brandi's theory of restoration, in which restoration is differentiated for objects as opposed to relevant works of art, restored monuments are by implication the latter. If indeed, as Rem Koolhaas claims, "preservation is prospective", the preservation of "everything" (built) would, applying Brandi's theory, render "everything"(built) works of art. Heidegger, in considering Hegel's statements regarding the end of art, queries, "is art still an essential and necessary way in which that truth happens which is decisive for our historical existence, or is this something that art no longer is?"[26] The Venice Charter, by its groundbreaking broadening of monuments as works not only of art but also of modest and socially useful character, has emancipated the monument. Adaptive reuse is its instrument in a changed world of shifting values. (fig. 9)

1 Articles VII & VIII, Project of an International Declaration Concerning the Laws and Customs of War. Adopted by the Conference of Brussels, August 27, 1874. *The American Journal of International Law*, Vol. 1, No. 2, Supplement: Official Documents (April 1907), p. 97. 2 "Convention (II) with Respect to the Laws and Customs of War on Land and Its Annex: Regulations Concerning the Laws and Customs of War on Land." The Hague, 29 July 1899, Articles 55 & 56. https://www.icrc.org/ihl/INTRO/150?OpenDocument (accessed November 23, 2015). 3 International Museum Offices in UNESCO Archives A to M catalogue, http://atom.archives.unesco.org/international-museums-office-imo (accessed November 23, 1915). 4 Le Corbusier (transl. Anthony Eardley), *The Athens Charter* (New York, NY: Grossman, 1973), accessed by https://modernistarchitecture.wordpress.com/2010/11/03/ciam's-"the-athens-charter"-1933/ 5 Ibid., Point 69. 6 Ibid., Point 70. 7 Manuel Martín-Hernández, "Time and Authenticity," *Future Anterior*, Vol. 11, No. 2, Winter 2014, p. 44. 8 http://www.iccrom.org/about/history/ (accessed June 18, 2015). 9 http://www.icomos.org/en/about-icomos/mission-and-vision/icomos-mission (accessed June 18, 2015). 10 Cesare Brandi (transl. Gianni Ponti with Alessandra Melucco Vaccaro), *Teoria del restauro* (Rome: Edizioni di Storia e Letteratura, 1963), in Price, Nicholas Stanely, M. Kirby Talley Jr. and Alessandra Melucco Vaccaro, eds., *Historical and Philosophical Issues in the Conservation of Cultural Heritage* (Los Angeles: The Getty Conservation Institution, 1996). 11 Ibid., p. 230. 12 Ibid. 13 Ibid., p. 231. 14 Jukka Jokilehto, *A History of Architectural Conservation* (Oxford: Butterworth-Heinemann, 1992), p. 4. 15 Brandi, p. 234. 16 Ibid., p. 341. 17 International Charter for the Conservation and Restoration of Monuments and Sites, "The Venice Charter—1964", Article 2. 18 Venice Charter, Article 3. 19 Venice Charter, Article 9. 20 Venice Charter, Article 5. 21 Venice Charter, Article 9. 22 Ibid. 23 Matthew Hardy, ed., *The Venice Charter Revisited: Modernism, Conservation and Tradition in the 21st Century* (Newcastle upon Tyne: Cambridge Scholars Publishing, 2008), p. xiii. 24 Rem Koolhaas, "Preservation Is Overtaking Us," in *Future Anterior*, Vol. I, No. 2, Fall 2004, p. 1. 25 Ibid. 26 Martin Heidegger (ed. and transl. Julian Young and Kenneth Haynes), *Off the Beaten Track* (Cambridge, UK: Cambridge University Press, 2002), p. 51.

Alois Riegl wrote that "[h]istorical monuments are unintentional ... in contrast to deliberate monuments."[1] Structures of historic significance unintentionally become monuments through preservation. The act of preserving transforms them from their previous use—as a temple, church, palace—to the new use of a historic site and, inadvertently, tourist destination. As such, historic monuments—from full-scale buildings such as the Pantheon in Rome, Italy, to semi-ruins such as the Parthenon in Athens, Greece,—are the first instances of adaptive reuse, albeit unintentional.

Centuries before the Athens Charter of 1931 and the Venice Charter that promulgated the use of monuments for a purpose, the 1560s conversion of the Baths of Diocletian in Rome to the Church of Santa Maria degli Angeli e dei Martiri was an intentional act of adaptive reuse. As a setting for such reuse, the 306 AD Roman baths were enormous ruins, missing much of their structure, including sections of roof and wall. Their architectural characteristics, in scale and grandeur, however, corresponded to those required for a cathedral and could, with some effort, translate directly to the inherent magnificence Pope Pius IV envisioned for a Renaissance church. Their adaptation required interventions of many different types. On the exterior, some new structure was needed to complete the missing elements of roof, walls and floors, and, on the interior, an entire retrofit to transform a ruined public theater of daily Roman civic life to a monumental celebration of religion. The reuse of the structure, despite the efforts required for its adaptation, was a decision that was not only economically sound but also embraced the continuity of character recommended in the Athens Charter of 1931. A precedent ahead of its time, the reuse of the Baths of Diocletian as the adapted church of Santa Maria degli Angeli e dei Martiri is an example of the complex relationship between an existing structure and its new use. (figs. 1a–b)

Hosts [and Guests] 07

FIG.0: *Dardanus calidus*: the hermit crab.

FIGS.1a–b: Santa Maria degli Angeli e dei Martiri as an intervention within the ruins of the Baths of Diocletian.

The Host Building

Hermit crabs, decapod invertebrates with soft abdomens that require protection, utilize discarded hard shell objects as fortification and dwelling. The hermit crab adapts to these imperfect surroundings, seeking larger ones as they grow and outgrow one shell after the next. In the same manner that a host is defined as a person who receives other people as guests, these objects—from empty clam casings to nautilus mollusks—host the hermit crab for a brief period of time. In the built environent, a host building is a structure that receives a new use for a defined or undefined period of time. The reuse of an existing structure for a new purpose requires similar adaptation to an imperfect host structure.

Host buildings are wrappers of different kinds, manifested as physical construction into which new life is introduced. Their ability to sustain a new use depends on many specific and individual factors: their condition, their potential to sustain additional load, their spatial fit with the demands of a new use, their memory, their placement in context. Host buildings can be classified by their various states of being; each type characterized by similar existing physical attributes. In turn, these attributes often determine the type of design intervention required in an application of reuse. The concept of the host building is not new; rather, it reflects "a clear difference between architecture and other artistic disciplines. It is not admitted, in principle, that a pictorial, sculptural, musical, cinematic or literary work of art could be modified by another author, but it has always been assumed that buildings can change use or be extended and transformed by other architects."[2]

All host structures are in many ways found objects, whole existing structures that have lost their relevance and are unused or underused. They share similarities with the French *objet trouvé*, a natural or discarded object "found by

FIG.2: Herzog & de Meuron's conversion of the Bankside Power Station to the Tate Modern, London.

an artist and displayed with no, or minimal, alteration as (or as an element in) a work of art."[3] Unlike the *objet trouvé*, host structures in adaptive reuse are characterized by alteration and transformation in the form of design interventions. For example, the transformation of the Baths of Diocletian to the Santa Maria degli Angeli or the Bankside Power Station to the Tate Modern Museum required significant alterations. In both examples, the entire host structure including its systems was transformed through a change of use and the necessary architectural interventions to accomplish such transformation. These particular projects are exemplary for the manner in which the implementation of the new use respects, acknowledges and even enhances the character of the host structure while introducing the elements of the new: in the Renaissance Santa Maria degli Angeli this is apparent in the grand vaults of the Romans; in the Tate Modern, in the remnants of an industrial character. (fig. 2)

Each host structure is an entity unto itself. "A thing with defined and independent existence,"[4] the definition of entity implies an object—large, small, built, found—that has its own specific character. While there are many examples of adapted and reused built structures, few transformed projects demonstrate a respect for the independent existence of their host. In not

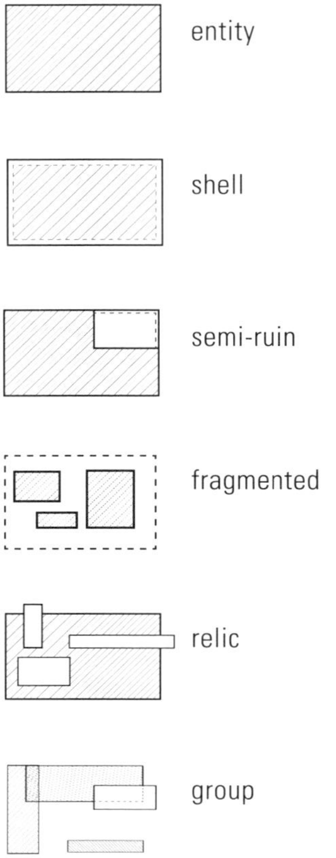

FIG.3: Host structure types.

doing so, they fall prey to the Frankenstein Syndrome. The purpose of this book lies in establishing the concept of the host structure as an entity and investigating the means by which alterations and interventions can be made in support of its independent existence.

Host Structure Types

The most common host structure is an existing whole and intact building that is available for conversion to new use. In this instance, design interventions can occur on both the exterior and the interior. Whole building conversions range from renovations to subtractions and additions. Carlo Scarpa's Castelvecchio Museum, a conversion of a previously altered medieval castle, is exemplary of a whole building host that is transformed for new use by renovation, subtraction and addition. But there are variants of host structures, many of which do not comprise a whole or intact building. The character of these variants determines the types of possible interventions.

Shell: Interior Conversion

A host structure as only the interior of an entire building differs dramatically from the whole building host. In this case, adaptive reuse comprises an intervention into a host building that engages with every part of the building except the building envelope. The host building simply acts as a shell to contain new and different activities. This type of host structure is often, though not exclusively, a heritage building with a designated protected exterior. While it does not intervene on the exterior, an interior conversion can engage the structural system within. The Selexyz Dominicanen bookstore in Maastricht, Netherlands, is an example in which new elements and furnishings, such as a set of bookshelves, a café and a mezzanine, are simply inserted into the 13th-century church without impacting the stone envelope or the internal structure. The MYU Bar in Beirut, Lebanon, is another such example located in a war-ravaged building in the now trendy neighborhood of Gemmayzeh. The design consists of the insertion of a textile structure into an industrial shell. The textile room negotiates the existing structural supports and systems while creating a chic atmosphere in a cohabitation of unfinished, derelict space. In contrast, the Cineteca Matadero in Madrid, Spain, is a conversion that includes interventions in the internal structure. The early-20th-century slaughterhouse and livestock market are converted to a cinema, film studio and archive. New interior elements—such as staircases or wide-span auditoria—are inserted, requiring some internal structural modification of the existing historic host. The use of woven irrigational hoses within a frame of steel tubing as internal structure introduces a new architectonic vocabulary within the old. With many variations, this type of host structure serves as a container of new designs that rely primarily on lightweight and minor structural interventions. (figs. 4, 5a–b, 6a–f)
A variant of the shell host, an interior segment of a whole building is the most common type of host structure. Occupying a portion of a floor or one or more floors, this type of host accomodates the interior retrofit, the most basic type of adaptive reuse. As part of a structure that is a complete and intact building, the interior retrofit is an insertion of space within one compartment of the shell rather than the whole shell. Its spatial limits are both the footprint of the compartment and the exterior structural system itself. Office and retail design with their characteristic frequent tenant turnover are common cases of interior retrofit. The open office plan is an example of a

FIG.4: The13th-century Dominican church is a shell-type host for the Selexyz Dominicanen bookstore in Maastricht.

FIGS.5a–b: In Paul Kaloustian's MYU Bar in Beirut, textile rooms are inserted into the industrial shell.

FIGS.6a–c: Virseda Vila Architects' interventions in the conversion of a slaughterhouse in Madrid.

FIGS.6d–f: Churtichaga + Quadra-Salcedo Arquitectos' intervention of woven industrial hoses introduces a new architectural sensibility to the interior spaces of the Cineteca Matadero.

structural grid as determinant of the interior space, as the placement of columns dictates the confines of possible interventions. Such intervention does not affect the integrity of the building nor that of the neighboring spaces. Primary design interventions include spatial manipulation through non-load-bearing means and the selection of furniture, finishes and equipment (FF&E). Retrofit projects typically include a change of use, for example, from office to retail or from retail to education. However, retrofit projects may not entail a change of use at all, as in the rapid turnover of one retail space for another and different type of retail. Such interior renovation nonetheless introduces change as new purpose and is, in that sense, an adaptive reuse intervention.

Incomplete Host Buildings: The Semi-Ruin Host

Interior retrofits and conversions assume a complete host building with functioning systems, structure and exterior envelope. There are instances, however, of host buildings that are not entirely intact and are missing elements of either the structure, the infrastructure or both, as is the case with the Baths of Diocletian. Design interventions in the framework of this type include not only interior insertions but also additions. The purpose of such additions are twofold: first, to bring the existing ruined structure back to a whole state and, second, to extend, if desired, the extent and the capacity of the host building in its new use. The former case can include sections of new structure, walls, floors, circulation elements and systems; the nature of these additions depends on the state of the host structure itself In the latter case, the extension is new construction that is limited by the load-bearing capacity of the host to directly sustain additional weight or to act as support for a new appendage. In either instance, the relationship of the addition(s) to the existing structure is the determinant of an adaptive reuse practice as maintenance or as art. At the Moritzburg Museum in Halle, Germany, a conversion from a semi-ruined roofless castle, the insertion of a new roof and top floors as a folded strctural platform is an example of both. (figs. 7a–c)

The reuse of "ruins" has made for some of the most interesting adaptive reuse projects due to the inherent need to consider the issue of time. Temporality, a crucial element in conservation practice, is a key determinant of different adaptive reuse strategies. How much or how little does one acknowledge the passage of time when engaging in adaptive reuse? Conversely, how far should adaptive reuse go in terms of expressing its presence in the language of materials and construction? These are the same critical questions that Viollet-le-Duc faced and that sparked the theories of

FIGS.7a–c: Nieto Sobejano Arquitectos' insertion of a self-supporting floor and roof structure into the Moritzburg Castle, Halle.

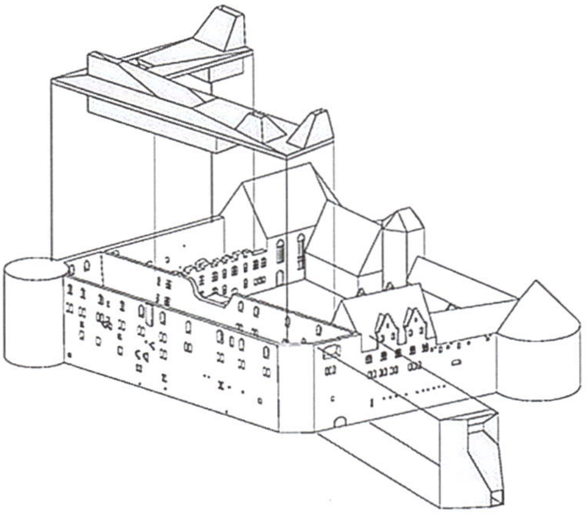

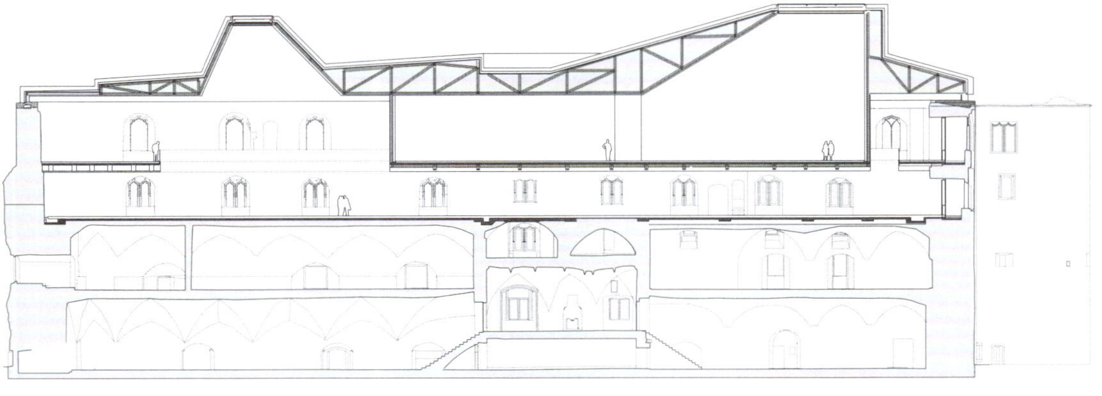

FIG.8: Sverre Fehn's Hamar Museum.

FIG.9: Linazasoro & Sánchez Arquitectura's Cultural Centre of the Piarists in Lavapiés.

FIGS.10a–b: David Chipperfield's Neues Museum in Berlin.

19th-century conservationists, which resulted in the ensuing international policies such as the Athens and Venice Charters. Three projects with incomplete structures as host buildings demonstrate the spectrum of viewpoints on this particular issue. At the Hedmark Museum, an archaeological site of Norwegian civilization, Sverre Fehn intervened only to enable the site to continue in time as a cold, living museum. The few additions are spare, of a modern vocabulary and used for a simple closure of the envelope or for the introduction of visitor circulation. They interfere little in the time clock of the site. At the bombed remains of the Neues Museum in Berlin, Germany, David Chipperfield instead recreated a past spatial experience in plan through the reconstruction of a stair in its exact previous location. In its realization, however, he delineated the passage of time through the introduction of modern materials and details. At the Centro Cultural Escuelas Pías de Lavapiés in Madrid, Spain, Linazasoro & Sánchez's new library co-inhabits the ruins of the ancient Piarist school of San Fernando with a comfortable convergence of the old and the new. Time, in this instance, moves forward in a newly combined time zone. (figs. 8, 9, 10a–b)

Fragmented Host

When the host building is characterized by an extent of incompleteness rendering it uninhabitable, adaptive reuse becomes an act of invention. Such hosts vary and range from a fragment of a building to its infrastructure, facade or structure. Adding to such fragments to achieve a new state of completion is charged. The addition must be justified by the importance of the fragment itself and such justification includes historic significance but also economy. The obsolete crane way in the port of Amsterdam, Nether-

FIG. 11: Existing infrastructure as the structural foundation for OTH Architecten's Kraanspoor Building in Amsterdam.

FIGS. 12a–c: An abandoned concrete structure was the point of departure for Studio Piva's Le Terrazze Hotel in Treviso.

lands, and the abandoned concrete skeleton in Carità de Villorba, Italy, are examples of the latter; their significance lies mainly in their potential as a resource for building structure. As structure constitutes a significant percentage of a construction budget, their reuse as structural support respectively for an office and archive complex and a four-star hotel, is based on sound economics. Despite taking on only structural roles, the hosts, in these projects, inspire the design vocabulary of the interventions. (figs. 11, 12a–c)

The reuse of historic fragments, on the other hand, translates to a different level of complexity. The significance of such remains dictates an adaptive strategy that can just as easily be an architecture inspired by history as one that falls prey to false historicism. The recognition and acknowledgment of history in the manifestation of a building's new design are fundamental to a successful reuse of fragments. In the transformation of the earthquake-ruined Chiesa Madre in Salemi, Italy, to a new urban plaza, the additions of a new

FIG.13: The ruins of the Chiesa Madre are reborn as Salemi's urban plaza in the project by Álvaro Siza and Roberto Collovà.

floor, circulation, structural improvements and new lighting are all dictated by the consideration of the 17th-century church. Completed with unobtrusive means and finishes, some of which utilize original materials and 17th-century methods, the additions focus on the architectural ruin itself. Its new use as an open piazza, in which young lovers find privacy in the remains of the church apse and skateboarders perform flips across the almost indiscernible outline of the past nave, is simply a continuation in the history of this small Sicilian hillside town. (fig. 13)

The preservation of historic facades as a fragment differs from facadism, a practice that retains and exploits an historic facade for its referential value

FIGS.14a–b: Insertion of a new atrium into the heritage facades at the Bibliotheca Hertziana, Rome, by Juan Navarro Baldeweg.

FIG.15: Facadism as unfettered development: the Bucharest Novotel with the exterior of the old Romanian National Theatre.

rather than the heritage value of its exterior. An example of adaptive reuse with a focus on heritage value can be found in the heart of Rome's center city, where facades are strictly under historic preservation. The new building for the Biblioteca Hertziana, designed by Juan Navarro Baldeweg, provides a distinctive insertion of a volume within the historic fronts that allows the 1912 palazzo to go forward in time with not only a new program of use but a fresh interpretation of the ancient courtyard typology. Facadism, by contrast, is a practice that produces a new building behind a facade and lacks any correspondence of time and place. (figs. 14a–b, 15)

Relic Host

Sometimes a host structure is simply a relic of the past. It is not transformed but rather serves as the catalyst for new construction. Its significance is in the recall of a memory: an event, history, a period of time. An example of this is the tiny fragment of wall and the statue of the Madonna of the St. Kolumba parish church that inspired the architecture of the new Kolumba Museum in Cologne, Germany. The spirit of these relics pervades the detailing of the new building, guiding a spatial experience that very much recalls the old one. Another example is the Long Museum West Bund in Shanghai, China, where a 110-meter-long coal hopper unloading bridge from the city's

FIG.16: The new grey brick unites the fragments of the St. Kolumba Church in the new Kolumba Museum, Cologne, by Peter Zumthor.

FIG.17: The Long Museum in Shanghai is built around a 1950s coal hopper unloading bridge.

industrial past forms the center of a new museum of contemporary art. Without function or even direct connection to the museum's exhibit spaces, the primary purpose of the industrial remnant is to recall the memory of this site as a wharf for the transportation of coal. Its form, however, inspired the use of concrete cantilevered vault umbrella structures in the design of the museum itself. (figs. 16, 17)

Group Hosts

A host structure is not necessarily bound to a single building. The reuse of more than one building as host engenders a grand scale of adaptive reuse. Group hosts are differentiated by whether these buildings are elements that comprise part of one single complex or individual elements in an overall urban environment. As a single complex, the aim will most often be the preservation of a historic event, community or moment in time, such as the heritage sites protected by UNESCO. The conversion of the Zollverein coal mine and coking plant in Essen, Germany, is such a case where the preservation of the history of coal mining has resulted in the complex's conversion to a museum showcasing this way of life. The adaptive strategy for these host structures is to produce enhanced versions of their original selves, as exhibits. (fig. 18)

FIG.18: At the Zollverein coal mine, the different elements of the coal mining process are unified through adaptive reuse as an industrial monument anc cultural center.

FIGS.19a–b: The different rooflines of the Royal Palace in Dresden are unified under the addition of one roof in the conversion to a museum by Peter Kulka.

Utilizing more than one building as a host structure has many challenges: the condition of the individual structures, the physical relationship between them, their individual place in history and their collective relationships. The existence of such conditions requires a unifying adaptive strategy that provides the various structures with a new and singular identity. Given the multiple factors that may exist, this type of host, even more than the others, requires consideration on a case-by-case basis. For example, the conversion of parts of the Royal Palace in Dresden, Germany, to a single museum complex is relatively less complicated due to the fact that the parts are all segments of the palace, albeit with different rooflines. The unifying strategy here was the addition of a single new roof to join the buildings as one. In the case of the Pixel Hotel in Linz, Austria, the different hosts were highly individual and unrelated spaces within the city. With vastly divergent characteristics from one to the next they included a part of a barge, the top of a crane, a passageway in a medieval corridor and a section of an art gallery. The adaptive reuse of these disparate spaces as one single project was not achieved by a physical strategy, as in Dresden, but by an abstract one. In a novel model of hospitality, the many different spaces spread across the city have become rooms unified by a concept in which the entire city serves as the hotel. (figs. 19a–b)

With the many opportunities to reuse and adapt different types of host structures, adaptive reuse practice is unique for "for its requirement of the taking of a stand in the transformation of architecture in space and time. The rehabilitation of works of the past forces us to read a building as the sum of different juxtaposed texts, in which the new intervention is another chapter of its long history."[5]

1 Alois Riegl, "The Modern Cult of Monuments: Its Essence and Its Development," in Nicholas Price, M. Kirby Talley, Jr., and Alessandra Melucco Vacarro, eds., *Historical and Philosophical Issues in the Conservation of Cultural Heritage* (Los Angeles: The Getty Conservation Institute, 1996), p. 72. 2 Luis Sacristán Murga, "Between Memory and Invention: An Interview with Nieto Sobejano Arquitectos," in *Int|AR Journal of Interventions & Adaptive Reuse*, Vol. 06, 2015, p. 98. 3 Ian Chilvers, *The Oxford Dictionary of Art and Artists* (Oxford: Oxford University Press, 2009), p. 448. 4 Oxford Dictionaries, http://www.oxforddictionaries.com/us/definition/american_english/entity (accessed July 14, 2016). 5 Sacristán Murga, p. 98.

We are defined by our genes—the basic units of heredity. Made up of DNA, genes are "instructions" inherited from our parents. While most genes are the same in all people, a few of them differ slightly between persons. These small differences in the varying forms of the same gene contribute to the individuality of each person.[1] The architectural elements of structure, circulation, systems and facade are the basic units that identify all buildings—their bones, blood vessels, organs and skin. As slight genetic differences differentiate persons from one to the next, differences in these architectural elements differentiate one building from the next. Eyes are differentiated by color, shape, size and even expression as windows are differentiated by shape, size, detail, style of frame and type of glass.

The human body, like the host structure, is often a site for rehabilitation and intervention. With new technologies in medicine, such interventions include prosthesis, organ transplant, skin graft and joint replacements, which each have their counterpart in adaptive reuse interventions such as addition, systems replacement, new facade and transfer beams. The success of operations such as organ replacement and prosthetic placement are dependent on a perfect match of the slight differences in defining characteristics such as blood type, size of skeleton and type of skin. Even a complete correspondence is no guarantee of success. Successful adaptive reuse in the form of renovations, extensions and additions similarly requires a correspondence between the new intervention and the defining and characteristic elements of the host structure.

In Shelley's novel *Frankenstein: Or the Modern Prometheus*, a monster resulted from an assemblage of random body parts. As a derivation of the Latin word *monstrum*, "monster" has the additional connotation of "portent," that Cicero defines as "a sign, usually some disruption of the natural order,

Considering DNA

08

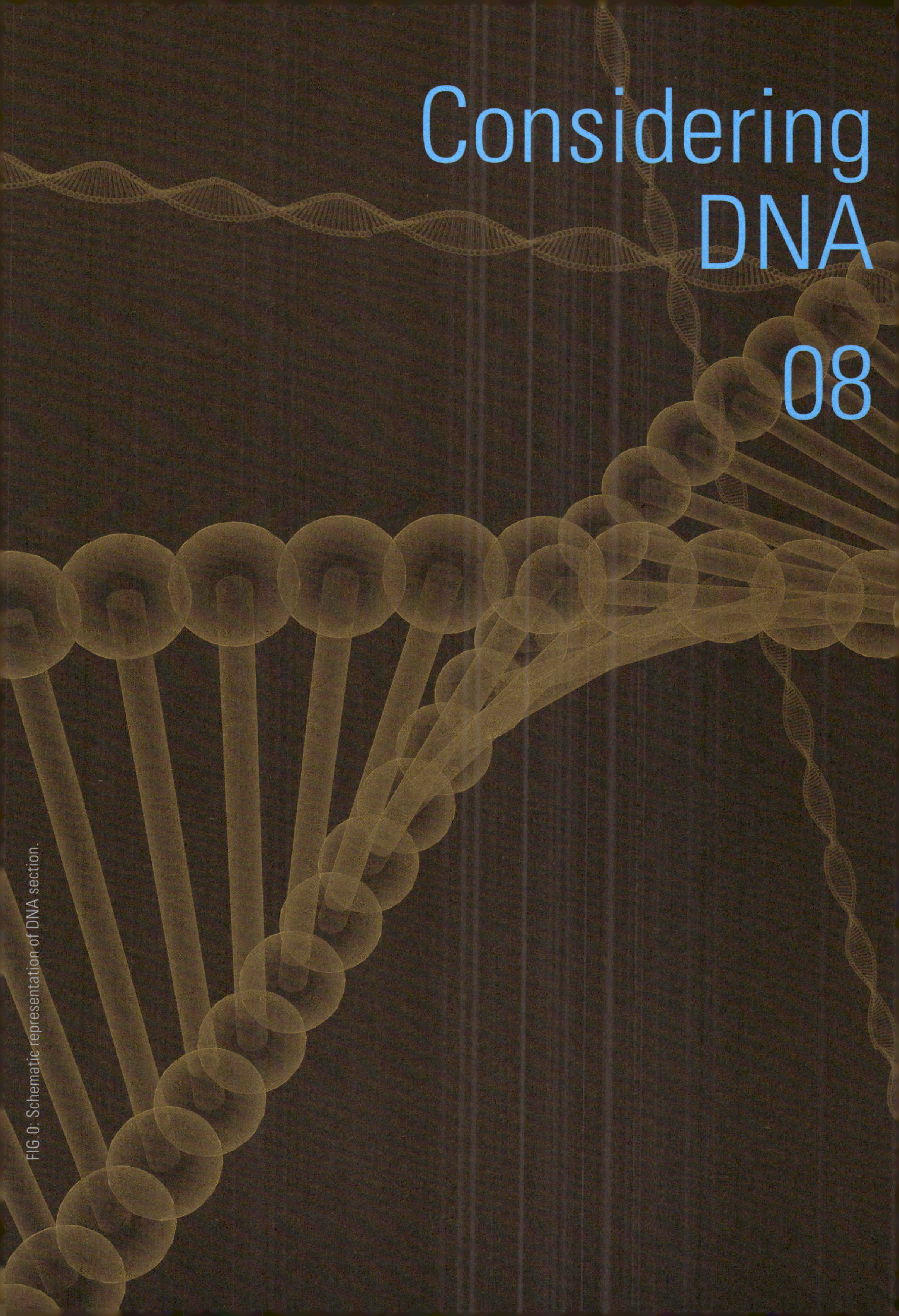

FIG. 0: Schematic representation of DNA section.

FIG. 1: No one would dream of adding to the work of Leonardo da Vinci.

sent by the gods to show that they were displeased."[2] In this sense, Frankenstein in an adaptive reuse analogy equates to an intervention strategy that disrupts the natural order of the host structure. There is no expectation that one should paint on the Mona Lisa, add a splatter to a Jackson Pollock or an appendage to a Noguchi. Yet we transform and add to buildings from nondescript warehouses to heritage such as Notre-Dame de Paris. If intervention to existing buildings distinguishes architecture from other arts, what in adaptive reuse constitutes a successful intervention within a building's natural order that is worthy of the arts? (fig. 1)

Rehabilitation, refurbishment and renovation (without a change of purpose) typically modernize an old structure. Varying in degrees of change, these operations take place within an existing confine and update a pre-established order. They are distinguished from adaptive reuse as interventions that assume and maintain the existing use of the building. Adaptive reuse, defined as the renovation and reuse of pre-existing structures for new purposes, requires the introduction of the new within the established order of the existing.

As a term of the 1970s, adaptive reuse not only references a time in which the scarcity of resources emerged as a global issue but also a turbulent one of change which witnessed the manifestation of many idealistic protests of the previous decade. In the realm of urban planning, it was a time of opposition to urban renewal programs introduced in the 1940s and 1950s that authorized "loans and grants to localities to assist locally initiated, locally planned and locally managed slum clearance and urban redevelopment undertakings"[3] "to aid in the ... elimination and prevention of slums."[4] While Jane

FIG.2: The Clock Tower Gallery on the top of the New York Life Insurance Company Building by McKim, Mead & White.

Jacobs' seminal 1961 *Death and Life of Great American Cities* voiced opposition to this type of urban renewal, which often affected the most disadvantaged, it was not until the early 1970s that this disaffection became action. In particular, the U.S. Department of Housing and Urban Development (HUD) enacted the Community Development Block Grant in 1974, which allocated funds for the rehabilitation of housing and commercial buildings. In this context, one of HUD's longest-running programs, large cities such as New York pursued various initiatives, including one to "Reuse Vacant Space in Existing Buildings."[5] Art entrepreneur Alanna Heiss pioneered adaptive reuse practice as we know it today in her efforts to rehabilitate "derelict warehouses and unused city-owned property in an environment reeling from blight and decay, creating nonprofit art spaces that blurred the lines between studio, gallery, theater and community center."[6] These initial instances of reuse included the 1972 founding of an artists' gallery in the clock tower of the 19th-century McKim, Mead & White New York Life Insurance Company Building in Lower Manhattan (that was subsequently designated a historic landmark in the 1980s), the reuse of a condemned pier beneath the Brooklyn

FIGS.3a–b: The abandoned Queens Public School No.1 is now MoMA PS1, one of the oldest contemporary art institutions in the USA.

Bridge and the reuse of the abandoned First Ward School or Queens Public School No. 1 (PS1) in Long Island City as the Institute for Art and Urban Resources, Inc., an organization devoted to organizing exhibitions in underutilized and abandoned spaces across New York City. As part of Heiss' 1971 Brooklyn Bridge Event, artists found "inspiration (and materials) from the gritty Manhattan waterfront ... and constructed their works over a period of three days."[7] *Rooms*, the first exhibit at PS1, was an invitation to 78 artists "to transform the building's unique spaces into site-specific art."[8] This included the work of artists such as Richard Tuttle, Sol LeWitt and Gordon Matta-Clark. Matta-Clark's installation consisted of cuts in the floor at the threshold of three doors, one on each of three floors, consecutively aligned one on top of the next. The cuts of the size and shape of a door created an illusion of door openings in an unexpected location. The intended confusion created by thresholds that led to openings in the floor is one that is dependent on its location. Such an installation is an instance of making informed responses to site-specific conditions, one that takes into account the building's DNA. It is a forerunner of the kind of informed intervention required in a significant adaptive reuse intervention to a host structure. (figs. 2, 3a–b)

Actions of Interventions

In adaptive reuse, design interventions as responses to the unique DNA of structures can best be understood as actions. These actions are operations that create a new user experience through very different types of interface with the host. Harkening back to the early site-specific art installations of the 1970s, these actions can be categorized as passive, performative and referential. These concepts are best illustrated in their purest form by projects of art and art installations in site-specific locations.

FIG. 4: Rachel Whiteread, *Ghost*, 1990, Plaster on steel frame, 106 × 140 × 125 in (269 × 35 × 318 cm).

The Passive

Rachel Whiteread's *Ghost* is a casting of the interior of a Victorian parlor in an abandoned building in North London. Part of an early body of work that included plaster castings of domestic objects, *Ghost* was a casting attempted at a much larger scale. The cast of each wall of the parlor resulted in a set of new plaster walls made of the negative space of each original wall. Assembled on a steel frame as a box, these four cast walls provide a new experience of the old parlor; one in which the user can only experience through the new. Without impingement upon the existing space, the new "object of walls" allows the spectator to create a different relationship with the past. *Ghost* is a metaphor for the interventions within host buildings that do not act upon the integrity of the structure. Rather, they transform the host structure to provide a novel experience while leaving the existing relatively unchanged. (fig. 4)

The interior retrofit as discussed in the chapter *Hosts [and Guests]* is a prime example of this type of action. Projects of tenant fit-up such as the Apple Store comprise the application of an interior template to building shells in ubiquitous locations. The iconic white interior of a sea of minimal tables displaying varying Apple devices is uniquely recognizable in shopping malls

FIGS.5a–b: The Apple Store, identifiable anywhere in the world, is exemplary of the interior retrofit.

around the world as well as in site-specific locations. Implementation of this standard requires a layout of FF&E *within* the structural grid of the host. The characteristic features of the host—with the exception of the structural system itself—have been suppressed in the service of the production of the new image. Most interior renovations of this type that take place within passive existing building shells similarly require little structural intervention, thereby leaving the "DNA" of the host intact. The retrofit is a temporary experience that is continuously reinvented within the brief and numerous cycles of the host's life. (figs. 5a–b)

FIG.6: *Splitting*, Gordon Matta-Clark, 1974.

The Performative

The host for Gordon Matta-Clark's project *Splitting*, like Whiteread's *Ghost*, is an abandoned domestic structure. Awaiting demolition, 322 Humphrey Street in Englewood, New Jersey, USA, was an ordinary 1930s two-story home with front and back porches. Matta-Clark's now iconic actions with a chainsaw, in which he cuts open the side of the balloon frame structure from top to bottom, revealing it from inside to outside, offer numerous interpretations. From a historic point of view, *Splitting* is a social commentary on conformity and the failure of architecture (and housing) in the era of post-war reintegration in America. As a work of sited art, *Splitting* symbolically severed the idea of home. As a film, *Splitting* documents the spectacle of a man physically engaged with a construction tool, a performance in which both Matta-Clark and the house perform. The house undergoes "a brief change of state executed with care and precision, which gives it a new life ... before the final destruction."[9] This "brief change of state" aptly applies also to those adaptive reuse interventions that require the host to transform; from an incomplete state to a whole one, from one programmatic use to a different one, from one type to another. Unlike the *passive* action, in which the character of the host is suppressed, the *performative* one requires participation of the existing structure. A term often embedded today in the culture of digital technology, the application of "the performative" in adaptive reuse may be understood as an analog interpretation: "Form [in performative action] is animated, acting and interacting with the surrounding object/forms

FIG.7: The *Yellow House* in Flims by Valerio Olgiati is white in its new life.

and the human subject, creating possibilities for the emergence of new realities."[10] (fig. 6)

Interventions that require a performative response of the host mandate a reckoning with its DNA. As host structures are entrenched in the principles of their own architecture—structural elements, material properties, spatial sequences, organizing lines, geometries, proportions—the reuse of an existing structure means to alter this architecture and modify its principles. From renovation to a new use to extension and addition, these modifications are visible signals of change through a physical expression of such intent. Viollet-le-Duc's decision to restore to a state that may never have existed was, in part, a response to the dilemma presented by the existence of several stylistically unique renovations and extensions within one existing structure. The Cathedral of Notre-Dame de Paris, for example, built between the 12th and 14th centuries, included many differing aspects of the developing Gothic style. This issue at the center of many critical discussions in the 19th century—which style to restore to—is at the heart of every extension and addition project today. How does a new form emerge from within the existing structure?

These issues are apparent in, for example, the extensions of facades. The whitewashing of the Yellow House in Flims, Switzerland, designed by Valerio Olgiati, intentionally signals the progression of time with the change of the iconic color of this alpine hut. The addition of a new glass skin over the existing 1908 masonry facade at the 185 Post Building in San Francisco, California, USA, instead further expands the role of the facade. The creation of a double wall system enabled the outmoded host building to meet energy efficiency requirements through natural light, thermal and acoustic

FIG.8: The 1908 facade is preserved in 185 Post Street Building in San Francisco, CA.

FIG.9: David Chipperfield's stone facade at Joachimstrasse 11 in Berlin responds to its neighboring context.

insulation, while establishing its identity as caretaker of the historic facade below. At the Chipperfield office in Berlin, Germany, the infill designed by the architect completes anew the deep plot of the site of an 1895 piano factory, severely bombed in the war. The new facade of the street block completes the street front with proportions and materials responding to the proportions of its neighbors while striking "a balance between re-establishing the typical pre-war courtyard structure, and a post-war configuration of solitary buildings."[11] Each intervention strategy, though uniquely different, reanimates its host through an acknowledgment of some part of its defining principles. (figs. 7, 8, 9)

While the first debates between the proponents of restoration and conservation are still relevant in this matter of intervention strategy, the architectural pluralism of the present day has expanded and further muddied the limit of possibilities. Extension "in the style of" recalls the same objections as "in the style of"-type restorations in the 19th century. The lack of truth in replicating a style of another time is universal. When designing 300 years later, how does one work within the regulating lines of an 18th-century facade? Within a facade in which the apertures were previously dictated by the confines of the then structural capabilities, how does one add openings today? What are the responsibilities for extending and adding when present-day structural capabilities allow the addition of a physical mass exceeding that of the host? How much of a host structure can be removed or obscured before its identity is entirely obfuscated? In approaching these questions, two critical issues face the architects and designers of the extensions and additions of adaptive reuse: first, the need to take a stance on time within a host structure already characterized by a form, material and organizational identity and, second, with already many authors within a single work, the weight of one's authorship on the host.

The Referential

Wounds and cracks have long been a focus of the work of Alberto Burri. These themes of trauma witnessed during the Second World War have been explored in his paintings in numerous media from paint to burlap to tar and Celotex. They are present in his life-size installation *Cretto di Burri* in Gibellina, Sicily, Italy. Upon the site of the 1968 Belice earthquake, in which the town of Gibellina was destroyed, Burri erected a series of concrete forms, the approximate height of a human being, that resemble a three-dimensional version of one of his canvases, spread onto a sloping countryside. Cracks are present in this labyrinth of concrete as "streets" that reference and memorialize the layout of the felled town. (fig. 10)

Cretto importantly demonstrates the relationship of the artist's concept to the confines of a specific site. In adaptive reuse this relationship is critical for an intervention that in its engagement with the structure is respectful of the host DNA. Herzog & de Meuron's project at the Park Avenue Armory in New York City, New York, USA, demonstrates such a relationship. Their work within the landmark building comprised the delayering and revealing of marks on the walls and surfaces within the many historic rooms. But it also included very subtle interventions in the form of gilt overprinting of pattern over pattern—their 21st-century interpretation superimposed upon the existing

FIG.10: *Cretto di Burri*, Alberto Burri, 1984.

FIGS.11a–b: Herzog & de Meuron's *delayering* at the Park Avenue Armory, New York City, NY (left, new; right, original).

layers. In this, their "microscopic" intervention, Jacques Herzog stated that "[w]e are treating the Armory like a monument, preserving it for the future and above all reinventing it."[12] (figs. 11a–b)
At a different scale, the discovery of 1st-century Roman ruins together with Celtiberian 2nd-century BC ruins in the site of a proposed parking lot in Daroca, Spain, inspired the design of an entire civic building focused on the presence of such history. The design is connected in an intricate sectional scheme referencing and revealing the layers of the city's visible histories. A series of glimpses lead the visitor through the building and to the ruins, including tiny pinprick openings in the surface of the plaza above, points that reference the exact placement of the ruins several layers below. (figs. 12a–d)
In contrast to the passive and performative actions, the referential action re-animates the host structure through design strategies and interventions that are co-dependent with its past, incorporating what was with what is.
Many factors make for a rich relationship between host structure and its new use, enabling a host structure's DNA to be perpetuated into the future. A disregard for these factors results in the end of the line, so to speak. An initial assessment of specific characteristics of the host must be a starting point of every adaptive reuse strategy. By examining such characteristics and acknowledging their presence in the host structures, we gain an understanding of how to alter its prevailing framework. As "[a]rt is the child of nature ... in whom we trace [t]he features of the mothers face...,"[13] so in an adaptive reuse project one should be able to trace the features of its host.

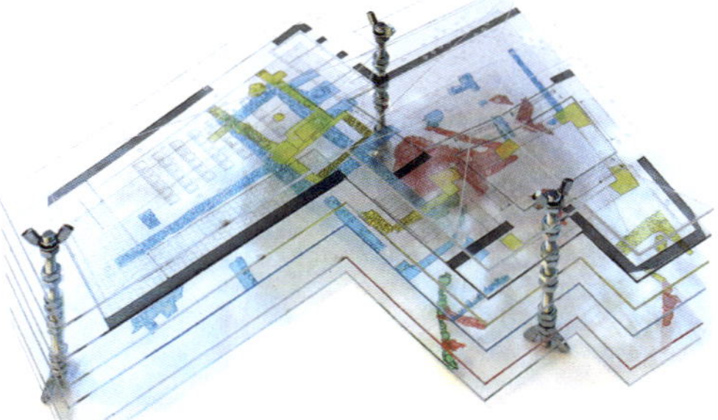

FIGS. 12a–d: Sergio Sebastián Franco's Archaeological Space in Daroca is an intervention that connects the DNA of thousands of years.

1 http://ghr.nlm.nih.gov/handbook/ 2 Cicero (transl. David Wardle), *Cicero: On Divination (De Divinatione)* Book 1 (Oxford: Oxford University Press, 2006), p. 102. 3 Summary of Provisions of the National Housing Act of 1949, Committee on Banking and Currency U.S. Senate, U.S. Government Printing Office, Washington, DC, 1949, p. 1. 4 Public Law 560—August 2, 1954, U.S. Government Printing Office, Washington, DC, 1954, p. 1. 5 Economic Recover, New York City's program for 1977–81, U.S. Department of Commerce NOAA, p. 48. 6 "Introduction," The Artist in Place: The First 10 Years of MoMA PS 1, https://www.moma.org/interactives/exhibitions/2012/artistinplace/ 7 Alana Miller, "From the Records of MoMA PS1: The 40th Anniversary of The Brooklyn Bridge Event," Collection & Exhibitions, Library and Archives, MOMA PS1, June 27, 2011. http://www.moma.org/explore/inside_out/2011/06/27/from-the-records-of-moma-ps1-the-40th-anniversary-of-the-brooklyn-bridge-event (accessed December 7, 2015). 8 MoMA PS1 Profile, http://momaps1.org/about/ (accessed December 7, 2015). 9 Imogen Racz, "Gordon Matta-Clark, *Splitting* and the Unmade House," The IB Tauris Blog, January 26, 2015 (accessed December 7, 2015). 10 Yasha Grobman and Eran Neuman, "Performalism: a manifesto for architectural performance," in Grobman & Neuman, eds., *Performalism: Form and Performance in Digital Architecture*, (Routledge, 2011), p. 4. 11 http://www.davidchipperfield.co.uk/project/joachimstrasse (accessed December 7, 2015). 12 Gerhard Mack, ed., *Herzog & de Meuron, Transforming Park Avenue Armory New York* (Basel: Birkhäuser, 2014), p. 314. 13 Henry Wadsworth Longfellow, *Kéramos & Other Poems* (Cambridge, UK: Houghton, Osgood & Company, 1878), p. 23.

Science claims genetic inheritance as a main determinant of who we are. Psychology, sociology, philosophy refute this claim in favor of the influence of environment. Disputing the merits of innate qualities to those of experience, the nature vs. nurture debate is an ongoing one, with truth on both sides. In the chapter *Considering DNA*, we discussed the DNA of host buildings as possible determinants of intervention strategies for new use. What of the *tabula rasa* of John Locke and the "EXPERIENCE. [I]n that all our knowledge is founded; and from that it ultimately derives itself"?[1] Many structures and spaces are renovated or reused in succession, as differing building programs, each independent of the previous. Does the experience derived from the use of a structure impress itself upon the structure, affecting the implementation of a different future use?
By definition, adaptive reuse is characterized by the DNA of an existing host structure and, with it, the physical evidence of a previous user or users. This physical evidence is found in renovation, refurbishment or extension with the demolition of any part of the existing structure. The removal of even a simple partition leaves a telltale trace on both the ground and the ceiling: a scar defined by the depth and thickness of framing members and finishes. In this sense, the host structure has been analogized to a palimpsest, in which ghost traces of writing are faintly perceptible within an old manuscript scraped for reuse. Traces of war, in the form of bullet marks and destroyed patches of plaster, form the basis of David Chipperfield's intervention strategy in the rebuilding of the Neues Museum in Berlin, Germany, from a burnt post-war semi-ruin. Preserving these scars of war through the meticulous salvage of bullet holes and bits of destroyed brick and plaster, woven with insertions of new large-format prefabricated concrete, is a "multidisciplinary interaction between repairing, conserving, restoring and recreating."[2] This

Ghosts 09

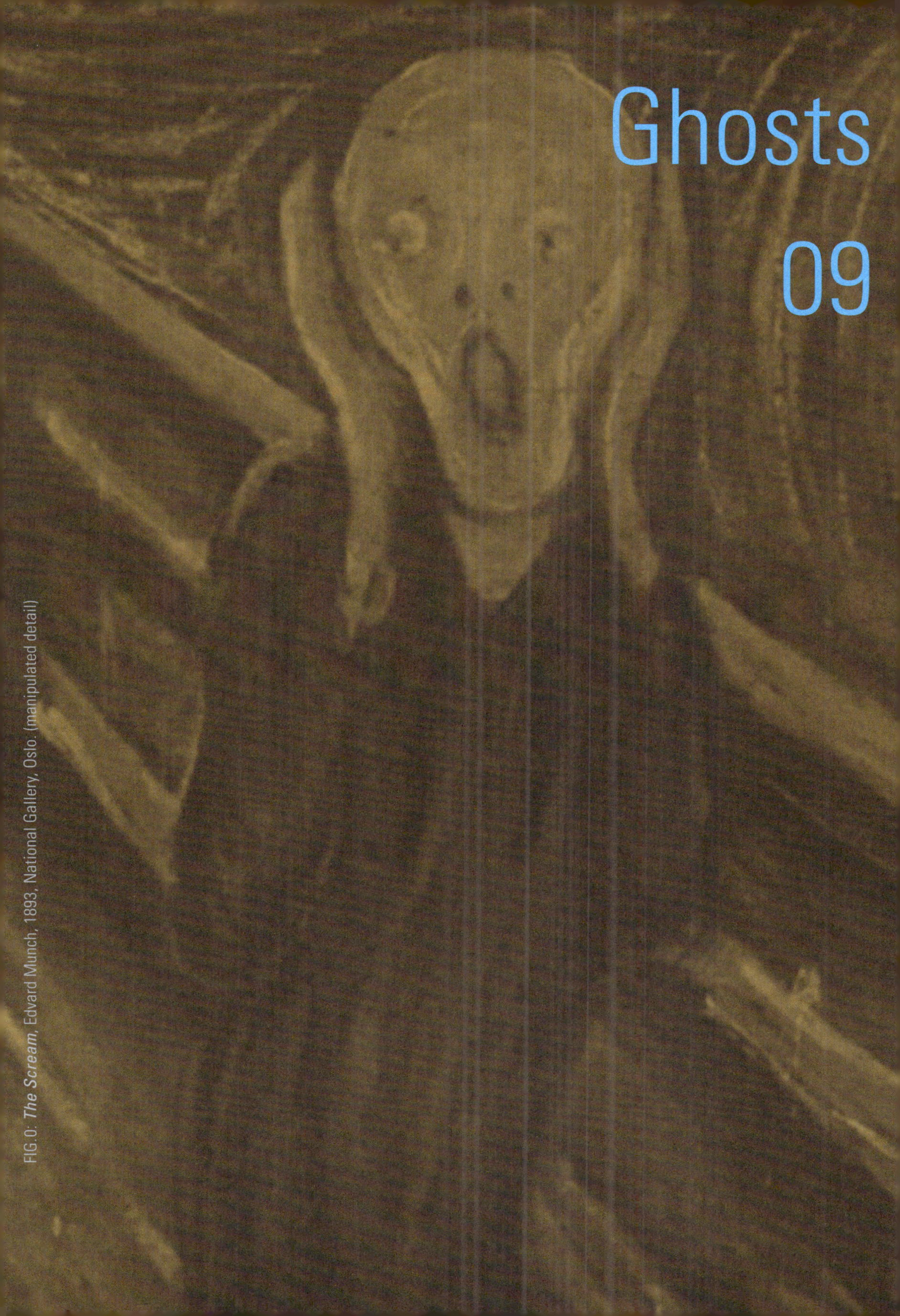

FIG.0: ***The Scream***, Edvard Munch, 1893, National Gallery, Oslo. (manipulated detail)

FIGS. 1a–b: David Chipperfield's intervention inside the Neues Museum, Berlin, embraces the traces of war.

juxtaposition, in which "the contemporary reflects the lost but without imitating it"[3] allows the past to co-inhabit the space of the present, without erasure or recriminations. (figs. 1a–b)

Programs of use with function-specific spaces also leave traces. Characterized by the particularity of a ritual of use, the spaces within any given program are interrelated to form a unified whole. An example is the program of a Christian church, one that culminates at the altar in a transformation of bread and wine to the body and blood of Christ. The architecture corroborates this ceremony with a choreographed sequence of procession, from west to east and from nave to transept, concluding at the altar and the radiating chapels. The main altar of the church, the site of transubstantiation, and the radiating chapels, the place for the miraculous relics of martyrs, are imbued with the liturgical implications of the Christian faith. This highly charged program of use, with its centuries-old significance, asserts its presence through time, space, and new use. The complexity of introducing a new purpose to such a space requires a synthesis of the significance of a previous use with the needs of a new program. In the conversion of the 13th-century Dominican church in Maastricht, Netherlands, to the Selexyz bookstore, the place of the altar is programmed as a wine bar, referencing in a boldly ironic move the transubstantiation of wine. The conversion of an Italian church to a mechanic's garage places the pneumatic hoisting jack at the site of the altar, where the transformed host is lifted to the heavens at the consecration. These instances re-appropriate meaning within a highly charged space. Such strategies are overlays that connect to previous traces of "writing" within a palimpsest. They acknowledge a past significance and engage it in a new context.

FIGS.2a–b: The Selexyz Bookstore wine bar, located at the altar of the former Dominican church.

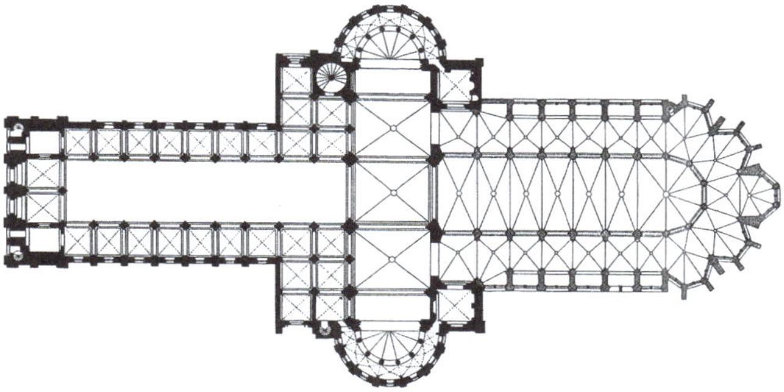

This reuse approach perpetuates the spirit of the host, allowing for a continuum through time. In contrast, the insertion of many new levels within the vast height of a sacred space in a church-to-condominium conversion denies the previous existence by obliterating the charged space itself. (figs. 2a–b)
The traces of a past existence as DNA within a host structure are tangible and therefore comprehensible. They are ghosts that make themselves known as faint outlines of the past. They can serve as parameters for the formulation of new interventions. What, however, of the intangible traces of experience within an existing space? Do structures absorb and retain the memory of events that take place within them? Do memories assert themselves when subject to a new context? Are these traces of a different nature that can inform the strategies of reuse?
Structures subjected to difficult experiences result in a unique form of afterlife, one in which the host dictates the parameters of future use. These too are ghosts—apparitions of the dead "believed to appear or become manifest to the living."[4] Offering a different immortality, ghosts roam for various reasons; some are stranded in time and others haunt. Popular culture and even religious practices address those spirits who wander as a result of devastating experience, with exorcisms and other attempts to lay such ghosts to rest. Buildings are also subject to destructive and devastating experiences, as prisons, torture chambers, concentration camps, hangman's scaffold. Do such deeds transcend time and materials? Can such structures be gainfully reused? How do these buildings haunt?
The conversions of two penitentiaries, each with its own lengthy history, demonstrate very different specters within one building typology. Incarcer-

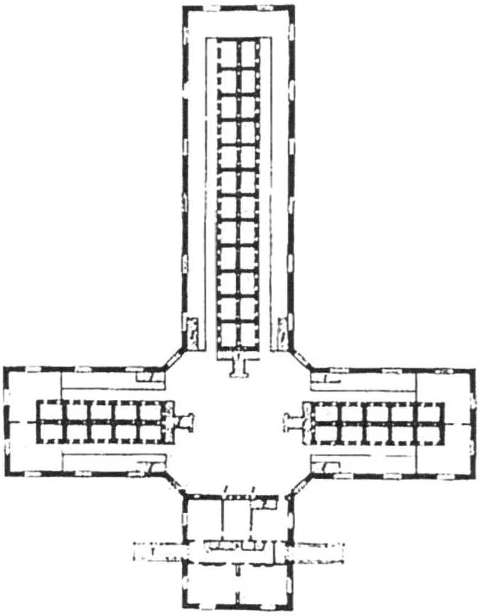

Massachusetts
Eye and Ear
Infirmary

FIGS.3a–e: The Charles Street Jail and the Liberty Hotel in Boston, MA, are connected in time through a transformation based on spatial typology and use.

ation is a product of a society and the penal code its social and legal system. With societies differing from one to the next, modes of incarceration reflect these differences. In Boston, Massachusetts, USA, the Charles Street Jail is part of a long history of American penal reform. Built in the era of prison development, the jail is most recognized as an example of the "Boston Granite Style." The octagonal building complex houses an atrium, catwalks, and jail cells in the centralized prison design style of the time. The new Liberty Hotel repurposes the historic 19th-century Romanesque Revival structure, exploiting its architectural characteristics with deliberation. Once the omniscient central space of a panopticon-like system of jail cells, the 27.4-meter-high atrium is reused as the heart of the hotel and the connective center of its many rooms. Clink, the hotel bar, draws upon the aesthetic of jail cell doors, using these features to place its users in the cells of its infamous past occupants. With spatial parallels drawn, at times, through functional similarities and, at times, through wit, the Charles Street Jail is a benevolent spirit that permits the experience of incarceration to be repackaged as a tool of commerce. As part of a penal system but without untoward incidents, the jail's conversion to luxury accommodations is an interesting example in which the physical remains of incarceration are treated as architectural typology rather than as reminders of a difficult past. (figs. 3a–e)

In contrast is the Carandiru Penitentiary of São Paulo, Brazil, the largest in South America. Built to meet the 1890 criminal code, the prison was the site of riot resulting from poor conditions and culminating in a police massacre of 111 prisoners. Parts of the prison complex were demolished to erase the site of what is noted in Brazil's history as one of the worst violations of human rights. The remaining buildings were converted for new use as programs that gave back to the community: a technical school, a library and a youth park. Elements of the penitentiary—certain walls, the guard tower—remain, scattered within the park and used as canvas for graffiti art. Unlike its counterpart in Boston, the Carandiru Penitentiary conversion was necessitated by the need to appease the ghosts of the massacre.

Structures that witness such acts of inhumanity are limited in reuse potential by their experience. Auschwitz or S-21, the jail cells of Pol Pot in Cambodia, for example, hold innumerable and different ghosts that haunt. Konzentrationslager Auschwitz became the largest of the death camps of the Second World War in Germany and has since "become a symbol of terror, genocide and the Holocaust."[5] Once a school built to the principles of Le Corbusier, the Chao Ponhea Yat High School was converted to S-21 (Security Prison 21), the torture chambers of the Khmer Rhouge, witnessing unspeakable acts. Today the remaining structures of S-21 and Auschwitz, saturated with the memories of brutality, are structures without the reprieve of reuse. They can only serve as witness. As living but immobilized history, they unwittingly become a place of remembrance. The death camps of Auschwitz, now

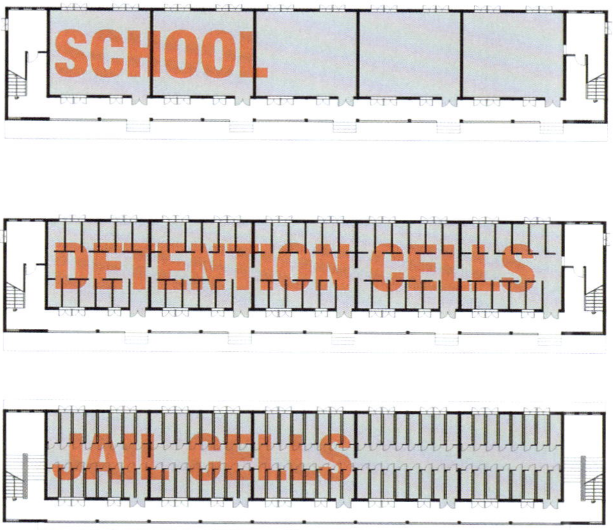

FIGS.4a–b: S-21, transformed from a school to a place of torture, can serve only one possible use today: a place of witness and remembrance.

Auschwitz-Birkenau Memorial and Museum in Poland, and S-21, now the Tuol Sleng Genocide Museum in Cambodia, are a unique category of Alois Riegl's unintentional monuments. As memorials they serve a redemptive role. (figs. 4a–b, 5a–b)

Until recently, this redemption equated to a convertibility limited to remembrance and memorial. In 2015, however, the humanitarian crisis created by the Syrian refugee exodus to Europe brought about a pioneering reuse of similar structures for a different program. Prompted by the housing shortage, the garden buildings of Dachau were converted to refugee accommodations, breaking a long and unspoken taboo. This reuse of buildings of the former concentration camp was controversial, tempered only by the plight of those

FIGS.5a–b: Auschwitz-Birkenau Memorial and Museum.

without shelter. In this sense, the need to alleviate even a small part of a human tragedy has helped to expand the role of an otherwise inconvertible typology. (fig. 6)

Ghosts of more distant trauma offer redemption of a different kind. The city of Nantes, France, was France's principal slave port in the 18th century, with more than 1400 voyages to Africa.[6] The Memorial to the Abolition of Slavery repurposes the understructure of the Quai de la Fosse, the wharves from which these ships sailed. A 7,000-square-meter pathway inserted below the wharves together with 2,000 glass plaques recall details of the slave trade in unbiased light. This information, from the names of the trading posts to personal accounts to abolitionist texts, brings a new awareness of this difficult past while recreating below ground the confinement of

FIG.6: Is there another possible use for the grounds or buildings of a former concentration camp?

FIGS.7a–b: The transformation of the former slave ship port in Nantes to the Memorial to the Abolition of Slavery.

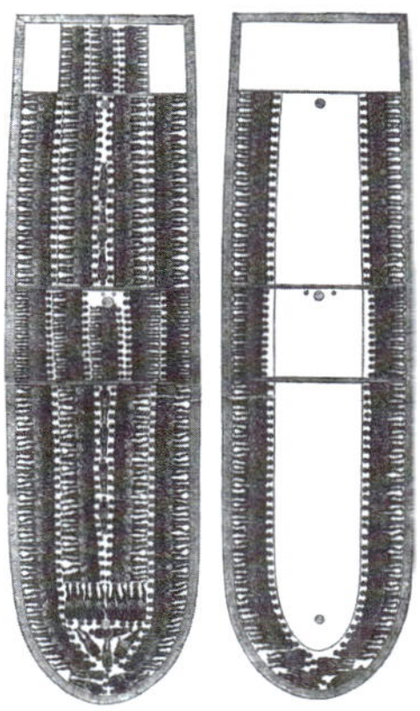

the ships. This project of adaptive reuse offers another form of redemption, in which new use serves a didactic role as well as that of remembrance. (figs. 7a–b)

Another example lies in the many ghosts conjured by the site of the Berlin Palace in Germany. Once the imperial residence of the last kings of Prussia, the palace lost its official purpose with the abdication of the monarchy in 1918. The fate of the structure perhaps would have been that of any other European imperial palace, as a national symbol, had it not been partially destroyed in the bombing of Berlin. Its significance as a symbol of Prussian rule in divided East Berlin, under the protection of the Soviets, eliminated the possibility of reconstruction, despite resistance from the West: it was razed in 1950 and 25 years later replaced by the Palace of the Republic, the

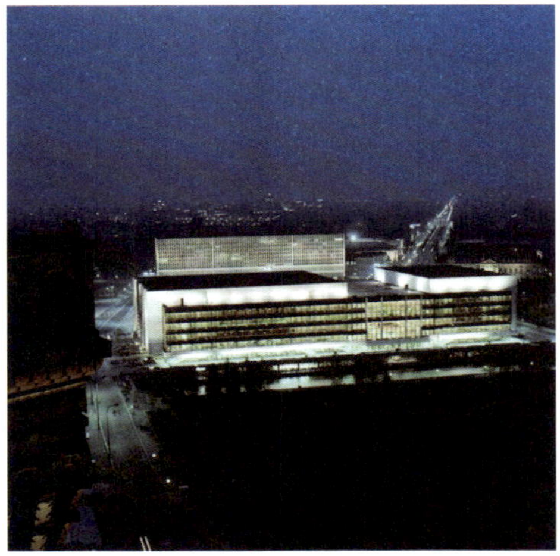

FIGS. 8a–b: The site of the Berlin City Palace once accommodated the seat of the Prussian kings and subsequently the Communists Palace of the Republic under the GDR.

seat of Parliament for the German Democratic Republic. With the reunification, the existence of the Palace of the Republic was now questioned as a remnant of Soviet rule. Like the Berlin Palace before it, the existence of the Palace of the Republic had become a reminder of a different past, maybe posing a symbolic threat to the newly reunified government. A ghost to be eliminated, the discovery of asbestos within the building justified its demolition amidst controversial and polarizing discussions on its significance in the new Berlin. The future Humboldt Forum will rise upon the footprint of the imperial residence, replicating three facades of the old palace. Without the need for a royal residence or a seat of government, it will instead serve the public as a cultural space. A modern facade design on the river's edge and functions within the palace courtyard are symbols of change stamped upon the old, as harbingers of a new phase of history. The ongoing tale of this site and the roles of the different ghosts it conjures demonstrate the complexity of experience and the longevity of its effect on a host structure over time. (figs. 8a–b)

According to the 20th-century philosopher Henri Bergson, pure memory or remembrance is in the past and separated from the body. In the example of the Berlin Palace, memories remain even when the matter has been destroyed, with potential repercussions reverberating into the future. The 9/11 Memorial in New York City, New York, USA, to remember and honor the victims of the 2001 terrorist attack, focuses on the preservation of absence. The memorial comprises a field of trees and two large pools set within the

FIG.9: The 9/11 Memorial in New York City, NY, by Michael Arad, in accordance with the master plan of Daniel Libeskind.

sunken footprint of the Twin Towers that were destroyed in the attack. These voids are surrounded by parapets, engraved with the names of the victims and serving as barriers at the water's edge. Named "Reflecting Absence," the memorial mediates between the present and what was lost. Homage to the invisible, this gesture demonstrates the power of ghosts that haunt from a distance. (fig. 9)

In adaptive reuse, where every project is premised on a pre-existing set of circumstances, the effect of past experience on new interventions of reuse is equally viable as physical traces of the past. Ghosts that haunt are opportunities for a particular type of architectural intervention, although these occasions, like the corporeal specters, are few and far between. Ghostly traces, however, exist in every project large and small. It is in the consideration of both types of ghosts that meaningful adaptive reuse strategies are found—ones that exemplify perception as "master of space in the exact measure in which action is the master of time."[7]

1 John Locke, *An Essay Concerning Human Understanding*, Book 2, Chapter 1 (London: Printed by Eliz. Holt, for Thomas Basset, MDCXC). 2 http://www. davidchipperfield.co.uk/project/neues_museum (accessed February 22, 2016). 3 Ibid. 4 Oxford Dictionaries, http://www.oxforddictionaries.com/us/definition/american_english/ghost (accessed February 16, 2016). 5 http://auschwitz.org/en/history/ (accessed February 16, 2016). 6 "Breaking the Silence: Learning about the Transatlantic Slave Trade," http://old.antislavery.org/breakingthesilence/slave_routes/slave_routes_france.shtml (accessed February 16, 2016). 7 Henri Bergson (transl. Nancy Margaret Paul and W. Scott Palmer), *Matter and Memory* (London: George Allen and Unwin, 1911), p. 11.

In 2015, the 100-year-old abandoned church of Santa Barbara in Asturias, Spain, was saved from demolition and transformed to a skate park with the insertion of wooden skating ramps that span from side of church to side of church. An escalator leading to the lobby of Copenhagen's Skt. Petri Hotel recalls its 2003 conversion from the 1930s Danish shopping mall Dælls Varehus. Change of use is at the heart of adaptive reuse practice that gives new purpose to an unused or underutilized structure. From the common conversion of residential space to the ubiquitous home-office, from the grand conversions of Roman baths to cathedral, or from grain storage facility to library, it is an operation both familiar and extraordinary. At many scales of transformation, change of use refers to the common process within a given structure of exchanging one type of activity for another or, in the case of an unused building or ruin, bringing it back to life. (figs. 1, 2)

Defined as the intended purpose (or purposes) of a building or part thereof, use is determined by the many spaces within a given structure. The design of these different spaces—their sizes and relationships to each other—is an interpretation of the architectural program, a document translating a client's needs for a building into spatial terms. It can be a simple set of square footage requirements determined by the client. It can also be a product of a programming service that includes an elaborate process of goal-setting, value identification and expert consultations. No matter its form or complexity, the architectural program defines a building's use by identifying all required spaces and their intended occupants, establishing the size of each space and the relationship between them and providing a framework of efficiency for accommodating these spaces within a building.

The architectural program document facilitates the design of a building or space, both as new construction and in adaptive reuse projects. The "bubble

10 Fitting In

FIG.0: The Nikolaj Kunsthal is a Contemporary Art Centre in the former Saint Nicholas Church in Copenhagen.

FIG.1: The entry to Skt. Petri Hotel in Copenhagen.

FIG.2: The converted church of Santa Bárbara in Asturias.

diagram" has traditionally been a method for understanding and visualizing the relationship between the various spaces described in the design brief. With each required space depicted as a circle relative to its intended size, these diagrams of interconnected circles are interpretations of how the different spaces of the building might relate to one another. They stretch in seemingly limitless space, often without acknowledgment of vertical adjacencies. In the last decades, diagramming architectural programs as a tool has expanded in scope. OMA's 1999 proposal for the Seattle Public Library introduced the concept of the architectural program as generator of form. In the now seminal section drawings of the library, the program elements are presented not as "bubbles" but as words of varying font sizes, color, and character that express the scale of each space and its relative adjacencies. While the "bubble diagram" expresses use as a sprawling two-dimensional abstraction, OMA's section diagram speaks to use as inhabiting a three-dimensional form with the limitations of volumetric parameters. This distinction between the two types of diagrams is expressive of the relationship of the architectural program to a new building as opposed to an existing structure. In the former, all is possible within the constraints of site. In the latter, design is dictated, in most part, by the confines of the host structure. (figs 3, 4)

While equally constrained by the limitations of budget and of site, the bases for design of new structures and for adapted existing structures differ in the making of form. In new construction, the form of the building is generated by the accommodation of program elements. The form of adaptive reuse projects

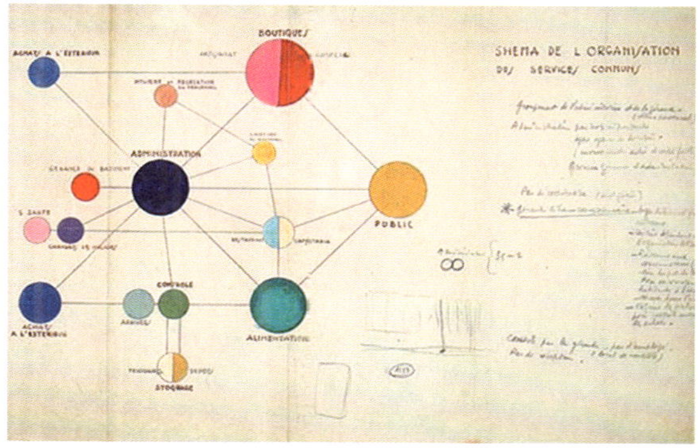

FIG.3: Unité d'habitation, Marseille, 1945, Schéma d'organisation des services communs, Le Corbusier.

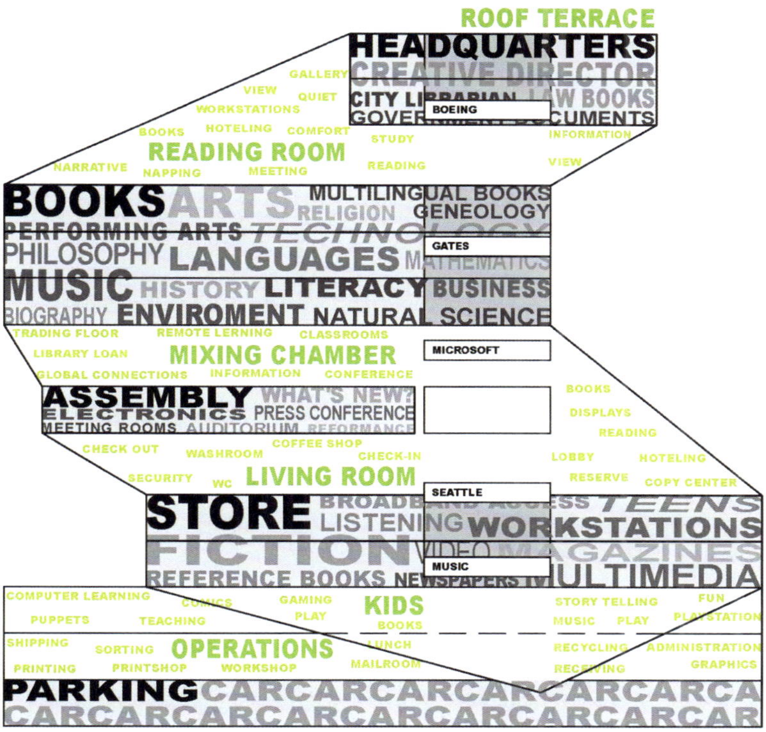

FIG.4: "Legibility Section," OMA's program diagram for the Seattle Central Library, WA, 1999.© OMA

FIG.5: Dresden Military History Museum by Daniel Libeskind.

FIG.6: Elbphilharmonie, Hamburg, by Herzog & de Meuron.

is, instead, primarily predetermined by the form of its host. The primary task lies in accommodating the program elements of use *within* this pre-existing form. Additions to existing structures can certainly transform an existing form in a most dramatic fashion, as exemplified by projects such as the Dresden Military History Museum or the Elbphilharmonie in Hamburg, Germany. Nonetheless, the extended and revised forms are derived from or in response to the host characteristics. In adaptive reuse, the unlimited and expansive nature inherent in the "bubble diagram" has less relevance. Rather, new spatial requirements must be carefully fitted into an existing form. (figs. 5, 6)
From gloves to political affiliation and from schedules to diversity, "fit" has multiple definitions and implications. The consideration of a new use in an existing structure is dependent on "fit" and the potential for intervention. In adaptive reuse, the concept of "fit" yields different interpretations, both objective and subjective. In the most basic sense, "fit" refers to size. The desired size of any architectural project is manifested in the total square footage of the architectural program described in the brief. With new construction, one designs directly to these spatial requirements. In the reuse of an existing structure, one needs to determine the feasibility of accommo-

dating all the necessary program elements within the host. As pre-existing space, this question of physical "fit" is partly determined by the intended use or occupancy. For a full investigation, one must begin with understanding "use" as defined by building regulations.

Building regulations classify all building uses through types of occupancies.[1] In the International Building Code, they are: Group A for Assembly, Group B for Business, Group E for Education, Group F for Factory and Industrial, Group H for Hazardous, Group I for Institutional, Group M for Mercantile, Group R for Residential, Group S for Storage and Group U for Utility and Miscellaneous. (fig. 7)

FIG.7: Assembly Group classifications of the International Building Code.

Assembly occupancies, or Group A, refer to buildings or spaces used for gathering. This group is divided into subgroups that address the act of assembling for social, civic, religious and entertainment purposes. These groups are differentiated by varying factors: the presence of fixed seating, the presence of food or drink, use as worship or amusement, whether the activity is indoors or outdoors. Assembly occupancies include theaters, sports facilities, bars, churches, restaurants, libraries, art galleries, waiting areas of transportation terminals.

Business occupancies, or Group B, refer to buildings or spaces used for offices, professional activities and service transactions. While this category is self-evident with uses such as post office, offices and car wash facilities, it does include airport control towers, outpatient clinics and educational facilities above the 12th grade.

Educational occupancies, or Group E, refer to buildings or spaces used for educational purposes of up to the 12th grade and for more than six occupants.

Factory occupancies, or Group F, refer to buildings or spaces used for different manufacturing activities such as fabricating, assembling, packing and processing, as long as these activities are not hazardous and do not contain a storage use. Such activities are subdivided into moderate and low hazards with critical differences of combustibility. For example, the space for a baker or a luthier, both with some degree of combustibility, is considered moderately hazardous while the space for the production of ceramics or ice is considered low hazard.

High Hazard occupancies, or Group H, similarly refer to manufacturing activities such as that of Group F but are distinguished as those that constitute a health hazard.

Institutional occupancies, or Group I, refer specifically to the use of a building or a space for the care of those who are not capable of self-preservation without supervision. This group is subdivided with differentiations of the user groups: hospitals, detention centers, rehabilitation centers, assisted living centers.

Mercantile occupancies, or Group M, refer to the use of a building or a space for the display and sale of merchandise with the inclusion of some storage of stock.

Residential occupancies, or Group R, refer to the use of a building or a space for sleeping, where it does not constitute a Group I designation. This group is subdivided with distinctions of transiency, numbers of units and numbers of occupants. This group includes hotels, dormitories, convents as well as the single-family home.

Storage occupancies, or Group S, refer to the use of a building or a space for non-hazardous storage. It is subdivided into moderate and low hazard.

Utility occupancies, or Group U, serve as a catchall for accessory buildings. They include airport hangars, barns and garages.

Understanding "use" as a product of occupancy group classifications permits the determination of "fit" in two ways: first, as the number of occupants an existing structure might accommodate for a particular use, and, second, as the size required to accommodate a specific number of occupants for a given use.
For a particular occupancy, a related allowable load factor can be determined through occupancy load charts such as IBC Table 1004.1.2, "Maximum Floor Area Allowances per Occupant."[2] The product of this load factor and the size of the host structure determine the number of occupants allowed within the existing space of the host structure for a particular program of use.

LOAD FACTOR (# OCC/SF) X SIZE OF HOST STRUCTURE (SF)
= ALLOWABLE OCCUPANTS

Conversely, with a pre-determined number of occupants and use, a version of the same equation can be used to calculate the size of host structure required for their accommodation.

DESIRED # OF OCCUPANTS / LOAD FACTOR (# OF OCC/SF)
= SIZE OF REQUIRED HOST STRUCTURE

These simple equations determine physical "fit" as the feasibility of a new program of "use" within a host structure. They can also serve as indicators of the types of interventions required for a project. If the allowable number of occupants or the square footage of the desired spaces exceeds that allowed in the host structure, an addition might be required. If the allowable number of occupants or the total square footage of the desired spaces is far less than that allowed in the host structure, additional program may be added or a subtraction can occur. Such subtractions are opportunities for atriums and other voids in the host structure.
Considering the physical "fit" of space through the lens of economics offers an entirely different outlook. When adaptive reuse is the product of fiscal incentives, the existing structure may serve a role other than host. Tax incentives are oftentimes the drivers of reuse in the conversion of non-heritage structures such as the reuse of schools for housing. In such cases, the viability of the conversion is premised on the potential profit of the venture, in this case, the greatest number of salable units. When the host structure is a landmark building, it may be valued for its authenticity, which in turn serves a role in marketing and branding. Viewed in economic terms, this authenticity is sometimes skin-deep, as space equates to revenue. With "fit"

FIG.8: This conversion of St. Teresa's Church in Watertown, MA, to a condominium complex ultimately distorted its original form.

FIGS.9a–c: The conversion of the Brutalist St. Agnes Church in Berlin to the König Galerie.

FIGS. 10a–b: Reversible interventions transformed the Montemartini thermoelectric center in Rome to the Centrale Montemartini museum.

defined as maximized square footage, the preservation of the assets of a host structure becomes secondary. The church-condominium conversion type illustrates this principle in which the assets of the host, its authenticity and character, are used as unique setting for the marketing of luxury condos. In reality, the maximization of revenue through the insertion of floors of apartment units into the grand church interior destroys this very authenticity itself. The General Principles of the Athens Charter of 1931 recommending "that the occupation of buildings, which ensures the continuity of their life, should be maintained but that they should be used for a purpose which respects their historic or artistic character"[3] was intended to safeguard against such types of reuse. A different conversion from church to gallery, on the other hand, views "fit" as one pertaining primarily to character rather than profit or size. The interior of the Brutalist St. Agnes Church in Berlin, Germany, with its windowless, toplit space was, by its architectural characteristics, a perfect "fit" for an art gallery, a program type specifically requiring windowless space and unique lighting conditions. This new use preserves the Brutalist heritage of the church and, in doing so, is an ideal interpretation of the Athens Charter recommendation. (figs. 8, 9a–c)
From the viewpoint of preservation and rehabilitation of historic property, "fit" might refer to a new use that "will be undertaken in such a manner that, if removed in the future, the essential form and integrity of the historic property and its environment would be unimpaired."[4] This requirement posits impermanence or reversibility as an aspect of "fit." An example is the 1912 Montemartini thermoelectric center, the first public power plant to produce electricity for Rome, Italy. Sited between the General Markets and the left bank of the Tiber, this industrial heritage building was transformed into the Centrale Montemartini museum for the exhibition of the Musei Capitolini's classical sculpture. The machinery remained in situ in the transformation of the

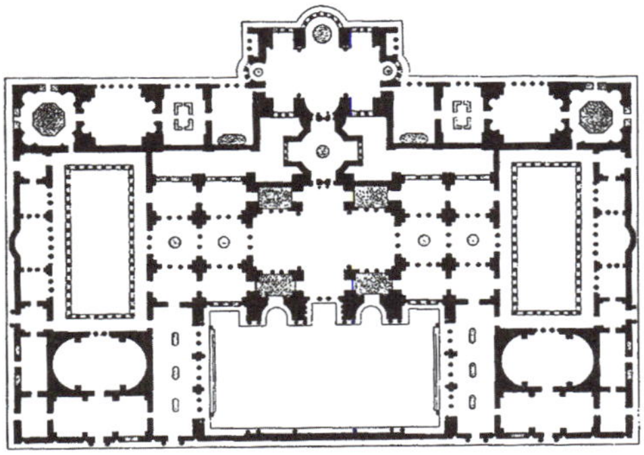

boiler rooms into art galleries. Low-impact, easily removable construction, such as half walls and partitions, enables this new use that juxtaposes the classical with the industrial. The introduction of a new use in this case safeguards for the future the integrity of the antique machines and their environment. (figs. 10a–b)

"Fit" can also refer to compatibility and appropriateness of size, character and shape. In the first adaptive reuse project to transform the *frigidarium* of the Baths of Diocletian in Rome, Italy, to a High Renaissance church, the vaulted bays of the existing host structure "fit" the needs of a church in terms of scale, shape, sequential circulation and appropriateness. The monumental remains of the vaulted *frigidarium* evoked a quality and scale desirable for a church. Its compatibility lay in the ease with which the existing space could be adapted for its new use. The amphitheater at Arles, France, with its repetitive structure of 120 arches "fit" the need for fortification in the 5th century AD after the fall of the Roman Empire. Its size, once accomodating 20,000 spectators of Roman games, was appropriate for housing a reduced population of approximately 200 households, with the open arena as town square. The compatibility of the program of arena for reuse as medieval town was complemented by the potential of the physical structure to support additional load. The existing stone construction supported the addition of four lookout towers, the hallmark of its converted use as walled city. The correlation of existing space to new use is critical in an adaptive reuse relationship, as evidenced by the "fit" between two seemingly disparate uses—a coliseum and a small town. This reciprocity is at the heart of a "fit" of compatibility. (figs. 11a–b, 12a–b)

In addition to the many nuances of "fit," "use" has direct and concrete implications. In building codes, change of use from one occupancy type to another (and even within the same occupancy from one sub-group to another)

FIGS.11a–b, 12a–b: There is a similar compatibility of fit in the use of the frigidarium of the Baths of Diocletian as the Church of Santa Maria degli Angeli e dei Martiri and the Arles Amphitheater as a fortified town.

triggers life, safety, and welfare issues. Critical building information— height and area limitations, types of construction and finishes, fire protection, means of egress, accessibility, systems—is dependent on use group designation. Therefore, any change in use and occupancy may result in a change in the design of these parts of a building. For example, the conversion of the Group H electrical power station to the Group A Centrale Montemartini museum is one that increases numbers of occupants. The change from designing for the few users of a mechanical space to accommodating large groups of museum visitors would affect occupancy-related criteria such as egress. Conversely, designing for the physical dangers of hazardous spaces would

FIGS.13a–b: The decommissioned Tempelhof Airport in Berlin is reused for multiple programs from park to fashion runway and temporary shelter for refugees.

differ dramatically from designing for a space of assembly, in particular with fire-resistive materials and fire ratings.

A change of use in a semi-ruin or ruin that requires complete renovation plus an addition triggers a consideration of all code categories, as one would do for a new building. A change of use within a shell-type host, an intervention that takes place primarily within the host building, might, on the other hand, require consideration of only key conditions pertaining to the interior. For the designer, occupancy-dependent criteria include occupant loads, egress, and fire resistance ratings. These elements determine, for example, how many occupants the new program of use can accommodate, the types of surfaces and materials, the required means of egress, the size of the egress components and even their placement in plan. These many critical parts of the code also contribute to the assessment of "fit."

Adaptive reuse transformations often include more than one type of use within any given structure. Mixed-use occupancy is defined as the co-existence of several use groups within a single structure. In such cases, the requirements of each occupancy type are calculated and the most stringent prevail, unless the uses are separated by fire-rated partitions. For example, the decommissioned Tempelhof Airport building in Berlin, Germany, is reused for various functions that take place concurrently in different areas of

the sprawling facility. The uses range from fashion shows to outdoor park and, most recently, as refugee housing. These functions, respectively occupancy groups A1, A5, and R1, could be considered in two ways: as individual uses each with its own requirements and separated from each other, or as a single multi-use group that conforms to the strictest requirements. (figs. 13a–b)

The implication of "fit" and "use" are complex and most often offer many interpretations. Mark Twain said: "A round man cannot be expected to fit in a square hole right away. He must have time to modify his shape." In adaptive reuse practice, it is the process of designing that round shape to fit into a square opening that creates a unique logistical, functional, and even poetic opportunity.

1 For the purpose of this discussion, all code regulations are derived from the International Building Code. 2 *2015 International Building Code* (Country Club Hills, Illinois: International Code Council, 2014), Section 1004.1.2. 3 The Athens Charter for the Restoration of Historic Monuments—1931, ICOMOS International Council on Monuments and Sites, http://www.icomos.org/en/charters-and-texts/179-articles-en-francais/ressources/charters-and-standards/167-the-athens-charter-for-the-restoration-of-historic-monuments (accessed February 16, 2016). 4 Kay D. Weeks and Anne E. Grimmer, *The Secretary of the Interior's Standards for the Treatment of Historic Property, with Guidelines for Preserving, Rehabilitating, Restoring & Reconstructing Historic Buildings* (Washington, DC: U.S. Department of the Interior, 1995), p. 62.

Hosts and guests are fundamental to each other's existence. This reciprocity also defines the relationship between host structure and new, or renovated, use. New use is implemented at many different scales, as dictated by the different host types, discussed in the chapter *Hosts [and Guests]*. As transformative architectural actions, these interventions range from those wielding minor impact on the host to ones in which the host structure is subsumed. To better understand the nature of this relationship, we further probe the actions discussed in the chapter *Considering DNA* and explore the degree of interface between new use and existing confines. We begin our examination of these different actions with those uses that require minimal interaction with the host structure.

The shell-type host structure permits both limited and unlimited actions within the confines of its infrastructure. Interior conversions typically respect the existing structural system, the floor plates and the envelope. Within these constraints, the host of this type acts as a blank slate for unlimited new design strategies. The shell-type host acts simply as a box for the introduction of new spatial experience, with a minimal degree of interface between its surfaces and the new use. This lack of embeddedness is characteristic of a temporary type of reuse noted for its brief life cycle. While there are many functional types of such temporary use, the most common are for exhibition and retail purposes.

As a type of shell host, the exhibition hall exemplifies best the idea of temporary inhabitation within an existing structure. It has a first instance in Joseph Paxton's Crystal Palace, erected in London, England, to house the Great Exhibition of 1851. The precursor to world's fairs and exhibitions, Crystal Palace featured a groundbreaking modular, cast iron and glass structure that provided 13 kilometers (8 miles) of display tables, accommodating 14,000 international

The Impassive Host

11

FIG.0: *String-a-Ling* installation, RISD MDES Summer Program 2011

FIG.1: The Alape exhibit by Heine/Lenz/Zizka for the ISH Trade Fair in Frankfurt.

FIG.2: The Art Gallery at Oklahoma State University, Stillwater, OK.

FIG.3: The converted Dacheng Flour Mills hosts exhibits such as the Shenzhen Biennale 2015.

exhibitors and their wares.[1] Within a simple open floor plan, a regular column grid created bays within which individual exhibitors showcased their goods: false teeth, carpets, ribbons, artificial legs, Colt's repeating pistol, the Koh-i-Noor diamond, Goodyear india rubber goods, statues, chewing tobacco. In the vast hall, exhibitors tailored their booths to the scale, shape, and character of their respective product. The exhibition hall as a host structure required little to no interaction, and exhibits were installed and uninstalled with relative ease. As a host structure, the exhibition hall is characterized by indistinctive DNA, features that simply act as background.

From expos to museums, today's exhibition spaces have not changed much from this standard. They remain host buildings with regular bays that allow for a succession of changing exhibits. As tools of commerce, the changing exhibits take on varying forms, inhabiting a finite space of temporary walls, reconfigurable lighting, paint and graphics. The host is an empty box for displaying these objects and the intervention an impermanent occupation. At the 2015 ISH in Frankfurt, Germany, a trade fair for water and energy

FIG.4: *corpus*, Ann Hamilton, 2003–2004, MASS MoCA, North Adams, MA.

FIG.5a: Lee Boroson's *Deep Current*, a recreation of a waterfall.

FIG.5b: *Uplift*, Lee Boroson, 2014, *Plastic Fantastic*, MASS MoCA.

products, the Alape display occupied a place in the vast exposition hall as a series of abstract boxes of different sizes. Showcasing various bath products, each box creates a weightless, precise and pristine atmosphere, intended to reflect the characteristics of the plumbing product on display. The display boxes float above the floor plane by way of a cantilevered construction detail. As a defined group, they are boxes within the larger box of the exhibition hall. They establish a brand presence among a sea of other displays, to be repeated at the next exposition. (fig. 1)
Museums are variants of shell hosts in which the different galleries are the small boxes within a large box that are reconfigured for each new show. In museums with clearly delineated permanent and temporary shows, the impermanent galleries transform through new interior partitions, lighting and paint, engaging the host through non-structural and removable construction to accommodate the type and style of art displayed. (fig. 2)
In recent decades, some notable exhibition halls and museums were themselves converted structures. The 1986 conversion of the Gare d'Orsay in

Paris, France, to the Musée d'Orsay by Gae Aulenti is one of the forerunners of this type. The intervention of low walls and a unique display system transformed the cavernous train station to a series of traditional picture galleries within a single space. At more recently converted museums such as MassMOCA in North Adams, Massachusetts, USA, previously an 18th-century manufacturing complex, there is no desire for the vast industrial spaces that once held enormous machines to conform to the standards of a traditional museum. Instead, the gigantic exhibition spaces, the size of football fields, inspire monumental and unconventional exhibits, from a re-creation of Niagara Falls in sheet plastic[2] to a sea of magenta-tinged sheets of onionskin paper.[3] These pieces derive their scale and character from the host structure and interface with it through art. Exhibitions such as the Shenzhen Biennale of 2015 took place in the "found space" of an old flour factory instead of the common exhibition hall or converted museum. In these instances, a temporary exhibit inserted into a raw space must contend with the traces of several past lives, the characteristic of a more complex "box" host. (figs. 3, 4, 5a–b)

The Pop-Up

The pop-up store is another variant of temporary occupation in an existing shell-type host structure. Defined as short-term retail, pop-ups are often seasonal and provide a transitory tenancy in otherwise vacant space. In recent years, they have also become a tool of high-end brands, as brief, three-dimensional advertising. As seasonal or one-off transitory space, pop-ups are, by nature, defined by an economy of means. They are often self-contained and do not engage the systems of the host interior. Like exhibits at an expo, the pop-up is often designed for ease of installation, with impermanent and inexpensive materials. For some brands, pop-ups are demountable, for reuse in another location.

The setting for pop-up retail varies. Pop-ups for malls or airports are in reality objects that float within a larger space. As in the exhibit hall, the host structure is indistinctive and offers little context for design. The Illy Pop-Up designed for the Venice Biennale is a self-contained unit that opens to include all equipment as well as furniture. It functions independently of the host structure. It provides the same coffee and a place to consume it whether it is sited in the Campo San Stefano or the Mojave Desert. By contrast, the Illy Pop-Up store in Milan, also in Italy, is a demountable system. Its design concept is premised on a 45-centimeter display cube with variations of storage capabilities that can be reconfigured through combinatory logic to 3,000 permutations. Easily assembled and disassembled, this design interacts with different simple host conditions of wall and ceiling to provide,

FIGS.6, 7: Pop-up stores for the Illy coffee brand by Adam Kalkin in Venice and Caterina Tiazzoldi in Milan.

in the end, variations of the same iconic store. In either case, there is little interaction between the host and the new use. The host becomes simply a stage for implementing brand image. (figs. 6, 7)

Prada Pop-Ups in Paris and in Venice demonstrate the importance of brand image to host context. Both stores are located in classical architectural settings with interiors typical of their respective locale; 19th-century Place Beauvau in Paris and 18th-century Calle Larga XXII Marzo in Venice. Within the graceful context of tall period windows and marbled floors, the designs nonetheless introduce new surfaces and partitions within the existing to establish a new identity. In the case of the Paris store, the walls—both external and internal—are covered in a trompe-l'œil of an iconic bridge. In Venice, a consistent set of low walls is introduced within the historic Vene-

tian palazzo, directly against the existing walls, to define the limit of the host and the intervention.

Alternatively, some pop-up stores, especially for high-end brands, thrive on a host context for their design. Set within intriguing hosts, from historic to sumptuous and shabby-chic, the pop-up derives added value from such association. The richness of the context therefore offsets the need for elaborate interventions. The Frame Store in Amsterdam, Netherlands, a six-month display of fashion, food, and design for *Frame Magazine*, illustrates this concept with a setting of a historic 18th-century interior inside the Felix Meritis building. With a long history as a center of art, science and culture, the Neoclassical temple-fronted building has also held other lives as concert hall, printing company, Communist party headquarters, and theater. Its interior, though faded and scarred, reflects its original grandeur in the classical windows and ornate millwork. With a need to introduce casework and display shelves, the interventions consist of mirrored surfaces and boxes, placed precisely within the room to engage this architectural past. The many reflections multiply the host features, visually juxtaposing old and new. Framing the new use visually as part of a continuum of change, these new interventions are freestanding and do not impact the historic interior. (figs. 8a–c)

FIGS.8a–c: i29 interior architects' interventions to the Felix Meritis Building in Amsterdam take full advantage of the context without impacting the historic host.

Interior Retrofit

Interior retrofit refers to a full and transforming renovation of an interior space. It often refers to use as retail or restaurant but can also be broadened in definition to include offices and residential projects. Similar to the exhibition and the pop-up, the interior retrofit temporarily inhabits a shell-type host as part of a continuum of interior transformations over time. While exhibitions work on a short cycle of change over weeks, and the pop-up of months, the interior retrofit operates on a longer cycle of years, one dependent on the success of the venture. With the primary goal of catering to consumption, these projects are based on design concepts to sell a product through spatial experience.

The Camper shoe brand offers insight into this relationship between product and interior retrofit. In partnership with global designers to brand through architecture, the stores range from the interactive to the sublime. In Barcelona, Spain, the Camper store is simply a giant message board where the design is the message. Clients are invited to write on the walls, and the resultant graffiti as message corroborates the brand idea: "Design elements are means to transmit a message and the content becomes as valuable as the aesthetics. Decoration is thus transformed into information and information into decoration."[4] While the Barcelona store exemplifies the latter, the

FIGS.9, 10: The different branding strategies for Camper Stores illustrate the nature of interior retrofit.

New York City 5th Avenue store exemplifies the former. Here, decorations in the form of cast shoes—walls of them—transmit the message for the few real shoes on display. In either case, the host provides the architectural framework for the implementation of design messages that, most often, have no relationship to the host. The host structure, in fact, is a means to a commercial objective. (figs. 9, 10)

Temporary occupation as pop-up or retrofit is implemented as different experiences within a box-like host. There are two types of boxes: the plain shoe box and the jeweled box. The former is unadorned, with either basic surfaces

FIGS.11a–b: Reversible interventions create small outdoor reading rooms at the landmark Redwood Library Athenaeum, Newport, RI.

or often open studs awaiting new surfaces. Interventions within it require a simple engagement of new non-bearing walls, finishes, furnishing and equipment, and a tie-in to the existing systems. Although these elements of the host are typically indistinctive, there is nonetheless a need to account for the peculiarities of existing column grids and systems. In this respect, these interventions are more complex than those of the exhibit booth or the pop-up. The jeweled box type host is instead a type of interior retrofit in which the architectural attributes of the host structure are used to enhance brand, as in the Frame Store. In this instance, the existing traces of the host shell add an aura to the products, and the concept of the design is entirely conceived around such distinctive DNA. The shoe box and the jeweled box illustrate two very different types of shell-host DNA and the interventions they inspire.

Heritage Interventions

Landmark structures are shell-type hosts because the entire host or some part of it is protected and cannot be changed. In landmark properties where existing architectural DNA is vital to their existence and heritage status, interventions must engage the host lightly. Most often these interventions harken back to the host structure itself and are limited by the pertinent preservation regulations. Despite such limitations, interventions in heritage properties are those within the shell-type host category that engage most with the host's features. (figs. 11a–b)

Landmark designation protects different parts of a historic building: the exterior shell, the interior or both. The 1928 International Magazine Building in New York City, New York, USA, is a six-story office building with an ordinary interior and an Art Deco stone facade. In this case, only the exterior was protected as a landmark. The Interior Landmark[5] designation, on the other

FIG.12a: Mies van der Rohe's Crown Hall, Chicago, IL, is a fully protected landmark.

FIG.12b: Only the facade of the International Magazine Building is preserved in the Hearst Tower, NY.

hand, pertains only to the protection of the interior of a space. This designation is a relatively recent type of protection and includes historic residences, courthouses, theaters, cinemas and the interiors of other extraordinary buildings such as Mies van der Rohe's Crown Hall in Chicago, Illinois, USA. In the example of the International Magazine Building that did not have an Interior Landmark designation, protective restrictions did not apply beyond the facade, enabling any and all changes within the interior. This is evident in the total gutting of the interior in the current, transformed Hearst Tower, a 46-floor skyscraper emerging from the preserved facades of the International Magazine Building. With Interior Landmark designation, change is instead permitted on the facade but not within the interior. By contrast, in fully protected heritage, like for example Crown Hall, both the exterior and the interior are designated landmarks. (figs. 12a–b)

Beyond the requirements of building regulations, heritage structures are also regulated by codes such as, in the USA, *The Secretary of the Interior's Standards for the Treatment of Historic Properties.* With the primary objective to preserve heritage as legacy, most of the regulations are aimed at retaining historic character in its many forms: material, detail, shape, use. The standards, however, are not opposed to the introduction of a new use as long as it wields minimal change to the monument's distinctive character. Similar to the international regulations of the Venice Charter, Clause 9 of *The Secretary*

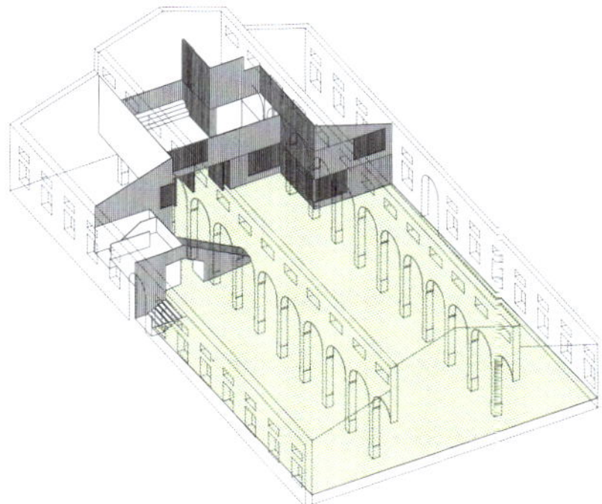

FIGS.13a–d: Within a heritage exterior, the market building in Alcaniz is converted to a Civic and Children's Center through non-invasive interior interventions by Miquel Mariné and César Rueda.

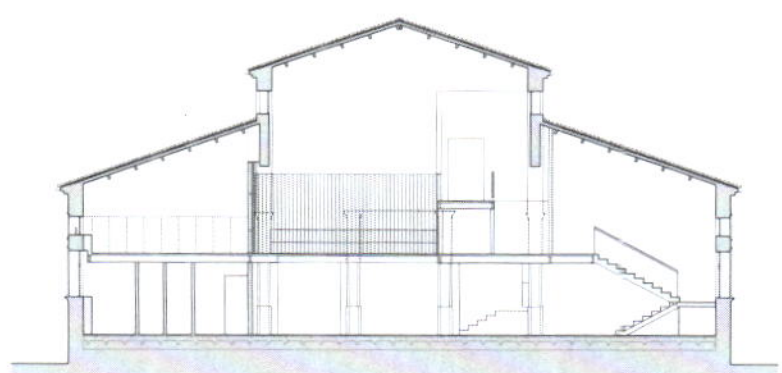

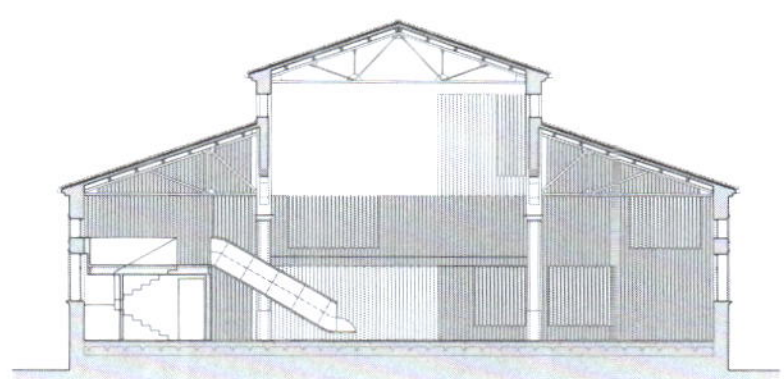

of the Interior's Standards for the Treatment of Historic Properties references new additions with the proviso that they are differentiated from and compatible with the existing. Clause 10 is unique in requiring new work to be reversible, that is, if the new intervention were to be removed in future the essential existing form would be unimpaired. These two clauses together provide an opportunity for creative interventions to historic hosts.

Within the range of interventions in heritage buildings, the Centro Infantil del Mercado in Alcañiz, Spain, demonstrates the potential for intervention within a protected historic exterior. Occupying a corner site in this Aragonese town, the abandoned market has been infused with new life through use as a child care center. The exterior shell is untouched, maintaining the urban context, while the interior is entirely transformed. Interior partitions dodge and weave themselves within and around the existing internal structure—the new architecture inspired by, but not interfering with, the distinctive features of the host. (figs. 13a–d)

By contrast, the 15th-century Church of San Felice in Guglionesi, Italy, is a protected interior that, over time, has undergone a series of devastating renovations. Originally noted for its colorful features, the church was subjected to many renovations that have left little trace of its original polychrome wall decorations. With insufficient evidence of these interior features, a liberal application of preservation regulations permitted the acknowledgment of the loss of the polychrome color of the walls through a whitewashing. Its past identity of polychrome surfaces was reintroduced as an intervention of a multi-colored tile composition in the floor. The insertion of the new floor demonstrates a reversible intervention that can be removed in future without impacting the original structure. (figs. 14a–b)

Herzog & de Meuron's intervention to the room for Company D of the Park Street Armory in New York City, New York, USA, extends the limits of preservation regulations. As a landmark exterior, the Armory comprises certain rooms such as the one of Company D that also received Interior Landmark designation. In the Company D room, the restoration of the wall surfaces revealed many layers of color and pattern superimposed upon each other, affirming the difficulty of establishing a clear authenticity. When posed with this dilemma at Vézelay, Paris and Carcassonne, Viollet-le-Duc elected to bring his work to a new reality, one that had not previously existed. Heir to this conservation dilemma, Herzog & de Meuron instead elected to place their mark on this long history by the addition of a newly invented pattern, one inspired by the materials and forms of the past that would provide a connection through material and time to the future. (figs. 15a–b)

From large-span exposition sheds to historic interiors, new interventions into the shell-type structure are defined by a minimal interface with the host. Wielding little impact on the existing structures, these architectural actions focus instead on the creation of brand and experience within an impassive host.

1 "Crystal Palace," *The Encyclopedia Britannica*. http://www.britannica.com/topic/Crystal-Palace-building-London. 2 The waterfall was part of the exhibition *Lee Boroson: Plastic Fantastic*, MASS MoCA, October 2014–May 2015. 3 The sea of paper was part of the exhibition *Ann Hamilton: corpus*, MASS MoCA, December 2003–October 2004. 4 On the Barcelona store by Martí Guixé, see the Camper website, http://www.camper.com/en_US/shops/stores (accessed February 21, 2016). 5 Interior landmark designations are determined by local commissions within individual cities, for example, Philadelphia's Preservation Alliance or Boston's Landmark Commission.

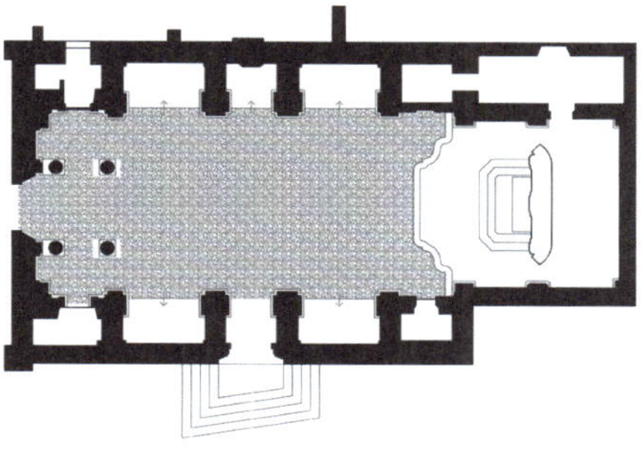

FIGS. 14a–b: Claudio Greco's tile floor intervention in the restoration of the St. Felice church in Avignonesi.

FIGS. 15a–b: At the landmark Park Avenue Armory in New York City, NY, Herzog & de Meuron have created a new authenticity.

Installation art is distinguished from other traditional art forms as a single unified experience rather than a display of individual pieces of art. Defined in part by its relationship to site, installation art as a group forms a subset of use for various types of host structures. As an art form that transforms space, installation art has several precedents. In Hanover, Germany, Kurt Schwitters' *Merzbau* was an abstract three-dimensional collage of ever-shifting found objects, placed inside a single space from 1923 to 1937. Defying definition, *Merzbau* was its own environment, created through many interventions over time. In May 1971, Alanna Heiss invited artists to create work inspired by the Brooklyn Bridge, New York, USA, and sited below its western base. This intervention that lasted for three days came to be known as the Brooklyn Bridge Event. Almost half a century and an ocean apart, these two works are early instances of the intervention as a response to site-specific characteristics and its extension into the larger, neglected urban context. (fig. 1)

Artist Ilya Kabakov said: "The main actor in the total installation, the main centre toward which everything is addressed, for which everything is intended, is the viewer."[1] Installation art places the viewer in a space, one transformed for a calculated experience that takes place in many forms and locales and at many scales. As an intervention within the host structure of a gallery, the relationship of the installation to the physical space varies. Some installations aim to create an "other world" experience within the impersonal, white gallery, transporting the viewer through a mental engagement. In *Cold Dark Matter: An Exploded View*, Cornelia Parker recreates the explosion of a wood barn inside a gallery of the Tate Modern by using the barn remains. Suspended from the ceiling, the pieces are transformed from charred wood to the idea of explosion through their reflections on the

Sited Interventions

12

FIG.0: *Blue Print*, installation by Sui Park in a former factory building in Philadelphia, PA.

FIG.1: *Merzbau*, Kurt Schwitters, 1923–1937, Hannover.

FIG.2: Cornelia Parker's *Cold Dark Matter: An Exploded View*, 1991, Tate Gallery.

FIG.3: Sol LeWitt's *Wall Drawing 51*, MASS MoCA Building 7.

surrounding gallery surfaces. The explosion is reinvented through shadow, which constitutes an intervention relatively independent of its context. The museum gallery as a host is neutral, intentionally without spatial cues. This type of intervention recalls the exhibition hall model in which the shell-type host structure provides a wrapper for the insertion of new experience. (fig. 2)

At the other extreme, installation art takes place as sited work within a charged room. Sol LeWitt's *Wall Drawing 51* is such an example in which the art is entirely premised on the pre-existing conditions of the space. Part of a series of wall drawings in which each is produced through a specific set of instructions, *Wall Drawing 51* is a product of the words "All architectural points connected by straight lines."[2] The resulting drawing, a work that differs with each installation, consists of a series of blue chalk construction snap-lines, each connecting the architectural elements within the space: door frame, door jamb, column, fire alarm. Relying on the particular architecture of a particular space, each installation of *Wall Drawing 51* is unique. Sol LeWitt's instructions transform the relationship between shell and new use to one of an interdependency of host and work. (fig. 3)

FIGS.4, 5a–b: The installations of Dan Flavin are entirely informed by the architectural characteristics of the space they inhabit: *Lights* at Museum of Modern Art, Vienna (MuMoK), Chiesa di Santa Maria Annunciata in Chiesa Rossa, Milan.

Sited art interventions derive their sole objective from the space itself, aided by the artists' "set of directions." The work of Dan Flavin, with its signature assemblages of fluorescent light tubes, demonstrates a development in which sited work began in the gallery context and evolved to a full engagement with specific sites. Early installations of light into "'barred corridors' and corner installations ... concentrated on the relationship between his sculptures and the spaces they inhabited,"[3] which at that time consisted of various museum galleries. Later work extended beyond the gallery to entire architectural sites in which the notable characteristics of site informed his compositions. At the Guggenheim Museum in New York, his light installations were placed between the curving ovoid concrete bands, highlighting the geometry of the volume. At the Chiesa Rossa in Milan, Flavin created central light elements within this unremarkable church as a part of a renewal and restoration project. Utilizing the simple light tube, he distinguished and highlighted separate architectural elements of the church interior through different color renditions. The color differentiation served as a visual guide through the church, emphasizing the sequence from entry to nave and altar. In a reciprocal manner, the art is informed by the host and the host is transformed by the art. (figs. 4, 5a–b)

Installations are not limited to the shell-type hosts of a single room or the interior of a building. The size and scope of potential sites are limitless, from all or part of a building to built infrastructure and entire built sites. Different types of host structures provide unique and distinct issues of engagement for sited art. The complexity of this relationship can be seen in three installations of Elise Morin's *Waste Landscape*. An installation of 60,000 unused or discarded CDs, sewn and draped over inflated mounds into an undulating landscape of metallic dunes, it has been installed in varying host sites from cultural art centers to public civic space. The placement of these mounds, comprising five small "hills," differs in each re-siting. Its first installation in the courtyard of the Centquatre, a 19th-century funeral service establishment converted to a cultural space, responds to the clearly delineated bays of the Halle d'Aubervilliers, Paris, France. The dunes are placed to provide cross-currents within the highly regular grid implied by the multiple industrial openings. Installed a second time in the courtyard of the city hall of The Hague in the Netherlands, the five dunes reveal a slightly different configuration. In a context without distinct architectural traces, the relationship between the dunes is derived from their proximity to each other rather than from the surrounding context. By contrast, its installation in the interior of a small church turned art center in Troy, New York, USA, entails a placement of the dunes that responds to the specificity of the church floor plan. So placed, they appear as separate objects co-inhabiting a space, rather than as a unified landscape. These iterations of *Waste Landscape* in three different sites speak to the effects of site specificity. (figs. 6a–b)

FIGS.6a–b: The configuration of Elise Morin's *Waste Landscape* differs from its first iteration #1 in Paris to #2 at The Hague.

FIGS.7a–c: Taturo Atzu's 2015 *The Garden Which is Nearest to God* is dependent physically on its host, the Oude Kerk in Amsterdam, for structural support and metaphorically on its context of church and Red Light District for symbolic reference.

The 13th-century Oude Kerk, Amsterdam's oldest building and parish church, served as host to Taturo Atzu's 2015 work, *The Garden Which Is the Nearest to God*. Atzu installed a temporary platform over the entire sloping roof of the church to provide a place for viewing the surrounding context of the Oudekerksplein, a district of the city known for its legalized prostitution. As in Marcel Duchamp's *Fountain*, a urinal reframed as a drinking fountain, implicit with implications, Atzu reframes the iconic image of a church with its sloping roofs and skyward soaring spires. These religious references to heaven are hijacked in a literal leveling of the playing field. The massive horizontal platform transforms the top of the church to a flat roof, giving access to the unattainable spires and the heavens with the aim to look downwards and to the red light district below. With a history that includes the expulsion by the Calvinists of the homeless sheltered in the church, Oude Kerk is an ideal host site for the juxtaposition of the sacred and the profane. It offers a unique combination of location and history, without which the intervention would not exist. While the platform depends on the church for structural

FIG.8: Water falls from the underside of the Brooklyn Bridge in Olafur Eliasson's 2008 *The New York City Waterfalls*.

support, the host in this case is crucial less for its physical attributes than for its symbolic references. (figs. 7a–c)

Installations are not bound to host structures of architecture or architectural spaces. Since the "Brooklyn Bridge Event [that] embodied a fascinating shift in the art world's awareness, appreciation and reclamation of neglected urban spaces,"[4] many bridges and old highways have been host to interventions, the High Line in New York City being a prime example. Infrastructure as host pro-

FIGS.9a–c: Subway infrastructure is transformed by nascent technology in Toyo Ito's 1986 *Tower of the Winds*, Yokohama.

vides a monumental scale, enhanced loading capabilities and a special relationship to the built environment. Perhaps it is these opportunities that inspire unique interventions pushing the boundaries of art, such as Olafur Eliasson's 2008 installation, *The New York City Waterfalls*. This work used the underside of the Brooklyn Bridge as one of four infrastructural hosts in New York City to create a man-made waterfall in an urban setting. (fig. 8)

Such conditions paved the way for the transformation of a mechanical subway ventilation shaft in the frenetic urban setting of Yokohama Station, Japan. Through the addition of full-height perforated aluminum screens and the use of then emerging digital technology to convert environmental conditions to image, Toyo Ito's *Tower of the Winds* project is an art installation entirely generated from its context. By day, the aluminum screen reflects the activity of Yokohama station as a quasi mirror. By night, the same activity, as intangible phenomenon of traffic intensity, direction of wind, traffic and pedestrian movement around the square, is projected in the form of light and sound onto the screened ventilation shaft. Emergent technology transforms data to performance and infrastructure to sculpture.

The *Tower of the Winds* installation in 1986 can be seen as a pivotal point of change, a herald of digital technology's incursion into daily modern life. Utilized

FIG.10: Olafur Eliasson's *The Weather Project*, Tate Museum, London.

FIG.11: Random International's *Rain Room*, Museum of Modern Art, New York.

in this project as an agent of adaptive reuse, technology provides the adapted host with a performative role. In comparison to the inert host structures of exhibitions halls and interior retrofits, technology is an enabler of a new relationship of host to reuse. (figs. 9a–c)

Two installation projects on the subject of weather illustrate the changing nature of this relationship. Olafur Eliasson's *The Weather Project* at the Tate Museum in 2003 created an artificial sun in the 150-meter-long Turbine Hall. Fabricated from an enormous backlit screen, the installation had as its aim the eventual revelation of these mechanics. The process of revealing the

FIGS.12a–d: Technology is at the heart of UN Studio's facade revitalization of the Galleria Department Store West, Seoul.

screen was one of discovery, in which the visitor traversed the Turbine Hall. As host, the Turbine Hall served as the inert monumental background in this commentary on the social effects of weather. (fig. 10)

Random International's *Rain Room* also addresses weather as phenomenon in society. Installed several times into conventional gallery space—London's Barbican, New York's MoMA PS1—the installation creates an indoor rainstorm. As with *The Weather Project*, a discovery is required; through a system of sensors, the rain ceases only where one walks and recommences as soon as one passes. Digital technology engineers the visitor interaction in an engagement with the space. Visitors are required to forge their own paths through the room in this staged simulation. In contrast to *The Weather Project*, where the Turbine Hall served as container of an event, the digital technology in *Rain Room* facilitates the host's participation in the installation. Enabled by technology, the box gallery host becomes an actor in the play. (fig. 11)

The proliferation of digital technology in art installation has activated existing structures, transcending the static relationship of host and new use. Incorporating current preoccupations with the mediatization of image, technology has given new life to the facade as host structure. In the renovation of the Galleria Department Store West in Seoul, Korea, a new facade was added on top of the existing skin. Employing more than 4,000 glass discs with dicroic foil that was placed directly on the concrete surface, the new facade displayed a mother-of-pearl effect by day and a landmark display of changing LED activated light and color media by night. UN Studio posited this facade intervention as a confrontation of image and society's preoccupation with it, in the context of the office's experiments with "combining different types of image constructions."[5] (figs. 12a–d)

FIG.13: *War Veteran Vehicle Project*, Liverpool 2009, Krzysztof Wodiczko.

FIG.14: Mette Ramsgaard's *Slow Furl*, Lighthouse Gallery, Brighton, June 2008.

Extending beyond effects of light to animation, the video mapping on the Amir Building of the Tel Aviv Museum in Israel further expands the collusion of architecture, art and technology. A solid surface of segmented, "folding" concrete panels, the facade became a stage upon which a projection of light and images revealed imagined porosity within the seams and surfaces of a seemingly impregnable mass. The mapping transformed the facade momentarily, imbuing it with new roles and interpretations.

The facade as host becomes the vehicle of activism in the work of Krzysztof Wodiczko. Through video projections onto the facades of civic buildings, city monuments are utilized as canvases to address the plight of the homeless, the exploitation of hotel workers, the relationship between private economic interest and public rights. With the belief that the facades themselves must serve more than a role of weatherproofing, Wodiczko maintains that "not to speak through the city monuments is to abandon them and to abandon ourselves losing both a sense of history and the present ..."[6] (fig. 13)

The appropriation of the facade as host to adaptive interventions is only one of many possibilities engendered by the proliferation of technology. As technology continues to evolve, it will give rise to new roles for the host structure. However, advancements may not necessarily equate only to an increase in importance of the host structure's role in adaptive reuse. In fact, quite the contrary. Developments such as robotic processes within the built envelope have reduced the need for the host structure to take on additional roles. *Slow Furl*, a research project by CITA of the Royal Danish Academy of Fine Arts, is one such responsive interior textile. Developed as a prototype in 2008, the textile is intended to react with the actions of the inhabitant. In response to human movements, the robotic membrane slowly reveals its many folds with quasi-imperceptible moves. "Rather than fixing the digital in a responsive relationship to the user, where every call defines a reply, *Slow Furl* finds its temporality outside the immediately animate."[7] As an intervention, *Slow Furl* relies only upon itself, and the host structure, once again, is relegated to spectator. (fig. 14)

Installation art in sited conditions reveals to us an ideal relationship of host to intervention in which one informs the other. The art intervention as opposed to the architectural intervention, has the advantage of a certain autonomy: without the demands of function and permanence, it indulges in the pure principle derived from the context. In the built environment, where the accommodation of function necessitates compromise, the art installation serves as a standard in adaptive reuse for an ideal union of host and intervention.

1 *Installation Art,* http://www.tate.org.uk/learn/online-resources/glossary/i/installation-art (accessed January 13, 2016). 2 *Sol LeWitt: A Drawing Retrospective,* http://www.massmoca.org/lewitt/wall-drawing.php?id=51 (accessed January 13, 2016). 3 Dan Flavin, http://www.guggenheim.org/new-york/collections/collection-online/artists/bios/704 (accessed January 13, 2016). 4 Alanna Miller, "From the Records of MoMA PS1: The 40th Anniversary of the Brooklyn Bridge Event," INSIDE/OUT Collection, Library and Archives, MOMA PS1, June 27, 2011. 5 Caroline Bos and Ben van Berkel, "After Image," in *Design Models*, 2006 (from UN Studio website). 6 Lois Ascher, "Krzysztof Wodiczko: Public Space: Commodity or Culture," in David Michalski, ed., *Streetnotes* 20: URBAN FEEL, Spring 2010, http://people.lib.ucdavis.edu/%7Edavidm/xcpUrbanFeel/ascher.html (accessed January 15, 2015). 7 *Slow Furl.* http://cita.karch.dk/Menu/Research+Projects/Behaving+Architectures/Slow+-Furl+(2008) (accessed January 15, 2016).

Interventions extend the capabilities of the host structure. New spatial experience is inserted into the envelope of the shell-type host structure as interior retrofit. Sited installations engage the host structure in a temporary transformation. Addition, as another and different type of intervention, expands the host structure through a change in size or scope. With a long history, addition as architectural practice has historically been overlooked. In reality, many of the great works of history are products of additions over time. St. Peter's Basilica at the Vatican, as we know it today, is an accretion of additions by many different architects, beginning with Bramante in 1506 to Michelangelo Buonarroti in 1564, Carlo Maderno in 1612, and Gian Lorenzo Bernini in 1667. (fig. 1)

Defined as the total of two or more amounts, addition is a quantitative process of increase in number or degree. In mathematics, this sum is absolute, with only one possible solution at any given time. In architecture, however, the expansion of an existing structure through addition results in more than an increase of space. An increase in size or scope equates to changes in many other aspects of the host structure; the worth of the building, its property value, its relationships within the context and its place in the continuum of time. Its revised worth is a product of the old, the new and the many implications of its adjusted identity.

Whole Numbers +

The addition of whole numbers (positive integers and zero) in mathematics has its equivalence in architecture as the addition of discrete volumes to an existing host structure. These additions include single elements, from a

The Mathematics of Reuse

13

FIG.0: Additive and subtractive operations define adaptive reuse practice.

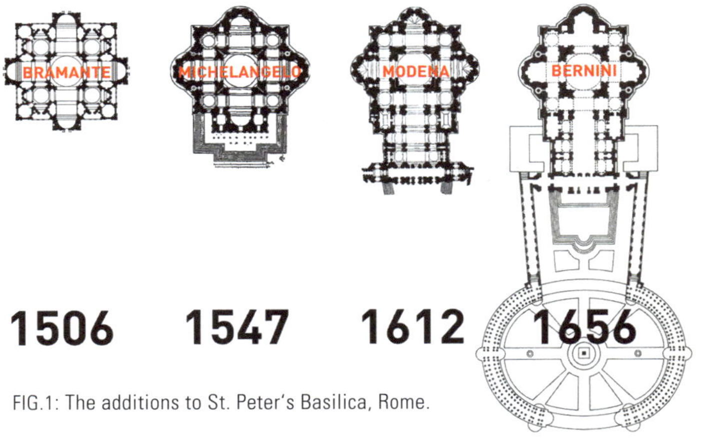

FIG.1: The additions to St. Peter's Basilica, Rome.

dormer to additional stories, but also a new facade or wing. Such additions naturally extend the spatial dimensions of their hosts. With the existing building and its inherent structural capabilities as a starting point, additions cantilever out from, perch on top of and wrap around their hosts in varying configurations. They are distinct volumes that expand the confines of the old.

The most basic outcome of additive interventions is increased square footage. The roof dormer, the most common of additions, for example, extends the head height of sloping attic spaces to create a room from otherwise unusable space. The rooftop addition is a variant, most often on a flat roof, in which an entire volume is added on top of the host structure. As an age-old strategy of expansion within the limits of an established footprint, vertical additions can significantly increase the square footage of a host structure. Vertical additions take place at different scales from a single floor on top of the roof to projects that increase the size of the host many times over. Nouvel's addition to the Lyon Opera House in Lyon, France, and Herzog & de Meuron's transformative addition to a 1960's warehouse as the Elbphilharmonie in Hamburg, Germany, roughly double the existing volume of their hosts. The scale of such additions places the relationship of old to new into question. The classical 1831 opera house topped with a gargantuan

FIGS. 2a–c: The Lyon Opera House is doubled in size by Jean Nouvel's addition.

metal barrel vault roof, though still recognizable, alters the skyline of Lyon's city center. The serviceable industrial brick warehouse topped with an enormous new "crystal" form transforms the context of Hamburg's working harbor. These additions, though large, clearly delineate old and new as distinct elements of a whole form. As such, they are part of a continuum in which buildings evolve while maintaining some semblance of their integrity. (figs. 2a–c, 3a–b)

FIGS.3a–b: An industrial warehouse is doubled in size in its new life as Herzog & de Meuron's Elbphilharmonie.

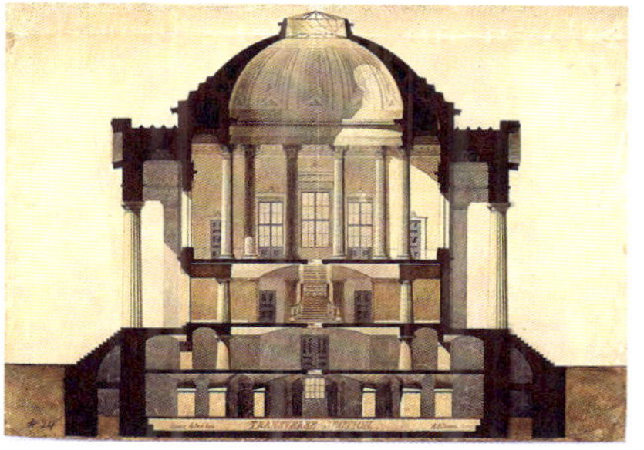

FIGS.4a–c: The dome of the U.S. Customs House in Boston, MA, is lost in the addition of a Campanile-styled tower.

In contrast to these examples are additions of a greater magnitude that have the potential to jeopardize the integrity of the host. Projects such as the addition of a tower onto the 1837 U.S. Customs House in Boston, Massachusetts, USA, or the 1928 International Magazine Building in New York City, New York, USA, illustrate these ideas. A product of the Greek Revival movement, the U.S. Customs House was the embodiment of American authority through its domed temple form. The 1915 addition of a multi-story tower in the style of the Venice Campanile, directly over the dome and obscuring it from view, dramatically transformed the character of the landmark building. The addition resulted in a hybrid that diluted its iconic presence. The Hearst Tower is also an addition that transformed the 1928 six-story landmark building to a high-rise. The 46-story tower is inserted within the landmark shell and emerges above the sixth floor in a new tectonic language. It asserts itself in the skyline of midtown Manhattan as an overt acknowledgment that the value of the host structure lay only in its Art Deco facade. When the scale of such transformations compromises the identity of the existing structure, they are no longer additions. Rather, adaptive reuse is a pretext for development. (figs. 4a–c, 5a–b)

Vertical additions transform the host without increasing the existing footprint. The addition of discrete volumes in a horizontal manner instead extends the host through an increase of the building footprint. Such additions assume sites with lot coverage potential for new wings and/or blocks. Added volumes have the potential for creating new urban relationships and for renewing connections that have shifted or been reduced or destroyed over time.

FIGS.5a–b: The Hearst Tower addition to the facades of the nternational Magazine Building asserts its presence into the New York City skyline.

In some contexts, such as in David Chipperfield's additions to a historic city block on Joachimstraße in Berlin, Germany, horizontal additions can renew areas of urban discontinuity. Sited in a war-damaged central neighborhood, the addition of three volumes, one on the street front and two in the rear, serves different purposes within the urban setting. The front addition completes the street facade while the rear additions, placed deep in the center of the plot, strike a balance between re-establishing the pre-war courtyard and responding to the post-war additions. (figs. 6a–b)

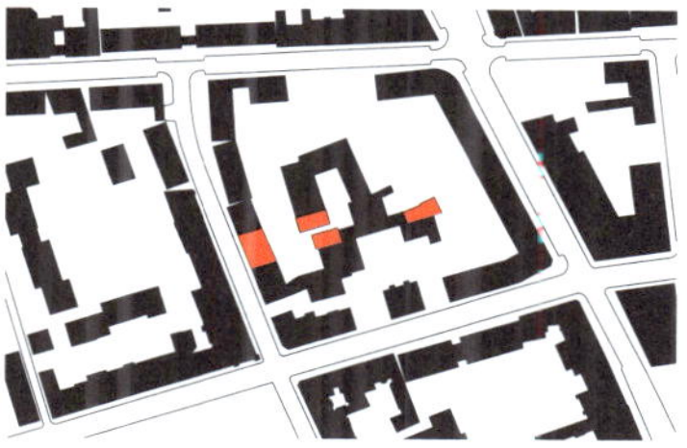

FIGS.6a–b: Urban infill additions such as David Chipperfield's Joachimstrasse 11 in Berlin are opportunities to address issues of context.

Additions require systems of support. Where feasible, smaller-scale vertical additions piggyback on the existing foundations of the host structure, which can support supplementary gravity loads of up to 5 per cent. The load of large-scale additions and wings typically exceed 5 per cent of the host's original design load and require supplementary structural support. For vertical additions where the magnitude of the new volume is greater than the host, such as the Hearst Tower, a new and separate structure is required. With the exception of small additions that can cantilever from the structural system of the host, horizontal additions, as extensions on the site, always require a new system of structural support.

Structural systems supporting additions are most efficient when they complement that of the host. Systems that utilize similar bay sizes and structural grids provide an organizational continuity from the old to the new. This continuity supports a connected flow of movement from host to addition. Similar materials also contribute to a continuity of construction and detail coherence. Structural systems that flow from the existing structure have an impact on the exterior expression of an addition, allowing for the new to be

FIG.7: Frank Gehry's addition to the Tower Records Building, Boston, MA.

articulated in relation to the host. This is not to say that additions should be made "in the style of." Gehry's 1987 roof addition to the Tower Records Building in Boston, Massachusetts, USA, for example, was a groundbreaking project of the time. Its controversial expression of cornice, roof and support were inspired by and a response to the classical structure of its early 20th-century brick Back Bay host. Together they formed a single dialogue of new and old. In contrast, Coop Himmelb(l)au's rooftop addition on Falkestrasse in Vienna, Austria, also of the late 1980s, was a deliberate deviation from its classical 19th-century host. Hailed as one of the first Deconstructivist projects, it used a "differentiated and differentiating constructional system, which is a cross between a bridge and an airplane."[1] This vocabulary is an intentional departure from the elements of load-bearing structure, both literally and figuratively. (figs. 7, 8)

FIG.8: Coop Himmelb(l)au's rooftop remodeling to the office at Falkestrasse, Vienna.

FIG.9: An obsolete craneway in Amsterdam Harbor serves as the foundations for OTH Architecten's Kraanspoor building.

The host can also serve a purely structural role. This is often the case with existing infrastructure that has lost its purpose. This vastly diverse category may include unfinished building frames, highways, bridges, gun batteries, defense fortifications. The Kraanspoor in Amsterdam, Netherlands, is an example of the reuse of infrastructure made obsolete by the city's development. A thriving port city since the 16th century, Amsterdam made use of the 1950s craneway in the harbor as the docking point of supertankers from the Dutch Docking and Shipbuilding Company. With present-day shipping commerce consisting primarily of bulk cargo and cruise ships, the craneway was slated for demolition. Instead, it was used as the foundations of a new lightweight office complex, placed directly on top of it. The host here serves to support the load of the new three-story building. The support system within the new bar building derives its order from that of the craneway below.

FIGS.10a–d: An unused blockhouse in Nantes serves as the foundation of Tetrarc's La Fabrique île de Nantes, a new arts and cultural space.

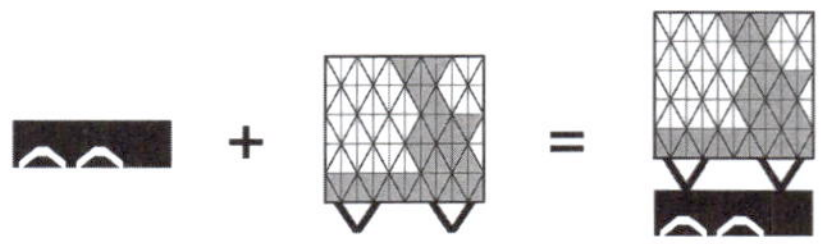

This association of old and new is clearly discernible in plan and in the expression on the facade. (fig. 9)
The thousands of blockhouses or pillbox wartime structures remaining in many European cities are another category of obsolete infrastructure. As military architecture, they are constructed of reinforced material to withstand invasion and the force of bombs. With walls of up to 9 meters thick, their very nature of impregnability renders these host structures nearly inconvertible. The addition of a lightweight tower on top of a World War II blockhouse in Nantes, France, enabled its conversion to an arts and cultural space housing several concert halls, recording studios, offices, and public spaces. The blockhouse serves as a foundation to support the addition of the tower above. Placed directly on the roof of the blockhouse, the new tower intersects it in an open terrace of columns en pilotis. The relationship of the host, as structural foundation, is made explicit by the expressed junction of these two volumes at the point where the weight of the tower is transferred to the concrete mass below. (figs. 10a–d)

Rational Numbers +

Whole numbers describe a universe in singular units. Rational numbers, those numbers that can be expressed as a fraction, instead address the many different increments in between: 1.5, 0.111, 25.3. Where whole numbers are analogous to discrete volumes added to the host structure, rational numbers offer us a view to the many nuances of additive interventions *within* the host.
Projects of refurbishment or renovation add to a host structure not only through extension but also through a process of renewal. Naturally this process pertains most to the semi-ruin or ruin-type hosts, structures that are incomplete. The fate of such heritage property inspired key points of the Athens Charter of 1931 and the Venice Charter of 1964. The establishment of a process for returning a ruin or semi-ruin to life yielded new interpretations of *anastylosis*, the re-instatement of fragments to a whole. In the Athens Charter, it is recommended that anastylosis be performed, where possible, with recognizably new materials. The controversial points of the Venice Charter further promulgate the need to distinguish between new intervention and its existing context. These points lead to diverse interpretations of restorative and reparative interventions through modern means.
The refurbishment of the Neues Museum in Berlin, Germany, demonstrates both types of additions—whole and rational numbers—that together result in a full renovation of the war-damaged ruin. The introduction of a new wing in place of the one destroyed intervenes with a discrete volume. The renewal of the damaged interior elements instead required many small interventions.

FIGS.11a–g: David Chipperfield's Neues Museum addition and renovation in Berlin unite past war wounds with present-day detailing.

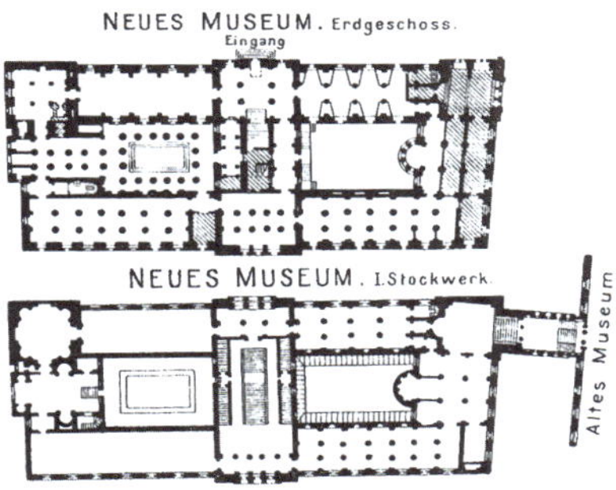
NEUES MUSEUM. Erdgeschoss.
Eingang
NEUES MUSEUM. I.Stockwerk.
Altes Museum

FIGS.12a–c: Linazasoro & Sanchez's conversion of the Piarist School to the Cultural Centre of the Piarists in Madrid.

The most noted of these interventions includes the insertion of a new staircase in the existing monumental entry hall and the meticulous reconstruction of the ruined surfaces, both wall and ceiling. The reconstruction of the destroyed staircase, precisely in its original location but in modern materials and construction, demonstrates one interpretation of the Venice Charter. The reconstruction of the interior surfaces—the wall and ceiling—through a painstaking mapping of the missing areas and the insertion of new material follows a similar strategy. With these efforts, the original pre-war spatial experience was restored. At the same time, this experience is differentiated from the past through contemporary materials that delineate past and present as a *unified* effort. (figs. 11a–g)

The Cultural Centre of the Piarists in the Lavapiés neighborhood of Madrid, Spain, completed in 2004, is also a project born of semi-ruins. Integrating the remains of the Piarist School of San Fernando, the Cultural Centre is, like the Neues Museum, an ensemble of both new construction and refurbishment. Founded in 1729 as the first of many Piarist schools, the complex included a church that was partially destroyed in the Spanish Civil War. Its renewal also included a new wing and a renovation within the bombed church. The semi-ruined church was converted to a library with interventions

FIGS.13a–c: Past and present are woven together through uniquely different viewpoints at the Cultural Centre of the Piarists (above) and the Neues Museum (below right).

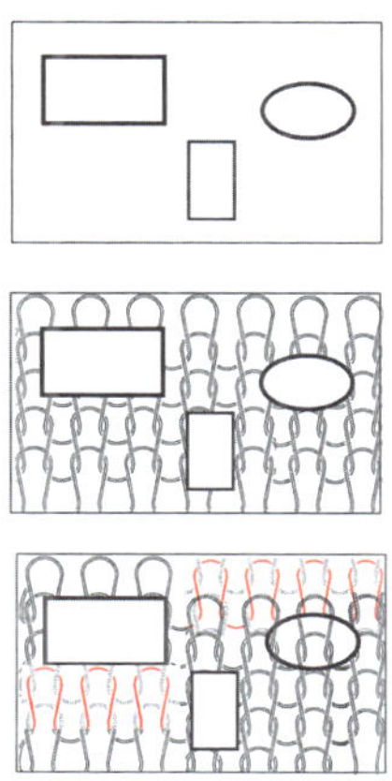

that included the addition of stairs, bookshelf and storage, reading rooms, new lighting, as well as insertions of glass and wood ceiling panels into the ruined dome. The newly added elements, detailed in a spare sensibility, stand out as deliberate insertions that delineate past and present as *distinct* efforts. (figs. 12a–c)

While both the renovated Neues Museum and the adaptation of the church of the Piarist school embrace the remnants of war as part of the buildings' history, their approaches for incorporating these marks through adaptive reuse diverge. With similar additions of stairs and new ceiling and surface treatments, both projects display a strategy for weaving the new within the old, both within and without. At the museum, the weaving of old to new, although with contrasting materials, is intentionally unified, resulting in a uniform surface. At the library, the weaving deliberately juxtaposes the new against the old, intentionally magnifying the differences as a passage of time. As strategies for interventions, these two projects clearly demonstrate two contrasting and viable interpretations; one darns a hole within the existing fabric using yarn of the same color, while the other purposefully weaves with a differently colored thread. (figs. 13a–c)

Summation Σ

Summation, another form of addition, is a sequence of numbers totaled as a single amount. Applied to architectural addition, it pertains to series of related elements—stairs, walkways, ramps, corridors, steps, balconies—that are not discrete volumes in and of themselves, but added together form a unified intervention to a host structure. These series of interventions occur both on the exterior and the interior, and at different scales.

FIG.14: Roberto Collovà's unifying intervention to the steeply sloping street in Salemi.

FIGS.15a–c: The conversion of the castle and fortifications in Verona to the Museo di Castelvecchio by Carlo Scarpa.

In a steeply sloping neighborhood in Salemi, Italy, the addition of a single front step of a uniform material to each house along the street mitigates the grade change from the urban front to the private domestic interior. While each step is its own height and shape, all the added steps along the street together form a series that constitutes a single intentional intervention of access. In the same material and style, the steps provide a new unity on the street. This domestic street step intervention has its equivalent at a grand scale in the renovation and conversion of a fortification complex to a cultural center in the Eisack Valley of Franzensfeste, Italy. New corridors, stairs,

FIGS.16a–f: Markus Scherer's intervention of new elements of circulation connects the many structures of Franzensfeste in Italy.

ramps were introduced to connect a sprawling set of buildings on a steeply sloping site. Fabricated from a uniform palate of galvanized patinated steel, this set of small interventions provides, in total, a unity to the site as a whole. Carlo Scarpa's conversion of the Castelvecchio castle and fortifications to a museum, also in Italy, offers an example of such additions applied simultaneously to both exterior and interior. With the architectural device of the cantilever, Scarpa introduced floating planes, small and large, all through the museum and in the junctures to the exterior. As support for sculpture both on the interior and the exterior, this device provides a unified gesture of weightlessness within the heavily fortified host. (figs. 14, 15a–c, 16a–f)

Subtraction –

Subtraction is the addition of negative numbers, whole or otherwise. In adaptive reuse, it refers to the removal of a part of the host structure. This removal can be deliberate or unintentional, the former a part of a choreographed design strategy, the latter an act of nature. Intentional subtraction takes place for various reasons: to make room for the new through demolition, to return a host to an original form, to appropriate the host structure for various intents, to bring an out-of-date host structure to current standards, to create double or multiple height spaces within the host. Residential renovations often begin with a subtraction to remove layers of additions and to bring a house back to its original state. Often preservation work also begins with subtraction. At the Park Street Armory, Herzog & de Meuron's work in the heritage rooms began with delayering the many finishes, placed one on top of the other. The complexity of this type of subtraction remains as it was

FIGS.17a–b: Cruz y Ortiz Arquitectos' return of the Rijksmuseum to its original design required a subtraction of the additions made over time.

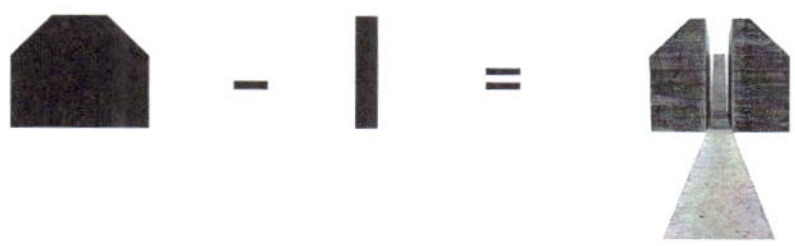

FIGS.18a–c: RAAAF and Atelier de Lyon's subtractive intervention to a Second World War bunker.

at the time of Viollet-le-Duc and his restoration projects at Vézelay and Paris. What is authenticity? Upon what criteria should such consideration be made? Which layer should one consider as authentic? Contemplation of this issue is ongoing without definitive conclusions.

These same questions were at the heart of the renovation of the Rijksmuseum in Amsterdam, Netherlands. Premised on the19th-century design of Pierre Cuypers, the winning proposal included a restoration to an original layout. This process required the removal of galleries added in the 1950s and 1960s from the inner courtyards and an elaborate procedure to sink this area below ground. This subtractive intervention allowed for the introduction of a new atrium as part of a redesigned entrance into the museum. Furthermore, as an intervention, it embraced the Cuypers design as authentic. For the city of Amsterdam, this embrace is a recognition that not all layers are precious, nor do they all contribute to a building's authenticity. While such decisions are case-specific, at the Rijksmuseum, this approach led to a restoration through a subtractive intervention. (figs. 17a–b)

Subtraction as appropriation most often occurs on host buildings without heritage designations. Such host structures are used as objects in service of activist agenda; to persuade through political content, to reveal history, to tell

FIGS.19a–b: Herzog & de Meuron's subtraction of the host structure's base at the Caixa Forum in Madrid.

FIGS.20a–c: In Salemi, Álvaro Siza & Roberto Collovà's interventions are in response to the earthquake that felled the Chiesa Madre in the center of town.

a tale. Such subtractive strategies tend towards the dramatic and include surgical interventions and major incisions within the host structure. Without the governance of landmark regulations, the host is bound to become *tabula rasa*. Bunker 599 is a prime example of an intervention to one of hundreds of unprotected World War II bunkers, built to defend Holland in the 1940s. Located in Culemborg, Netherlands, the project intervenes by splitting a reinforced-concrete pillbox structure, removing parts of its center and exposing the interior of a typically inaccessible military building. A long boardwalk inserted into the resulting fissure gives direct access to a flooded plain. This natural reserve is part of the New Dutch Waterline, a military line of defense used from 1815 to 1940 to flood eastern Netherlands against encroaching invaders. The subtractive intervention here is an act of revelation to disclose this long-time military secret. More importantly, this revelation demonstrates the present state of a Netherlands at peace. The ironic consequence of this subtraction was that the site, with its incision, earned it the status of Dutch national monument. (figs. 18a–c)

The Caixa Forum in Madrid, Spain, is another example of subtraction as appropriation. As a late 1890s power station without notable historic significance, the brick shell of the host was retained as a remnant of the early industrial age in Madrid. The stone base of the building was removed in its entirety, leaving a deliberate void at the entrance level. A feat of structural manipulation, the new building is noted for an entry that levitates from its site. In contrast to Bunker 599, where history played an important role, the agenda of the subtractive intervention here was to create spectacle out of

the ordinary. Both cases demonstrate that host buildings rooted in history but without the confines of landmark designation are opportunities as canvas of daring architectural feats, with adaptive reuse as a tool. (figs. 19a–b)
Subtraction as an act of nature can be a catalyst for change. The unexpected destruction of buildings or parts of them has repercussions that impact relationships in the surrounding context. In the case of the earthquake that severely damaged the Mother Church of Salemi, Italy, the devastation wreaked havoc not only on the church but on the plan of the hill town. The placement of the church at its apex reflects a long history that includes a feudal fiefdom. The subtractive act that felled the roof and left only partial elements of apse, subchapel and side altars created a ruin of the center of the town. The reuse of the ruin as an urban plaza is fitting as a new heart of town, especially in this age of secularization. The remaining elements double as outdoor furniture while the almost invisible interventions of Siza and Collovà, of which there are many, from the reinforced masonry to the metal struts, attend to the structural integrity and safety of the users. (figs. 20a–c)

Absolute Value

Subtractive interventions are not necessarily reductive. As in the mathematical principle of absolute value, where the magnitude of a number is independent of its sign, most subtractive interventions yield an eventual addition. As a variant of subtraction, this type of intervention does not result in a removal of matter in the ultimate balance. In this spirit, the Rijksmuseum project, with its objective to restore the plan to the original 19th-century layout, required a subtraction but only in order to implement an addition, a new atrium. In sum, the subtractive interventions enabled the creation of a new entrance for both museum visitors and the public at large.
Absolute value also prevails in the extension of the library for the Max Planck Institute for Art History, the Bibliotheca Hertziana, in Rome, Italy. Expansion of the building, situated in a historic neighborhood above the remains of a 60 BC Roman villa, was severely limited by the many constraints of heritage protection. With the need to work within the historic facades, the expansion project required the intricate removal of an interior space so as to insert a new atrium as part of the new library renovations.
Facade replacement is a unique category for the application of the absolute value function. The introduction of a new facade through the removal and replacement of the old is necessarily both subtractive and additive. An important intervention for the establishment of a different identity, it is an opportunity that requires consideration of how the new is woven into the existing. In addition to the issues of weaving into the host, the consequence of facade interventions reverberates outside the limits of the building structures

FIG.21: Valerio Olgiati's whitewashing of the *Yellow House* in Flims.

into the surrounding context. The impact of facade replacement is ultimately one that is positive in moving the project forward in time.

The facade replacement as an intervention is a renewal of the building skin. As a facelift, it updates a worn and outdated host building. It can be as minimal as a change of color, as in the Yellow House at Flims, Switzerland. The traditional farmhouse was transformed by a change of its iconic color to white and by interior interventions of a similar minimalism. Together they constitute a subtractive "whitewashing" of its agrarian associations for its new life as a museum. (fig. 21)

In residential projects, the addition of new cladding directly over the existing is a common practice. Removal of those added layers of cladding is, in reverse, a subsequent subtractive intervention. These additive and subtractive processes are at the heart of the 185 Post Street Building in San Francisco, California, USA. Originally built in 1908, this classically composed turn-of-the-century facade occupies a prominent corner in the Union Square neighborhood. In the 1950s, aluminum panels were introduced as a facelift that transformed the stone-clad building to a metal-clad one. What was in vogue in mid-century, however, was worn by the millennium. The 2008 renovation, in turn, consisted of the removal of the 1950s aluminum panels, a restoration of the 1908 facade and the addition of a glass skin over the restored stone. These interventions together culminate in the addition of a curtain wall assembly and an air gap that, in mitigating the temperature differential of the interior and exterior, increased the host's energy efficiency. The glass skin

FIG.22a: An outmoded aluminum skin covered the 1908 facade of the 185 Post Building, San Francisco, CA.

FIG.22b: Koonshing Wong's 2008 intervention at 185 Post Building reveals and protects the 1908 facade.

also protects the restored stone facade, encasing and preserving it from environmental damage. At night, the stone facade is visible behind the glass, displayed as a jewel of this historic quarter. Through the multi-layered intervention, the building is retained and preserved for the future while re-establishing urban relationships of the past. (figs. 22a–b)

The design of any facade is an opportunity to engage in the question of style. In projects of addition, this opportunity is moreover complex due to the existence of one or more previous authors. Depending on its age and the number of previous additions, a host building may be a canvas of many different styles. At St. Peter's Basilica in the Vatican, distinctive differences in the details of the various additions represent architectural styles from Renaissance to Baroque. Despite these differences, the church may appear unified to the layman; it is a work of one material and the styles are expressed in the language of similar architectural elements. This fundamental condition no longer exists; since the end of Neoclassicism, the emergence of a stylistic pluralism has muddied the process. With the possibility of many different languages of architectural elements, the design of the facade is now a charged opportunity. As the outer skin and face of a building, it can also serve as a canvas for acts of assimilation, historicism, or activism.

In many historic neighborhoods, zealous local preservation efforts perpetuate the consistent continuation of the urban fabric, without the acknowledgment of time. These attempts can result in false historicism. Gwathmey

FIGS.23a–b: Gwathmey Siegel's new facade at Princeton University's Whig Hall reinterprets the past and its historic temple host.

Siegel's 1974 intervention to Whig Hall at Princeton University in New Jersey, USA, spearheads this issue. One of twin 1893 Ionic temples on campus housing the university's debating societies, Whig Hall suffered damage from a 1969 fire that destroyed the interior and one of the facades of the temple. The addition comprised an insertion into the wrapper of three remaining facades. The new facade retains the base and cornice as a datum line for maintaining the integrity of the temple form. But within this datum, a new language of pure white geometric volumes emerges to expose the renovated spaces within. In a language of modern architecture, the new facade is an abstract composition inspired by the regulating lines of Neoclassicism. The renovation of Whig Hall and its missing facade retains the 19th-century legacy of the twin temples. At the same time, it signals a new era for the institution and the campus. As an addition resulting from a subtractive act of nature, Whig Hall demonstrates the use of the facade as expression and a messenger of change. (figs. 23a–b)

Since the 1970s, many facade interventions have served a similar purpose. They are messengers of change and other messages as well. Robert Venturi's 1976 addition to Cass Gilbert's Allen Memorial Art Museum at Oberlin College, Ohio, USA, is a vehicle for exploring his concept of the decorated shed in a historic context. Daniel Libeskind uses this strategy in several projects. At the Jewish Museum in Berlin, Germany, the facade of the addition is part of a narrative on loss and the disappearance of the Jewish people

during the Second World War. At the Dresden Military History Museum, the addition expresses itself as a violent form piercing the Neoclassical host structure. Libeskind describes the intent behind such an expression as an "architecture [that] will engage the public in the deepest issue of how organized violence and how military history and the fate of the city are intertwined."[2] Messages of change, however, do not always serve ulterior motives. Chipperfield's facade addition at Joachimstraße 11 simply expresses a clear and forward direction in which the choice of materials, the style and the detailing bridge the gap of years between the adjacent neighboring buildings. (figs. 24, 25)

While facade replacement facilitates a concrete interpretation of absolute value, absolute value as a concept can also apply to the abstract. Bunny Lane, an enormous industrial shed used in a residential application, illustrates such implementation. The inside of the shed holds a traditional suburban house, relocated and reused as a large interior element. Removed from the context of its New Jersey neighborhood of similar homes and placed in an entirely different scale, the house is transformed to a stand-alone object with exterior facades, roof and a porch. In the vast interior, the house becomes a room, a piece of furniture, a toy. The relocation is a subtractive act that removes

FIGS.24, 25: Venturi, Scott Brown's addition to the Allen Memorial Art Museum at Oberlin College, OH, and Daniel Libeskind's Jewish Museum in Berlin are facades that serve as messengers of change.

FIGS.26a–c: Adam Kalkin's use of a relocated house at Bunny Lane, NJ.

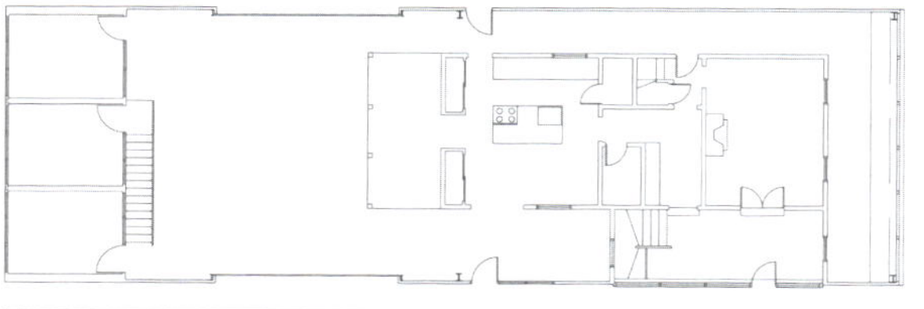

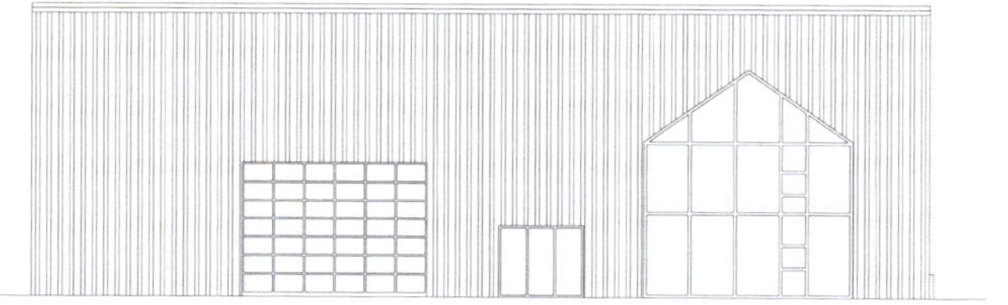

the house's natural identity and permits it to take on a different role in a new environment. (figs. 26a–c)

In a broader sense, the concept of absolute value is critical to understanding adaptive reuse. As a practice that implements change, adaptive reuse necessarily begins with demolition of some form. Its sum total effect will always require a consideration of both subtraction and addition. As interventions, additions of all types fundamentally provide extra space and enhanced use in a host structure. They interface with the existing structure in a spatial intersection of wall, ceiling or floor as appendages to an existing structure. These new intersections have ripple effects on the previously established systems of circulation and use, impacting the internal workings of the host. They also wield an impact on their host and host context that is not always evident and/or easily quantifiable. Applying an analysis akin to the absolute value function serves as a tool for evaluating the ultimate impact of each project of reuse.

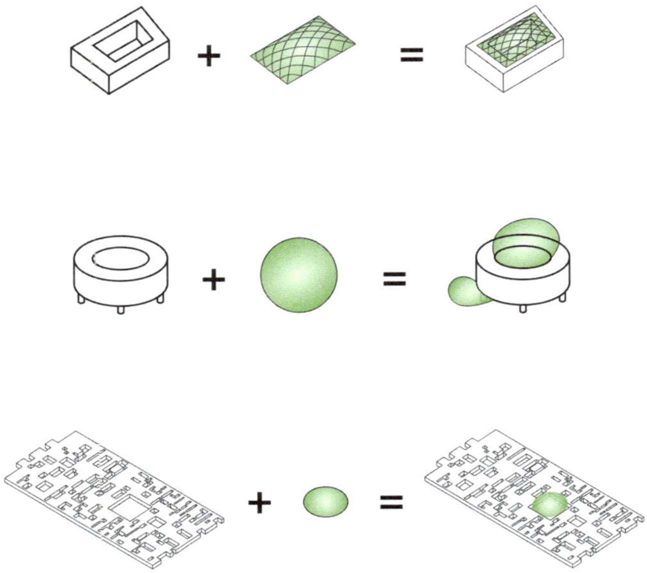

FIGS.27a–c: From top: Residenzschloss, Dresden, by Peter Kulka Architektur; The Hirshhorn Bubble Proposal by Diller Scofidio + Renfro; Free University Philology Library, Berlin, by Foster & Partners.

In such an evaluation, applying the brackets of the absolute function to a project might be to ask some of the following questions:

- What is the purpose of the host before the addition?
- What is the purpose of the addition?
- How does the purpose of the addition impact the purpose of the host structure?
- What is the purpose of the newly adapted project?
- What, if any, change does the addition make on the previous patterns of use, both within the host and its context?
- Are the critical elements of use of the host still intact with the addition?

Together, the answers to such questions provide a whole picture based on both new and old circumstances. They consider what is lost, gained and ultimately altered.

Diller Scofidio + Renfro's Hirshhorn Bubble proposal for Washington, DC, USA, Foster & Partners' Free University Philology Library in Berlin, Germany, and Peter Kulka's Residenzschloss in Dresden, Germany, are, by typology, three projects of addition, each involving an ovoid form inserted within an architectural void. The Hirshhorn Bubble is a proposed insertion of an inflatable textile room within the void of the Hirshhorn Museum. The Free University Philology Library is the insertion of an entire ovoid-shaped library into a campus plan based on an ideology of open communication manifested in a "continuous building complex organized around built and non-built zones ... along an orthogonal street system or a diagonal path system from courtyard to courtyard."[3] The Residenzschloss Museum is a consolidation of several royal residences by the addition of a single, connecting semi-ovoid roof. While typologically similar in concept, the same questions applied to each of these projects would yield entirely different answers; the same typological design strategy of adaptive reuse would impact entirely different aspects of each host and host context. In adaptive reuse practice, where the existence of singularities in the individual host structures constitutes the only certainty, a pure reliance on principles derived from typology would not be advisable. Rather, a clear understanding of the impact of each design strategy is crucial to a successful adaptive reuse project. Viewing adaptive reuse as mathematics is to adopt an objective lens in the often subjective world of design. Albert Einstein tells us that "[p]ure mathematics is, in its way, the poetry of logical ideas." (figs. 27a–c)

1 Website of Coop Himmelb(l)au. http://www.coop-himmelblau.at/architecture/projects/rooftop-remodeling-falkestrasse (accessed January 30, 2016). 2 Richard Waite, "Libeskind Completes Redesign of Dresden Museum of Military History," *The Architect's Journal*, October 12, 2011. 3 Candilis, Josic, Woods, Schiedhelm, *Free University Berlin* (London: AA Publications, 1999).

Mention of restoration conjures Eugène Viollet-le-Duc and his much-quoted 1875 definition "that [t]o restore a building is not to preserve it, to repair, or rebuild ... [but] to re-instate it in a condition of completeness which could never have existed at any given time."[1] The ensuing anti-restoration sentiments, which subsequently led to the beginnings of the conservation movement, focused in great part on Viollet-le-Duc's reliance on conjecture. In the face of unknown territory, without documentation of what existed before, the speculative nature of such restoration prompted a discourse on authenticity that continues, more than a century later, today. In the often overlooked continuation of his definition, Viollet-le-Duc cautions that "[i]t is only since the first quarter of the present century that the idea of restoring buildings of another age has been entertained; and we are not aware that a clear definition of architectural restoration has as yet been given. Perhaps it may be as well to endeavour at the outset to gain an exact notion of what we understand, or ought to understand, by a restoration ..."[2] Writing in 1875, Viollet-le-Duc would have encountered the 1832 definition of restoration in the writings of his countryman and Secretary of the Académie des Beaux-Art, Quatremère de Quincy, equating restoration generally to "the re-establishment of parts of a building more or less damaged ..."[3] He would also have been acquainted with the advocacy of Ludovic Vitet and Prosper Mérimée, who both held the position of Inspector General of the *Commission des monuments historiques*, for a critical approach to restoration based on architectural surveys and measured drawings. But in the latter half of the 19th century, such information was scant, as this type of documentation was the product of laborious and intensive tasks. (figs. 1a–b)

In the first quarter of the 21st century, restoration and conservation have dramatically evolved, especially through technology and the many tools it has

A New and Distant Frontier

14

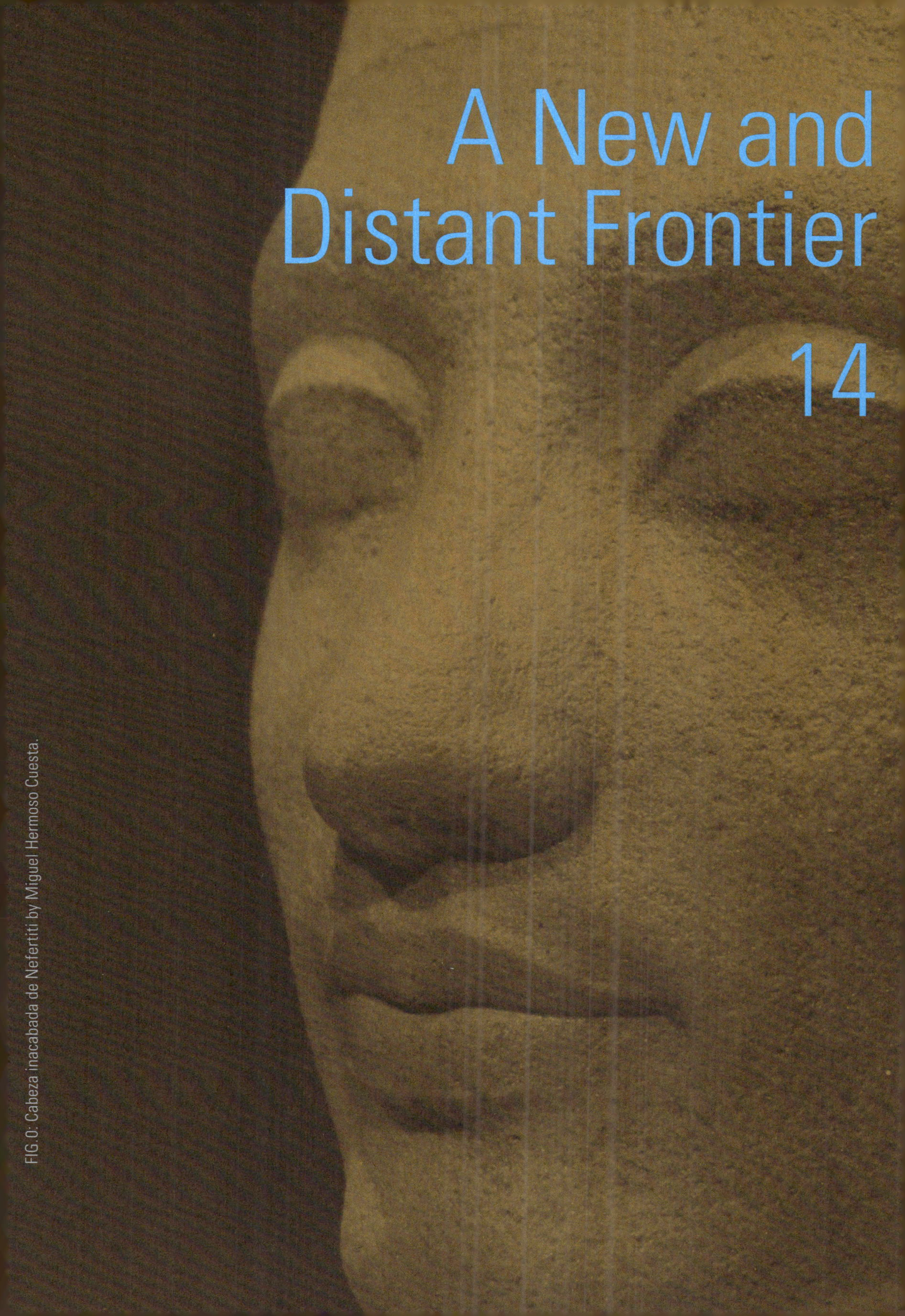

FIG.0: Cabeza inacabada de Nefertiti by Miguel Hermoso Cuesta.

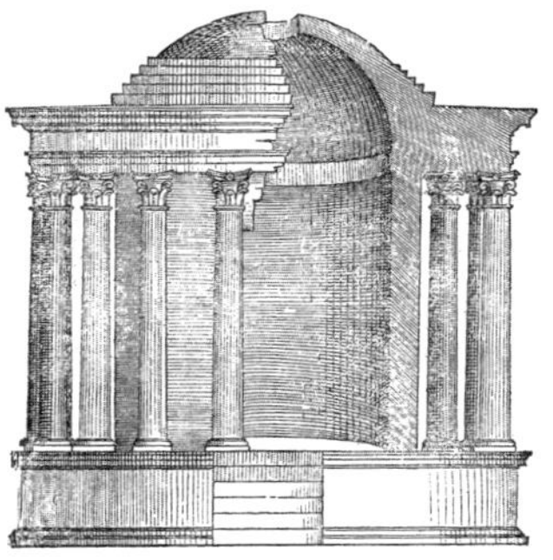

FIGS.1a–b: The engravings and writings of Serlio and Palladio are examples of resources available in the 19th century.

engendered. With changed methods, the notion of what we preserve and how we do it has greatly expanded since the late 19th century. Together, the means and the mind-set of our time redefine the acts of preservation.

Adaptive reuse, the legacy of these debates on restoration and conservation, has also evolved since the latter half of the 20th century, when key legislation such as the Venice Charter of 1964 first addressed the need for "some socially useful purpose" in the conservation of monuments. If the 20th century established an adaptive reuse practice based on alterations that bestow new use within the built existing environment, today we confront the possibilities of an adaptive reuse practice at a new frontier. (figs. 2a–b)

Restoration's first opponents focused on the confines of the era and the impossibility of "this kind of forgery."[4] William Morris stated in his 1887 *Manifesto* that in this respect, "knowledge failed the builders."[5] By the 1920s, the advances of the 20th century presaged a metamorphosis as expressed by French poet and philosopher Paul Valéry: "Our fine arts were developed, their types and uses were established, in times very different from the present, by men whose power of action upon things was insignificant in comparison with ours. But the amazing growth of our techniques, the adaptability and precision they have attained, the ideas and habits they are creating,

FIGS.2a–b: Thermography and augmented reality are examples of the many new means enabled by today's technology for restoration, duplication and visualization.

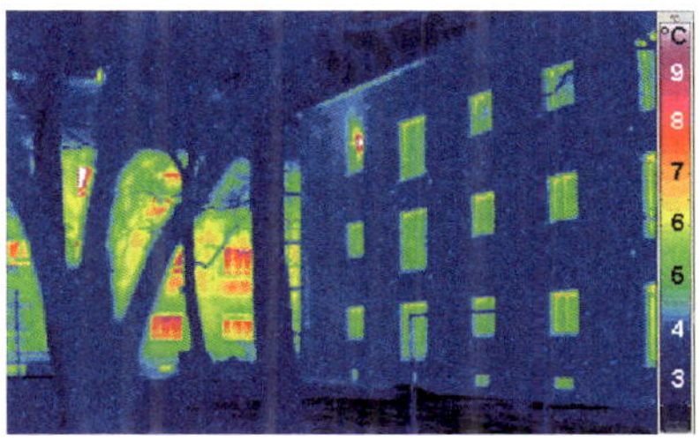

make it a certainty that profound changes are impending in the ancient craft of the Beautiful ... We must expect great innovations to transform the entire technique of the arts, thereby affecting artistic invention itself and perhaps even bringing about an amazing change in our very notion of art."[6] These sentiments are entirely applicable today, where the innovations of the late 20th and the early 21st centuries have led to unprecedented developments affecting much of modern life. In conservation and adaptive reuse, completely altered building construction practices expand the limits of practice. The

FIGS.3a–b: The UNESCO heritage site of Hallstatt in Austria, and its duplicate in Luoyang, China.

technological advances of the recent decades have indeed transformed not only the art but also the *notion* of art. In adaptive reuse, this manifests itself physically through innovative construction means and conceptually through the interpretation of the field in new realms. If early conservation resulted from imperfect means such as those defined by Quatremère de Quincy, in which "it suffices for one to know some fragments of columns, entablature and capitals of columns of a Greek architecture to rediscover at least the order of the temple ...,"[7] then what are the implications of the new tools and methodologies that enable a more perfect means, informed by precise and readily available information?

In "The Lamp of Memory," John Ruskin asked: "What copying can there be of surfaces that have been worn half an inch down? The whole finish of the work was in the half inch that is gone ..."[8] In the 19th century of Morris and Ruskin, the knowledge of a structure required for its replication was derived primarily from publications such as those of Vitruvius, Serlio, Palladio and, in the late 18th century, Stuart and Revett. These books documented works of antiquity and perpetuated Classical ideals. Neoclassical works of architects such as Robert Adam, William Chambers and John Soane, by no means replications, also reflect this influence. Today, technology such as digitization, 3D laser and infared radiation expands the possibilities of replication far beyond the inspiration of period pattern books. A wealth of new and smart tools have emerged for building scans, materials diagnostics, physio-mechanical and non-invasive testing, surveying and general heritage science. Digital reconstructions are based in three-dimensional measurements, scanning and modeling. There is now a very real potential for producing full and accurate copies of existing objects and structures. Today the knowledge that "failed" Morris' stone chiseling builders exists.

In 1997, the Austrian town of Hallstatt, an ancient salt mining and production town in an extraordinary Alpine setting, received UNESCO World Heritage

FIGS.4a–c: Housing blocks on Boulevard Haussmann in Paris serve as the mold for the cast facade of Édouard François' Fouquet's Barrière Hotel.

designation as a "cultural landscape [that] has retained a degree of authenticity in nature and society."[9] In 2012, a duplication of Hallstatt opened in Luoyang, China, as a housing development. In 2006, several buildings in an urban block of Paris known as Triangle d'Or were renovated as Fouquet's Barrière Hotel. The upgrade of the building facades, including one from the 1970s, constituted a major part of this project. Referencing a 19th-century vision of Paris, a new concrete facade in the form of a molded casting that replicated nearby Haussmannian facades was directly applied to the existing structure. New apertures were subsequently placed within these duplicated concrete facades, dictated by the interior functions and unrelated to those of the Haussmann duplicates. In 2012, artist Do Ho Suh reconstructed the house in which he lived as a student in Providence, Rhode Island, USA, at full scale and in silk. Replicated to the minutiae, this ghostly translucent house

FIG.5: *Home Within Home* by sculptor Do Ho Suh recreates his temporary home in Providence, RI, in silk and at full scale.

floats in different galleries, including the Museum of Modern and Contemporary Art in Seoul, Korea. Through the new possibilities of technology, these 21st-century projects demonstrate and thereby redefine the ability to replicate existing structures with unerring accuracy. (figs. 3a–b, 4a–c, 5)

The matter of authenticity, central to the 19th-century controversy to "restore" damaged French monuments to their earlier and whole existence, does not exist in these examples. The replications are not attempts at preserving a physical object or structure. They embrace Walter Benjamin's belief that "[t]he presence of the original is the prerequisite to the concept of authenticity,"[10] and thus the clear absence of the original in these examples already negates all such claims. Instead, the replicated structures exist as new structures through the reuse of the existing ones as symbols. They gain a new "aura"[11] through such reuse. In China, where knock-offs are the norm, the aura of the replicated village lies in Hallstatt's authenticity as a UNESCO site; in the 8th arrondissement of Paris, the hotel's aura is established through a connection to the Haussmannian past in a facade that acts as a physical demonstration of time, past and present; in the galleries, the aura of the house lies in the act of recall. These replications embrace the sentiments of Viollet-le-Duc in creating a new state of "completeness which could never have existed at any given time." Benjamin speaks of mechanical reproduction as "the desire of contemporary masses to bring things 'closer' spatially and humanly."[12] In reproducing an ideal of an existing structure rather than the structure itself,

FIGS. 6a–b: The residence of an SS commandant at Kamp Westerbork, transformed to a museum and education center.

these projects, through new use, extend the metaphysical distance between what was and what is.

In 2015, the former residence of the SS commander at Kamp Westerbork, a former Nazi concentration camp in the Netherlands and since declared a national monument, was converted to an educational center. This conversion was achieved by encapsulating the clapboard house within an inhabitable glass box, as both an act of preservation and of reuse. Objectified within a colossal, climate-controlled vitrine, the residence is preserved *in situ* and in perpetuity. In contrast to the projects of replication, the original exists in this project, fulfilling Benjamin's prerequisite for authenticity. Yet it remains imprisoned in time, serving a symbolic life sentence as a witness to history. While not by any means a replication, this type of preservation, made possible by new notions of art, also detaches an original from the past. (figs. 6a–b)

Distance is at the heart of another strategy for heritage preservation: translocation, the process of moving a structure from one location to another. An age-old strategy, translocation consists of lifting a structure and transferring it onto a movable platform. With low-tech means such as wood cribbing and jacks, structures have been relocated for thousands of years.[13] Most often, this process is a last-resort measure of protection when a structure is physically threatened in its original site. Some known examples are: the Marble Arch in London, Great Britain, moved in 1851 from the edge of Buckingham Palace to Hyde Park due to the palace's expansion; and the 1999 move of

FIGS.7a–b: The translocation of the Cape Hatteras Lighthouse in North Carolina.

the seven historic structures of the 1870 Cape Hatteras Lighthouse & Station in North Carolina, USA, 885 meters from the original site, due to the impact of shoreline erosion on their foundations. An alternate method of translocation transports disassembled structures, rather than whole ones, that are reassembled on their new sites. This method was used with moves such as that of the 1244 BC Abu Simbel complex in southern Egypt. The temple was cut into pieces and transported higher up the bank of the Nile River to save it from the imminent inundation caused by the construction of the Aswan Dam. In these examples, translocation is an act of preservation that introduces a physical distance between the original and the moved structure. (figs. 7a–b, 8a–b)

Enhanced means of construction today permit translocation of not only a single building but also of high-rises and large structures, while enhanced modes of transportation permit translocation from afar. With such newfound potential, the use of translocation as a strategy has expanded beyond heritage protection. In 1968, John Rennie's 1831 London Bridge was deemed structurally insufficient to support the demands of the future and auctioned off to the highest bidder, Robert McCulloch. An entrepreneur, McCullough founded the town of Lake Havasu City, Arizona, USA, in 1963 out of 67.3 square kilometers of desert. With great hopes that the historic bridge would lend a validity to this newly founded town, the bridge was transported in pieces, reassembled, reconstructed on ground and connected to the lake through a dredged canal. In its transatlantic relocation, London Bridge was transformed from infrastructure to a means for legitimacy. In 1997, the 18th-century Yin Yu Tang House, a relocated late Qing Dynasty merchant residence from southwestern China, was disassembled and transported in pieces to the USA. Its relocation to the Peabody Essex Museum in Salem, Massachusetts, as a

FIGS.8a–b: The translocation of the Abu Simbel complex in Egypt.

FIGS. 9a–b: The 1831 London Bridge in its original location in London and in its new location at Lake Havasu in Arizona.

permanent cultural exhibit, transformed it from an abandoned domestic structure to museum object. (figs. 9a–b, 10)

With present-day means and methods such processes, once unimaginable, unleash a new breed of actions in the name of preservation. The reuse of the Yin Yu Tang as both exhibit and object, the reuse of London Bridge as pedigree, the reuse of a Haussmann facade as "wallpaper," the reuse of a house as memory, the use of a house as witness—these are transformations in space and time. How do we classify such work? Is it preservation? Is it restoration? Is it reuse? How do we justify such acts? What are we preserving? What of authenticity? How do we determine when extraordinary means are required and justify the enormous expense involved? What are the ethics in this new frontier?

FIG.10: The Yin Yu Tang House within its new context of the Peabody Essex Museum, Salem, MA.

While qualification of such recent endeavors are difficult to place within the context of history, as new directions do they in fact parallel developments in preservation practices since the latter half of the 20th century? Since the seminal adoption of the Venice Charter in 1964, the definition of heritage has expanded to include much more than monuments. The United Nations Educational, Scientific and Cultural Organization (UNESCO), for example, whose mission since its inception in 1945 is "in building intercultural understanding through protection of heritage,"[14] has expanded its interpretations of this heritage. Today, UNESCO protection includes everything from "our cherished historic monuments and museums ... to traditional practices and contemporary art forms" but also "intangible and underwater heritage, museum collections, oral traditions and other forms of heritage ..."[15] Recent interpretations of conservation from around the world reflect similar change: ICOMOS New Zealand Charter's 2010 definition that "[t]he purpose of conservation is to care for places of cultural heritage value"; the Burra Charter's 2013 definition that "Conservation means all the processes of looking after a place so as to retain its cultural significance"; INTACH's (Indian National Trust for Art and Cultural Heritage) 2016 Charter that "[t]he objective of conservation is to maintain the significance of the architectural heritage or site. Significance is constituted in both the tangible and intangible forms." In such a broadened arena of definition lies the possibility of novel interpretations.

As in artist Do Ho Suh's re-creation of physical domestic structures in ephemeral materials, artist Edoardo Tresoldi has re-created a similar object but

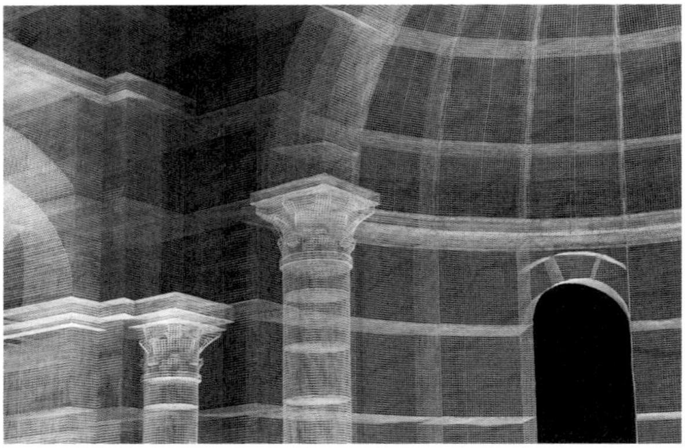

FIG.11: Artist Edoardo Tresoldi recreates in wire a full-scale interpretation of the 11th-century basilica that once stood on the site of Santa Maria di Siponto, Foggia.

within an archaeological site in Apulia, Italy. Constructed from seven tons of wire mesh and placed directly above its archaeological remains, the artist's installation is an interpretation of an 11th-century Paleo-Christian basilica that once stood upon the site of Santa Maria Maggiore di Siponto.[16] A conjecture, albeit with detailed architectural elements such as columns and arches, Tresoldi's reconstruction in insubstantial material has been likened to "a hologram projected onto the site."[17] Apropos of conjecture, the wire mesh wields an ethereal presence that is almost invisible from a distance. In contrast to Viollet-le-Duc's full reconstruction of Carcassonne with similarly scant remaining evidence, Tresoldi's concept and choice of materials resurrect the past lightly as a distant reinterpretation. Supported by the Minister of Culture with the objective to raise awareness of Siponto's significance as a Roman colony and port from 194 BC, this re-creation of the basilica has revived an interest in this part of Foggia's history. (fig. 11)

In contrast is the "reconstruction," currently in fabrication, of a Roman triumphal arch from Palmyra, Syria, that was destroyed in 2015 by ISIS militants. In the marble quarries of Carrara, Italy, a full-scale 120-ton replica is in the process of being carved out of Egyptian marble from a 3-D digital model generated from photos taken over the years. Intended for an installation in London demonstrating such reconstruction as propaganda, this model reinforces the idea of the Institute of Digital Archaeology that "[e]very time we resurrect from the rubble one of these monuments, it undercuts the mes-

FIGS. 12a–b: The city of Palmyra in Syria, including the Marble Arch, prior to destruction by ISIS.

sage of fear and ignorance that these people are trying to spread."[18] With the 2016 ouster of the ISIS militants from Palmyra, Syria, there is speculation of placing the duplicate onto the actual site of the destroyed arch. In comparison to Tresoldi's installation at the Santa Maria Maggiore di Siponto, the installation of the replicated arch in its original location and material reawakens questions of authenticity. How does technologically enabled precision change this ongoing debate? Does the political urgency at Palmyra justify a reproduction of destroyed heritage? What is its significance as a copy on the original site? Would the replica serve a new use as a symbol of fortitude and resilience in the face of terrorism? (figs. 12a–b)

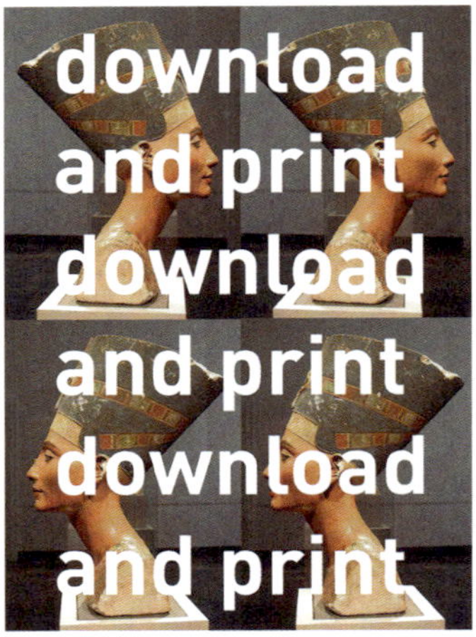

FIG.13

In the wake of ISIS' destruction at Palmyra, cultural organizations now engage in prophylactic documentation of ancient sites in threatened locations. In such information and its inherent potential lies a promise of resurrection. What are the implications in the greater world? In the era of Internet activism, artists recently visiting the Neues Museum in Berlin, Germany, scanned the bust of Nefertiti, in secret, using mobile devices. The release of these files on the Internet under a Creative Commons license enables anyone to download and 3D-print accurate copies of the head of Egyptian Pharoah Akhenaten's royal wife. Is such action the realization of Benjamin's "masses" "overcoming the uniqueness of every reality by accepting its reproduction"[19]? Are these reproductions that "substitute plurality of copies for a unique existence" and promote a "liquidation of the traditional value of the cultural heritage"[20]? Or is this trend akin to an iteration of the flowering of the Roman world between the 1st and the 3rd centuries AD that witnessed a wholesale replication of Greek sculpture from 500 years earlier? Replication in turn is a product of a variety of approaches, as many Roman sculptures were "purely Roman" while others were "carefully measured, exact copies or variants of Greek prototypes ..."[21] Millennia later, the unabashed replication of Greek culture and beauty "often provide our primary visual evidence of masterpieces ..."[22] (fig. 13)

At a time when people inhabit not only physical but virtual spaces in their everyday lives, these new possibilities of replication in the early 21st century may well in the near future become virtual ones, where distances between the original work and the replication become physically nearer and metaphysically farther apart. Prompted by events in the world today, the questions of authenticity, and ultimately authority, once raised and responded to in the mid- to late 19th century, are resurfacing in a new dialogue. Technology complicates the debate with the existence of the knowledge that "failed" Morris' builders. We now stand at the edge of a new frontier. New steps forward are full of potential but also grave implications.

1 Eugène Viollet-le-Duc, *On Restoration* (London: Sampson Low, Marston, Low and Searle, 1875), p. 9. 2 Ibid. 3 Quatremère de Quincy, *Dictionnaire Historique d'Architecture* (Paris: Librairie d'Adrien Le Clere, 1832). 4 William Morris, "The Manifesto," SPAB Society for the Protection of Ancient Buildings, 1887, from SPAB website, https://www.spab.org.uk/what-is-spab-/the-manifesto/ (accessed March 13, 2016). 5 Ibid. 6 Paul Valéry, "La conquête de l'ubiquité, Une édition électronique réalisée à partir du texte de Paul Valéry, « La conquête de l'ubiquité » (1928)", in *Œuvres, tome II, Pièces sur l'art*, Nrf, Gallimard, Bibl. de la Pléiade, 1960, pp. 1283–1287. 7 "Restauration. On sait qu'il suffit très-souvent de quelques framens de colonnes, d'entablemens et de chapiteaux d'une architecture grecque, pour retrouver du moins l'ensemble d'une ordonnance de temple." Quatremère de Quincy, *Dictionnaire Historique d'Architecture* (Paris: Librairie d'Adrien Le Clere, 1832), English translation by Veronica Dewey. 8 John Ruskin, *The Seven Lamps of Architecture* (Kent: George Allen, 1889), p. 195. 9 Hallstatt-Dachstein/ Salzkammergut Cultural Landscape, UNESCO website, http://whc.unesco.org/en/list/806 (accessed April 7, 2016). 10 Walter Benjamin, "The Work of Art in the Age of Mechanical Reproduction," (1936) in Hannah Arendt, ed., *Illuminations*, (New York, NY: Schocken Books, 1969), p. 222. 11 Walter Benjamin in "The Work of Art in the Age of Mechanical Reproduction" defines aura as "uniqueness." Other definitions include "distinctive quality" or "force emanating from somebody or something." 12 Benjamin, p. 223. 13 Definition of "relocation" from "The Appleton Charter for the Protection and Enhancement of the Built Environment", ICOMOS Canada, August 1983. 14 UNESCO website, http://en.unesco.org/about-us/introducing-unesco (accessed November 4, 2016). 15 Ibid. 16 Paolo Conti, "Siponto: con la rete metallica ricostruita basilica del XII secolo," *Corriere della Sera*, March 12, 2016. 17 "A Significant Wow Factor: Airy Resurrection of an Ancient Basilica," *Detail* Blog, http://www.detail-online.com/blog-article/a-signifcant-wow-factor-airy-resurrection-of-an-ancient-basilica-27317/ (accessed April 14, 2016). 18 Stephen Farrell, "If All Else Fails, 3D Models and Robots Might Rebuild Palmyra," *The New York Times*, March 28, 2016. 19 Benjamin, p. 223. 20 Benjamin, p. 221. 21 Department of Greek and Roman Art, "Roman Copies of Greek Statues," in *Heilbrunn Timeline of Art History* (New York, NY: The Metropolitan Museum of Art, 2000–), http://www.metmuseum.org/toah/hd/rogr/hd_rogr.htm (accessed October 2002). 22 Ibid.

What is time-honored at the edge of a new frontier? Innumerable publications through history address the principles of architecture from the *Ten Books* of Vitruvius and of Alberti to the *Four* of Palladio, from Ruskin's *Seven Lamps* and Tschumi's *Six Concepts* to Le Corbusier's *Five Points*, from Durand's systematization to Frank Lloyd Wright's organic system, from Louis Sullivan's *Tall* to Rem Koolhaas' *S, M, L, XL*.[1] They provide era-specific viewpoints on the design principles of buildings. What of adaptive reuse, understood very broadly as design interventions within the existing built environment? Do the principles that guide the creation of new form also guide the revision of such form in another iteration in time? Are the principles of the host structure those of the intervention?

An intervention such as the transformation of the craneway to the Kraanspoor Building in Amsterdam, Netherlands, demonstrates a visible adherence to the principles of the host structure. By contrast, the addition and subtraction at the Caixa Forum in Madrid, Spain, march to the "beat of a drummer"[2] other than its industrial host shell. Similarly, the insertion of a folded platform roof into the Moritzburg castle ruin in Halle, Germany, introduces an entirely new structural system for its conversion to museum. And the woven interior interventions to a brick abattoir for its conversion to the Cineteca Matadero in Madrid, Spain, a cinema and film archive, are instead based on the architect's memory of times past. Although conditioned by their context, these interventions are, in fact, often the products of new agenda. If adaptive reuse projects are by no means constrained by an adherence to the principles of their host, what governs the reuse of existing structures? (figs. 1, 2, 3, 4)

In Book III of *De Architectura*, Vitruvius speaks of harmony through the idea of symmetry, the principle of the day. In comparing the temple to the human

Second Violin

15

FIG.1: Kraanspoor Building, Amsterdam, by OTH Architecten.

FIG.2: Caixa Forum, Madrid, by Herzog & de Meuron.

FIG.3: Moritzburg Art Museum, Halle, by Nieto Sobejano Arquitectos.

FIG.4: Cineteca Matadero, Madrid, by Churtichaga + Quadra-Salcedo Arquitectos.

body he speaks archetypically through the most sacred building type of his time. This analogy of building to body probes the relationship of parts—be it building parts or body parts—in that "there ought to be the greatest harmony in the [symmetrical] relations of the different parts to the general magnitude of the whole" as without such "there can be no principles ..."[3] Within the framework of such an analogy, adaptive reuse as subtractions, additions, facade interventions and insertions into a host structure equates to a medical intervention—surgery, prosthetic, skin graft, organ transplants. These are interventions that invariably change the harmonious relationships of the original whole. (fig.5)

With the present-day implications of financial and legal liability, modern medicine and its interventions often prescribe to a mechanistic philosophy[4] as if "the body was a machine that could be fixed."[5] Within this sense of efficiency and efficacy, if an organ failed it would be removed and replaced through transplant; if part of the skin were destroyed a new piece would be grafted onto the body; if the hip broke a new joint would be inserted. Analogously, within an existing structure, if an elevator broke, it would be removed and

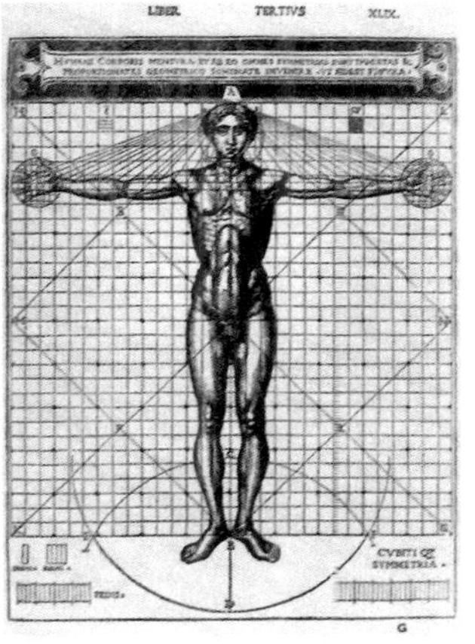

FIG.5: Illustration in the edition of Vitruvius' *De Architectura* by Cesare Cesariano ("Vitruvian Man"), c. 1521.

replaced; a deteriorating facade would be replaced with a new one; and a need for space might result in a building addition. In adaptive reuse, this medical approach provides a clear logic that accounts for projects of day-to-day refurbishment, renovation and renewal. Application of such logic, however, might, in the guise of efficiency, sanction the division of a large underused building into small spaces such as in the church-condo conversion. But this pragmatic logic alone would not account for the loss of the church's defining monumentality.

Vitalism, as opposed to mechanism, also has a history in medical philosophy as "the theory that the origin and phenomena of life are dependent on a force or principle distinct from purely chemical or physical forces."[6] Now discounted by modern medicine, this approach assumed the existence of a vital life force such as Hippocrates' Four Humors. "For vitalists, the body was not a machine. They believed that life had something special about it that science could never duplicate."[7] Adaptive reuse, seen through this view of medicine, acknowledges the existence in a building of some *anima* that must be respected. It is a logic that recognizes a vital type of life within an existing

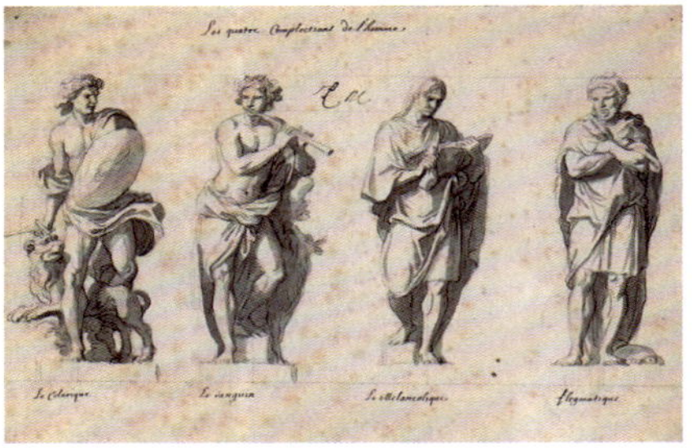

FIG.6: *Les quatre complexions de l'homme* ("The Four Temperaments"), Charles Le Brun, c. 1674.

structure distinct from that which pertains purely to its operation. In this view, a conversion of a 30.5-meter-high church interior through its division into six levels of condominiums would result in the loss of its *anima*. Such a view unites exemplary works of adaptive reuse that capture the essence of their host buildings while introducing the new within the existing: for example, the incorporation of water in Scarpa's Fondazione Querini Stampalia in Venice, Italy; the embrace of war wounds in Chipperfield's Neues Museum in Berlin, Germany; and the modesty of new forms within the archaeological presence of time in Fehn's Hedmark Museum in Hamar, Norway. Together, these two opposing approaches to medicine—mechanism and vitalism—viewed through Vitruvius' analogy of building to body, yield an understanding of adaptive reuse as a practice of quotidian change and of poetic intervention. (figs. 6, 7, 8, 9)

Applied to the 1931 James Whale film *Frankenstein*, these two contrasting views yield an understanding of the creature as a mechanical success but a failure as a man. A personal phantasmagoric vision, the experiment was less of science than of ambition. The true intentions of Dr. Frankenstein, as an architect of life reused, are revealed during the drama of a thunderstorm in which Frankenstein proclaims: "I created it ... now I know what it feels like to be God." While this is Hollywood at its best, in the analogy of building to body, the depiction of Dr. Frankenstein holds similarities to literature's frequent portrayals of the architect as self-interested. If self-interest and blind ambition account for the creature's ultimate failure, how does one avoid the pitfalls of the Frankenstein Syndrome? How must one approach the second act of a creation's existence?

In modern-day performance, the second violin describes a group of 14 to 16 musicians that make up the strings section of an orchestra. As musicians,

FIG.7: Fondazione Querini Stampalia, Venice, by Carlo Scarpa.

FIG.8: Hedmark Museum, Hamar, by Sverre Fehn.

FIG.9: Neues Museum, Berlin, by David Chipperfield.

second violins are equally skilled as first violins but play separate and different parts of the score. The first violins play the melody and the second violins play to support the melody through harmonic and rhythmic parts. "If truth be known, a lot of what is required of the second violins is difficult, even at times treacherous! They often have to play rapid intricate rhythms on the lower strings, which is difficult and tiring, and harmonies sometimes create awkward passages. They also have to play syncopated and other very difficult rhythms underneath the soaring melodies of the first violins."[8] But a melody by itself remains simply that—whereas an opus is always the product of both sections of musicians blending seamlessly as one.

The practice of adaptive reuse is much like playing the second violin to the melody of the host building. It is a song of redaction in which the minor keys humbly and sweetly negotiate between existing context and new content.

1 The books referred to are: Vitruvius, *De architectura*; Leon Battista Alberti, *De re aedificatoria*; Andrea Palladio, *I quattro libri dell'architettura*; John Ruskin, "The Seven Lamps of Architecture," in *The Stones of Venice*; Bernard Tschumi, "Six Concepts," in *Architecture and Disjunction*; Le Corbusier, *Vers une architecture*; J. N. Durand, *Précis des leçons d'architecture données à l'Ecole polytechnique*; Frank Lloyd Wright, *The Natural House*; Louis H. Sullivan, *The Tall Office Building Artistically Considered*; O.M.A., Rem Koolhaas and Bruce Mau, *S, M, L, XL*. 2 Refers to an expression found in Henry David Thoreau's *Walden*. 3 Vitruvius (transl. Morris Hicky Morgan), *The Ten Books on Architecture* (New York, NY: Dover Publications, Inc., 1960), p. 72. 4 The *Oxford English Dictionary* defines 'mechanism' as "The doctrine that all natural phenomena, including life and thought, allow mechanical explanation by physics and chemistry." http://www.oxforddictionaries.com/us/definition/american_english/mechanism#mechanism__8 (accessed April 29, 2016). 5 Victoria Sweet, *God's Hotel* (New York, NY: Riverhead Books, 2012), p. 112. 6 *Oxford English Dictionary* (accessed April 29, 2016). 7 Sweet, p. 112. 8 Jennifer Jones, Assistant Concertmaster of the Nova Scotia Symphony. https://symphonynovascotia.ca/faqs/symphony-101/whats-the-difference-between-first-violins-and-second-violins/ (accessed April 20, 2016).

Index of Subjects

Index of Buildings, Works and Projects

Page numbers in italics refer to illustrations

Index of Persons, Firms and Institutions

Page numbers in italics refer to illustrations

Bibliography

Alberti, Leon Battista (translated by Joseph Rykwert, Neil Leach, Robert Tavernor). 1988. *On the Art of Building in Ten Books*. Cambridge, MA: The MIT Press.

"Appleton Charter for the Protection and Enhancement of the Built Environment." 1983. ICOMOS Canada.

Arendt, Hannah. 1954. *Between Past and Future*. New York: Penguin Books.

Arrhenius, Thordis. 2012. *The Fragile Monument – On Conservation and Modernity*. London: Artifice Books.

"Articles VII & VIII, Project of an International Declaration Concerning the Laws and Customs of War. Adopted by the Conference of Brussels, August 27, 1874." 1907. In *The American Journal of International Law*, 1 (2), Supplement: Official Documents (April).

Ascher, Lois. 2010. "Krzysztof Wodiczko: Public Space: Commodity or Culture." In *Streetnotes 20: Urban Feel*, edited by David Michalski.

Benjamin, Walter (translated by Harry Zohn). 1968. *Illuminations*. New York: Schocken Books.

Berducou, Marie. 1996. "Introduction to Archaeological Conservation." In *Historical and Philosophical Issues in the Conservation of Cultural Heritage*, edited by Nicholas Price, M. Kirby Talley, Jr., and Alessandra Melucco Vacarro. Los Angeles: The Getty Conservation Institute.

Bergson, Henri (translated by Nancy Margaret Paul and W. Scott Palmer). 1911. *Matter and Memory*. London: George Allen and Unwin.

Bergson, Henri. 2007. *Creative Evolution*. New York: Palgrave Macmillan.

Boito, Camillo. 2009. "Questioni pratiche di belle art: restauri, concorsi, legislazione, professione insegnamento," translated by Cesare Birignani as "Restoration in Architecture: First Dialogue." In *Future Anterior*, University of Minnesota Press, 6 (1).

Bos, Caroline and Ben van Berkel. 2006. *Design Models*. London: Thames and Hudson.

Boudon, Phillipe (translated by Gerald Onn). 1969. *Lived-In Architecture – Le Corbusier's Pessac Revisited*. Cambridge, MA: The MIT Press.

Brandi, Cesare (translated by Gianni Ponti with Alessandra Melucco Vaccaro). 1963. *Teoria del restauro*. Rome: Edizioni di Storia e Letteratura.

"Breaking the Silence: the Transatlantic Slave Trade Education Project." UNESCO UNESDOC Digital Library. Accessed July 8, 2024. https://unesdoc.unesco.org/ark:/48223/pf0000137805.

Burke, Tony. 2016. "Principles of Building Adaptation and Conservation." *Open Resources for Built Environment Education*. Accessed March 5, 2016. https://www.scribd.com/document/118235853/1314451638-Learning-Pack-1-Building-Adapt-Conserv-Principles

Byard, Paul Spencer. 1998. *The Architecture of Additions: Design and Regulation*. New York: W.W. Norton.

Carbonara, Giovanni. 1996. "The Integration of the Image: Problems in the Restoration of Monuments." In *Historical and Philosophical Issues in the Conservation of Cultural Heritage*, edited by Nicholas Price, M. Kirby Talley, Jr., and Alessandra Melucco Vacarro. Los Angeles: The Getty Conservation Institute.

Cicero (translated by David Wardle). 2006. *Cicero: On Divination (De Divinatione) Book 1*. Oxford: Oxford University Press.

Conti, Paolo. 2016. "Siponto: con la rete metallica ricostruita basilicadel XII secolo." In *Corriere della Sera*, March 12.

Danto, Arthur C. 1997. *After the End of Art – Contemporary Art and the Pale of History*. Princeton: Princeton University Press.

De Quincy, Quatremère. 1832. *Dictionnaire Historique d'Architecture*. Paris: Librarie d'Adrien Le Clere.

Dillon, Brian (ed.). 2011. *Documents of Contemporary Art*. Cambridge, MA: The MIT Press.

Douglas, James. 2006. *Building Adaptation*. Chennai: Elsevier.

Drury, Paul and Anna McPherson. 2008. *Conservation Principles Policies and Guidance*. London: English Heritage.

Durand, Jean-Nicolas-Louis (translated by David Britt). 2000. *Précis of the Lectures on Architecture*. Los Angeles: The Getty Research Institute.

"Economic Recovery New York City's program for 1977–81. U.S. Department of Commerce NOAA." 1977. U.S. Government Printing Office. Accessed July 8, 2024. https://www.gpo.gov.

Elefante, Carl. 2007. "The Greenest Building is One That is Already Built." In *Forum Journal*, 21, (4) Summer.

Farrell, Stephen. 2016. "If All Else Fails, 3D Models and Robots Might Rebuild Palmyra." In *The New York Times*, March 28.

Fawcett, Jane (ed.). 1976. *The Future of the Past – Attitudes to conservation 1147-1974*. New York: Watson-Guptill Publications.

Feld, Gabriel. 1999. *Free University Berlin: Candilis, Josic, Woods, Schiedhelm*. London: AA Publications.

Fitch, James Marston. 1990. *Historic Preservation: Curatorial Management of the Built World*. Charlottesville: University of Virginia Press.

Fjeld, Per Olaf. 2009. *Sverre Fehn The Pattern of Thoughts*. New York: The Monacelli Press.

Giebeler, Georg, Rainer Fisch, Harald Krause, Florian Musso, Karl-Heinz Petzinka and Alexander Rudolphi. 2009. *Refurbishment Manual. Maintenance Conversions Extensions*. Basel: Birkhäuser.

Glendinning, Miles. 2013. *The Conservation Movement – A History of Architectural Preservation, Antiquity to Modernity*. London: Routledge.

Grobman, Yasha and E. Neuman(eds.). 2011. *Performalism: Form and Performance in Digital Architecture*. New York: Routledge.

Hardy, Matthew (ed.). 2008. *The Venice Charter Revisited: Modernism, Conservation and Tradition in the 21st Century*. Newcastle upon Tyne: Cambridge Scholars Publishing.

Hearn, M.F. (ed.). 1990. *The Architectural Theory of Viollet-le-Duc – Readings and Commentary*. Cambridge; MA: The MIT Press.

Hegel, G. W. F. (translated by T.M. Knox). 1975. *Hegel's Aesthetics: Lectures on Fine Art*. Oxford: Clarendon Press.

Heidegger, Martin (edited and translated by Julian Young and Kenneth Haynes). 2002. *Off the Beaten Track*. Cambridge, UK: Cambridge University Press.

Huxtable, Ada Louise. 1988. *Kicked A Building Lately?* Berkeley: University of California Press.

Issues in the Conservation of Cultural Heritage. 1996. Los Angeles: The Getty Conservation Institute.

Jacobs, Jane. 1961. *The Death and Life of Great American Cities*. New York: Vintage Books.

Jokilehto, Jukka. 1999. *A History of Architectural Conservation*. Oxford: Butterworth-Heinemann.

Koolhaas, Rem. 2004. "Preservation Is Overtaking Us." In *Future Anterior*, I, Winter.

Koshar, Rudy. 1998. *Germany's Transient Pasts: Preservation and National Memory in the 20th Century*. Chapel Hill: University of North Carolina Press.

Le Corbusier (translated by Anthony Eardley). 1973. *The Athens Charter*. New York: Grossman.

Le Corbusier (translated by Frederick Etchells). 1974. *Towards a New Architecture*. London: Architectural Press.

Lee, Pamela. 2000. *Object to Be Destroyed – The Work of Gordon Matta-Clark*. Cambridge; MA: The MIT Press.

Locke, John. 1690. *An Essay Concerning Human Understanding*. London: Elizabeth Holt, for Thomas Basset.

Longfellow, Henry Wadsworth. 1878. *Longfellow, Kéramos & Other Poems*. Cambridge, MA: Houghton, Osgood & Company.

Loos, Adolf. 1985. "Architektur" (1910 translation). In *The Architecture of Adolf Loos: An Arts Council Exhibition*. London: The Arts Council.

Mack, Gerhard (ed.). 2014. *Herzog & de Meuron, Transforming Park Avenue Armory New York*. Basel: Birkhäuser.

Martín-Hernández, Manuel. 2014. "Time and Authenticity," In *Future Anterior*, 11 (2) Winter.

Miller, Alana. 2011. "From the Records of MoMA PS1: The 40th Anniversary of The Brooklyn Bridge Event." *Collection & Exhibitions, Library and Archives, MOMA PS1*. Accessed December 7, 2015. http://www.moma.org/explore/inside_out/2011/06/27/from-the-records-of-moma-ps1-the-40th-anniversary-of-the-brooklyn-bridge-event.

Morris, William. 1877. "Manifesto of the Society for the Protection of Ancient Buildings." From "The Principles of the Society [for the Protection of Ancient Buildings] As Set Forth Upon Its Foundation." In *Builder 35* (August 25).

Murtagh, William J. 2006. *Telling Time, The History and Theory of Preservation in America*. Hoboken: John Wiley & Sons, 3rd ed.

Nietzsche, Friedrich (edited by Bernard Williams, translated by Josefine Nauckhoff). 2001. *The Gay Science*. Cambridge, UK: Cambridge University Press.

Palladio, Andrea. 1965. *The Four Books on Architecture*. Mineola: Dover Publications, Inc.

Philippot, Paul. 1996. "Historic Preservation: Philosophy, Criteria, Guidelines, I." In *Historical and Philosophical Issues in the Conservation of Cultural Heritage*, edited by Nicholas Price, M. Kirby Talley, Jr., and Alessandra Melucco Vacarro. Los Angeles: The Getty Conservation Institute.

Price, Nicholas, M. Kirby Talley, Jr. and Alessandra Melucco Vacarro, (eds.). 1996. *Historical and Philosophical Issues in the Conservation of Cultural Heritage*. Los Angeles: The Getty Conservation Institute.

"Public Law 560 — August 2, 1954." 1954. U.S. Government Printing Office, Washington, DC.

Racz, Imogen. 2015. "Gordon Matta-Clark, Splitting and the Unmade House." In The IB Tauris Blog, January 26, 2015. Accessed December 7, 2015. https://theibtaurisblog.wordpress.com/2015/01/26/gordon-matta-clark-splitting-and-the-unmade-house/

Rieff, Daniel D. 1971. "Viollet Le Duc and Historic Restoration: The West Portals of Notre Dame." In *Journal of the Society of Architectural Historians* 30, no. 1 (1971): 17–30. Accessed July 8, 2024. https://doi.org/10.2307/988670.

Riegl, Alois. 1996. "The Modern Cult of Monuments: Its Essence and Its Development," in Nicholas Price, M. Kirby Talley, Jr., and Alessandra Melucco Vacarro, eds., *Historical and Philosophical Issues in the Conservation of Cultural Heritage*. Los Angeles: The Getty Conservation Institute.

Riegl, Alois. 2000. "The Main Characteristics of the Late Roman Kunstwollen" (1901). In Christopher S. Brown(ed.). In *The Vienna School Reader, Politics and Art Historical Methods in the 1930s*. New York: Zone Books.

Riegl, Alois (edited and translated by Andrew Hopkins and Arnold Witte). 2010. *The Origins of Baroque Art in Rome*. Los Angeles: Getty Research Institute.

Ruskin, John. 1889. *The Seven Lamps of Architecture*, 6th ed. Kent: George Allen.

Ruskin, John. 1901. *The Works of John Ruskin*. London: George Allen.

Sacristán-Murga, Luis. 2016. "Between Memory and Intervention: An Interview with Nieto Sobejano Arquitectos." In *Int|AR Journal of Adaptive Reuse*, Vol. 6.

Scott, Fred. 2012. *On Altering Architecture*. London: Routledge.

Simpson, James. 2016. "The Anatomy of Theory." Accessed March 5, 2016. www.buildingconservation.com

Slow Furl. The Royal Danish Academy. Accessed July 8, 2024. https://royaldanishacademy.com/en/case/slow-furl

"Sol LeWitt: A Wall Drawing Retrospective." Accessed July 8, 2024. https://massmoca.org/sol-lewitt/

Stubbs, John H. 2009. *Time Honored: A Global View of Architectural Conservation*. Hoboken: Wiley & Sons.

"Summary of Provisions of the National Housing Act of 1949, Committee on Banking and Currency U.S. Senate." 1949. U.S. Government Printing Office, Washington, DC.

Sweet, Victoria Sweet. 2012. *God's Hotel*. New York: Riverhead Books.

"The Artist in Place: The First 10 Years of MoMA PS." MoMA.org. Accessed July 8, 2024. https://www.moma.org/interactives/exhibitions/2012/artistinplace/

"The Athens Charter for the Restoration of Historic Monuments — 1931," ICOMOS International Council on Monuments and Sites. Accessed February 16, 2016. http://www.icomos.org/en/charters-and-texts/179-articles-en-francais/ressources/charters-and-standards/167-the-athens-charter-for-the-restoration-of-historic-monuments

"The Greenest Building: Quantifying the Environmental Value of Building Reuse." 2011. The Preservation Green Lab, National Trust for Historic Preservation.

"The Nara Document on Authenticity." 1994. ICOMOS International Council on Monuments and Sites.

"The Venice Charter." 1964. In International Charter for the Conservation and Restoration of Monuments and Sites. Accessed July 8, 2024. https://www.icomos.org/en/participer/179-articles-en-francais/ressources/charters-and-standards/157-thevenice-charter

Tschumi, Bernard. 1996. *Architecture and Disjunction*. Cambridge, MA: The MIT Press.

Valéry, Paul. 1960. "La conquête de l'ubiquité, Une édition électronique réalisée à partir du texte de Paul Valéry, « La conquête de l'ubiquité » (1928)." In *Oeuvres, tome II, Pièces sur l'art, Nrf*, Gallimard, Bibliothèque de la Pléiade.

Vidler, Anthony. 2000. "The Paradoxes of Vandalism." In Jeremy D. Popkin and R. H. Popkin (eds.). *The Abbé Grégoire and His World*. Dordecht: Springer.

Viollet-le-Duc, Eugène. 1875. *On Restoration*. London: Sampson Low, Marston, Low and Searle.

Vitruvius (translated by Morris Hicky Morgan). 1960. *The Ten Books on Architecture*. New York: Dover Publications, Inc.

Waite, Richard. 2011 "Libeskind Completes Redesign of Dresden Museum of Military History." In *The Architect's Journal*. Accessed July 9, 2024. https://www.architectsjournal.co.uk/archive/libeskind-completes-redesign-of-dresden-museum-of-military-history

Watson, Paul. 2009. "The Key Issues When Choosing Adaptation of an Existing Building over New Build." In *Journal of Building Appraisal* 4, 215–223. Accessed July 9, 2024. https://doi.org/10.1057/jba.2008.39

Weeks, Kay and Anne Grimmer. 1995. *The Secretary of the Interior's Standards for the Treatment of Historic Properties with Guidelines for Preserving, Rehabilitating, Restoring and Reconstructing Historic Building*. Washington DC: US Dept of the Interior.

Zucconi, Guido. 2014. "Gustavo Giovannoni: A Theory and a Practice of Urban Conservation." In *Change Over Time*, 4, (1), Spring.

2015 International Building Code. 2014. Country Club Hills: International Code Council.

About the Author

Liliane Wong is Professor at the Rhode Island School of Design, where, for more than a decade, she was Chair of the Department of Interior Architecture, which focuses on architectural interventions to existing structures. Her interest and teaching in this subject led her to co-found the Int|AR Journal on design interventions and adaptive reuse, which promotes creative and academic explorations of sustainable environments through exemplary works of reuse. She was recognized by Design Intelligence for 2018–2019 and 2019–2020 as one of the top twenty-five most admired design educators in the US.

She is the author of *Adaptive Reuse in Architecture: A Typological Index* and *Adaptive Reuse: Extending the Lives of Buildings*, co-author of *Libraries – A Design Manual* (with Nolan Lushington and Wolfgang Rudorf), co-editor of *Interventions and Adaptive Reuse: A Decade of Responsible Practice* (with Markus Berger), a contributing author to *Designing Interior Architecture* (Sylvia Leydecker, ed.) and *Flexible Composite Materials in Architecture, Construction and Interiors* (Rene Motro, ed.)—all published by Birkhäuser.

Wong has been a long-time volunteer at soup kitchens, and her teaching emphasizes the importance of public engagement in architecture and design. Other teaching and research areas include design as social activism, preservation and sea-level rise, the mathematics of curved space, affordable modular housing, and technical textiles. Recent projects include *Crossing the Pell*, an interactive/experiential exhibition on adapting infrastructure; *Don't You Sit Down*, an installation on segregation and Jim Crow laws; *Projecting Change*, a community exhibition on the future of coastal neighborhoods in the era of sea-level rise; and *Saving Superman*, a collaboration with the Providence Preservation Society on the plight of the city's heritage Art Deco high-rise, the Industrial Trust Building.

Wong received her BA in Mathematics from Vassar College and her MArch from the Harvard University Graduate School of Design. A registered architect in Massachusetts, she has practiced through her own firm, Mahon Wong Associates, as well as with the Boston firms of Perry Dean Rogers and FHCM. Key projects include the American Embassy in Jordan, Montclair Public Library, Hartford Public Library, and the design of the Kore Library Furnishings Line.

Illustration Credits

In cases where illustrations and the rights to reproduce them were available via internet websites, the crediting follows the indications provided by the respective website, accepting a wide range of formats and limiting adaptations for consistency to a reasonable minimum.

Cover Image

Photographer: Liliane Wong

Chapter 00

Fig. 0_Public domain, via Wikimedia Commons

Chapter 01

Fig. 0_United Archives GmbH/Alamy Fig. 1a_Noclip (at English Wikipedia, transferred from en.wikipedia to Wikimedia Commons), Public domain, via Wikimedia Commons Fig. 1b_Photographer: Paul Taylor, Flickr Fig. 2_Toni Castillo Quero (Flickr: [1]) [CC BY-SA 2.0 (via Wikimedia Commons)] Fig. 3_By Benh (Own work) [GFDL (http://www.gnu.org/copyleft/fdl.html), CC-BY-SA-3.0 (http://creativecommons.org/licenses/by-sa/3.0/) or CC BY 2.5 (http://creativecommons.org/licenses/by/2.5)], via Wikimedia Commons Fig. 4_© 2016 Estate of Gordon Matta-Clark/Artists Rights Society (ARS), New York Fig. 5_Ungaroo—Udo Ungar (Own work) [CC BY-SA 3.0 (http://creativecommons.org/licenses/by-sa/3.0)], via Wikimedia Commons Fig. 6a_y Jleon (English Wikipedia) [Public domain], via Wikimedia Commons Fig. 6b_Andrew Ellicott, revised from Pierre (Peter) Charles L'Enfant; Thackara & Vallance sc., Philadelphia 1792—Library of Congress, Public domain, https://commons.wikimedia.org/w/index.php?curid=1519774 Figs. 7, 8_Diagrams by Liliane Wong Fig. 9_http://commons.wikimedia.org/wiki/File:Kette_und_Schu%C3%9F.jpg Figs. 10a, c_Courtesy of Zaha Hadid Architects Fig. 10b_http://www.geographicus.com/mm5/cartographers/sduk.txt [Public domain], via Wikimedia Commons Fig. 11a–b_Photographer: Plusea, (from 2015 E-textile Swatch Exchange), Flickr Fig. 12_Hans A. Rosbach (Own work), CC BY-SA 3.0, https://commons.wikimedia.org/w/index.php?curid=4567317 Figs. 13a–b, 15_Diagrams by Yue Zhang Fig. 14_Ibagli (Own work) [Public domain], via Wikimedia Commons

Chapter 02

Fig. 0_© V. Korostyshevskiy Figs. 1a–i_[Public domain], via Wikimedia Commons Fig. 2_Diagram by Yue Zhang Fig. 3a_Jensensderivative work: Ptyx (talk)—Portico_Octavia_Rome.jpg, Public Domain, https://commons.wikimedia.org/w/index.php?curid=10308745 Fig. 3b_[Public domain], via Wikimedia Commons Fig. 4a_J.B. (Jean Baptiste?) Guibert—postcard of old engraving, scanned by Robert Schediwy, Public domain, https://commons.wikimedia.org/w/index.php?curid=11470312 Fig. 4b_Paul-louis de la société MEROPS-Photo http://merops-photo.com (Own work) Paul-Louis FERRANDEZ http://merops-photo.com, CC BY 3.0, https://commons.wikimedia.org/w/index.php?curid=18456487 Fig. 5a_Unknown—from the Nordisk familjebok (1916), band 23, artikeln "Rom" [1], upload to Swedish wikipedia 23.10.2003 by Den fjättrade ankan, Public domain, https://commons.wikimedia.org/w/index.php?curid=1326053 Fig. 5b_Public domain Fig. 6_Bundeswehr-Fotos Wir.Dienen.Deutschland. (Flickr: Militärhistorisches Museum Dresden) [CC BY 2.0 (http://creativecommons.org/licenses/by/2.0)], via Wikimedia Commons Fig. 7_Diagram by Yue Zhang Fig. 8a_JN_Sylvestre 1847–1926—Historia No121, Public domain, https://commons.wikimedia.org/w/index.php?curid=8890011 Fig. 8b_Photo by Mirrorpix for Alamy Fig. 9a_Fair use, https://en.wikipedia.org/w/index.php?curid=47621633 Fig. 9b_Isabella Lynn Lee (Own work) [CC BY-SA 3.0 (http://creativecommons.org/licenses/by-sa/3.0)], via Wikimedia Commons Fig. 10_Paul Mannix [CC BY 2.0 (http://creativecommons.org/licenses/by/2.0)], via Wikimedia Commons Fig. 11_Achates (Own work) [CC BY-SA 3.0 (http://creativecommons.org/licenses/by-sa/3.0)], via Wikimedia Commons Fig. 12a_Louis Thümling (19th century: http://d-nb.info/gnd/14032366X) nach Hermann Krone (1827–1916)—http://www.schmidt-auktionen.de/12d_artikel_details.php?nr=16&mode=k&knr=177&kuenstler=2631, Public domain, https://commons.wikimedia.org/w/index.php?curid=9103184 Fig. 12b_© Ad Meskens/Wikimedia Commons Fig. 13_Bob Jagendorf from Manalapan, NJ, USA (A Day To Remember Uploaded by Trycatch) [CC BY 2.0 (http://creativecommons.org/licenses/by/2.0)], via Wikimedia Commons Fig. 14a_Photographer: Andy, Flickr Fig. 14b_Arland B. Musser—United States Holocaust Memorial Museum, courtesy of National Archives and Records Administration, College Park, Public domain, https://commons.wikimedia.org/w/index.php?curid=430483 Fig. 14c_Mstyslav Chernov (Own work) [CC BY-SA 4.0 (http://creativecommons.org/licenses/by-sa/4.0)], via Wikimedia Commons

Chapter 03

Fig. 0_Public domain Fig. 1_Andrew Balet (Own work) [CC BY-SA 2.5 (http://creativecommons.org/licenses/by-sa/2.5)], via Wikimedia Commons Fig. 2_Photographer: Reizergerin, Flickr Fig. 3_[Public domain], via Wikimedia Commons Fig. 4a_User:Jensens (Own work) [Public domain], via Wikimedia Commons Fig. 4b_Stian Haklev w:en:user:Houshuang (Own work (own photo)), [Public domain], via Wikimedia Commons Figs. 5a–b_Public domain Fig. 5c_Guillaume Speurt from Vilnius, Lithuania (The Old Town market square of Warsaw) [CC BY-SA 2.0 (http://creativecommons.org/licenses/by-sa/2.0)], via Wikimedia Commons Fig. 6a_Warburg (Own work) [Public domain or CC BY-SA 3.0 (http://creativecommons.org/licenses/by-sa/3.0)], via Wikimedia Commons Fig. 6b_© Raimond Spekking / CC BY-SA 3.0, via Wikimedia Commons Fig. 7_Photographer: Bert Kaufmann, Flickr Fig. 8a_Udey Ismail (Flickr: Hallstatt town, Austria) [CC BY 2.0 (http://creativecommons.org/licenses/by/2.0)], via Wikimedia Commons Fig. 8b_Hanno Böck (Own work) [CC BY-SA 4.0 (http://creativecommons.org/licenses/by-sa/4.0)], via Wikimedia Commons Fig. 9_Diagram by Minhee Kim Fig. 10_[Public domain], via Wikimedia Commons Fig. 11a_August Mau [Public domain], via Wikimedia Commons Fig. 11b_[Public domain], via Wikimedia Commons Fig. 11c_Courtesy of rome101.com. Rome101 is a registered DBA of LiveSky, Inc. Fig. 12_ Coyau [Public domain], via Wikimedia Commons Fig. 13_ [Public domain], via Wikimedia Commons

Chapter 04

Fig. 0_Diagram by Liliane Wong Fig. 1a_Gustave Le Gray (Gallica) [Public domain], via Wikimedia Commons Fig. 1b_Christophe EYQUEM from Vientiane (Laos) (Carcassonne) [CC BY 3.0 (http://creativecommons.org/licenses/by/3.0)], via Wikimedia Commons Fig. 2_Diagram by Yue Zhang

Chapter 05

Fig. 0_[Public domain], https://commons.wikimedia.org/w/index.php?curid=1020146 Figs. 1–4, 8–9_Diagrams by Liliane Wong Fig. 5_Nyotarou (Own work), CC BY-SA 4.0, https://commons.wikimedia.org/w/index.php?curid=39352102 Fig. 6_Jondu11 (Jondu11) [GFDL (http://www.gnu.org/copyleft/fdl.html) or CC BY-SA 4.0-3.0-2.5-2.0-1.0_(http://creativecommons.org/licenses/by-sa/4.0-3.0-2.5-2.0-1.0)], via Wikimedia Commons Fig. 7_Bernard Gagnon (Own work), CC BY-SA 3.0, https://commons.wikimedia.org/w/index.php?curid=20916502

Chapter 06

Fig. 0_Department of Defense. Department of the Army. Office of the Chief Signal Officer (http://research.archives.gov/description/5757187) [Public domain], via Wikimedia Commons Fig. 1_Diagram by Yue Zhang Fig. 2_U.S. Department of Defense. Department of the Army. Office of the Chief Signal Officer. [2]—http://www.archives.gov/research/arc/ ARC Identifier: 531287; U.S. Defense Visual Information Center photo HD-SN-99-02996 [1], Public domain, https://commons.wikimedia.org/w/index.php?curid=5811 Fig. 3, 4a_unknown author, Public domain Fig. 4b_M. Swierczynski—Stanisław Jankowski, Adolf Ciborowski, Warszawa 1945 i dziś (Wydawnictwo Interpress, Warszawa, 1971, p. 66) – Wiesław Głębocki; Karol Mórawski (1985), "Kultura Walcząca 1939–1945" (Warsaw: Wydawnictwo Interpress, p. 64) – Antoni Przygoński (1980), "Powstanie Warszawskie w sierpniu 1944 r."; Tom 1 (Warsaw: Polskie Wydawnictwo Naukowe), Public domain, https://commons.wikimedia.org/w/index.php?curid=2255273 Fig. 4c_Adrian Grycuk (Own work) [CC BY-SA 3.0 pl (http://creativecommons.org/licenses/by-sa/3.0/pl/deed.en)], via Wikimedia Commons Fig. 5_Mouagip (Based on the previous version of Madden), [Public domain], via Wikimedia Commons Figs. 6, 8, 9_Diagrams by Yue Zhang Fig. 7_ Diagram by Liliane Wong

Chapter 07

Fig. 0_Photographer: Rushen, Flickr Fig. 1a_Courtesy rome101.com. Rome101 is a registered DBA of LiveSky, Inc. Fig. 1b_Artwork from University of Toronto Wenceslaus Hollar Digital Collection, [Public domain], via Wikimedia Commons Fig. 2_MasterOfHisOwnDomain—Eget arbejde, CC BY-SA 3.0, https://commons.wikimedia.org/w/index.php?curid=4576074 Fig. 3_Diagrams by Clara Hernandez Lopez Fig. 4_Photographer: Jorge Franganillo, Flickr Fig. 5a–b_Courtesy of Paul Kaloustian Figs. 6a–c_Photographer: Matadero Madrid, Flickr Figs. 6d–f_Courtesy of photographer, Javier1949, Flickr Fig. 7a_ M*tth.K (Own work) [CC BY-SA 3.0 (http://creativecommons.org/licenses/by-sa/3.0)], via Wikimedia Commons Figs. 7b–c_Courtesy of Nieto Sobejano Arquitectos Fig. 8_User:Jensens (Own work), [Public domain], via Wikimedia Commons Fig. 9_Por Tamorlan—Obra do próprio, CC BY-SA 3.0, https://commons.wikimedia.org/w/index.php?curid=19338871 Fig. 10a_Liliane Wong Fig. 10b_Jean-Pierre Dalbéra, [Creative Commons Attribution 2.0 Generic], via Wikimedia Commons Fig. 11_Photographer: David van der Mark, Flickr Figs. 12a–c_Courtesy of Studio Marco Piva Fig. 13_Photographer: Liliane Wong Fig. 14a_Sailko (Own work) [CC BY-SA 3.0 (http://creativecommons.org/licenses/by-sa/3.0)], via Wikimedia Common Fig. 14b_Victor Andrade—Own work, CC BY-SA 4.0, https://commons.

wikimedia.org/w/index.php?curid=45628284 Fig. 15_User:Olahus1 [Creative Commons Attribution-Share Alike 2.5 Generic, 2.0 Generic and 1.0 Generic license], via Wikimedia Commons Fig. 16_Raimond Spekking, via Wikimedia Commons Fig. 17_Photographer: Trevor.patt, Flickr Fig. 18_Von Tuxyso/ Wikimedia Commons, CC BY-SA 3.0, https://commons.wikimedia.org/w/index.php?curid=43795147 Fig. 19a–b_Courtesy of Peter Kulka Architektur; photographer: J. Schöner

Chapter 08

Fig. 0, 1_Public domain Fig. 2_Unknown (http://www.nyc-architecture.com/SOH/SOH022.htm), Public domain, https://commons.wikimedia.org/w/index.php?curid=12101897 Fig. 3a_Jim.henderson (at English Wikipedia, transferred from en.wikipedia to Commons by Gerardus using CommonsHelper), [Public domain], https://commons.wikimedia.org/w/index.php?curid=15915713 Fig. 3b_準建築人手札網站 Forgemind ArchiMedia, Flickr Fig. 4_© Rachel Whiteread; Courtesy of the artist, Luhring Augustine, New York, Lorcan O'Neill, Rome, and Gagosian Gallery Figs. 5a–b_Photographer: Liliane Wong Fig. 6_© 2016 Estate of Gordon Matta-Clark/Artists Rights Society (ARS), New York Fig. 7_Adrian Michael [Creative Commons Attribution-ShareAlike License 3.0 Unported], via Wikimedia Commons Fig. 8_Courtesy of Koonshing Wong; photographer: Mariko Reed Fig. 9_© Simon Menges, Courtesy of David Chipperfield Architects Fig. 10_Boobax—Own work, CC BY-SA 3.0, https://commons.wikimedia.org/w/index.php?curid=27846951 Fig. 11a_Terrycohn (Own work) [CC BY-SA 4.0 (http://creativecommons.org/licenses/by-sa/4.0)], via Wikimedia Commons Fig. 11b_Jack Boucher [Public domain], via Wikimedia Commons Figs. 12a–d_Section drawing by Arturo Cebollero, María Sánchez, y Pilár Giménez Images: Courtesy of Sergio Sebastián Franco

Chapter 09

Fig. 0_[Public domain], via Wikimedia Commons Figs. 1a–b_Photographer: Liliane Wong Fig. 2a_[Public Domain], via Wikimedia Commons Fig. 2b_Photographer: Diueine Monteiro, Flickr Fig. 3a_Library of Congress (http://www.loc.gov/pictures/search/?q=Drawing:%20ma1642&fi=number&op=PHRASE&va =exact&co%20=hh&st=gallery&sg%20=%20true) Fig. 3b_WBUR Boston NPR's News Station, Flickr Fig. 3c_By Unknown (survey information not yet digitized).—Historic American Buildings Survey (Library of Congress), Survey number HABS MA-1259, Call Number HABS MASS,13-BOST,143-1. Public domain, https://commons.wikimedia.org/w/index.php?curid=1949963 Fig. 3d_Photographer: Wally Gobetz, Flickr Fig. 3e_WBUR Boston NPR News Radio Station, Flickr Fig. 4a_Floor plan courtesy of Barbara Stehle; Diagram by Yue Zhang Fig. 4b_Nefelimhg [Creative Commons Attribution-ShareAlike License 3.0 Unported], via Wikimedia Commons Fig. 5a_By Michel Zacharz AKA Grippenn[1]—Own work, CC BY-SA 2.5, https://commons.wikimedia.org/w/index.php?curid=1083901 Fig. 5b_y Marcin Białek—Own work, CC BY-SA 3.0, https://commons.wikimedia.org/w/index.php?curid=21470481 Fig. 6_T/4 Sidney Blau, 163rd Signal Photo Company, Army Signal Corps—U.S. Holocaust Museum photograph #37255 (also here)Credit: SC 206310, Credit NARA, College ParkSubject Classification: MAJOR CONCENTRATION CAMPS 1940–45—Dachau—LIBERATION—Views—GeneralKeywords: DACHAU, CONCENTRATION CAMPS, BARRACKS, VIEWS, SURVIVORS, Public Domain, https://commons.wikimedia.org/w/index.php?curid=542794 Fig. 7a_Photographer: Groume, Flickr Fig 7b_Public domain Fig. 8a_Public domain Fig. 8b_Kohls, Ulrich [Creative Commons Attribution-Share Alike 3.0 Germany], via Wikimedia Commons Fig. 9_Saschaporsche (Own work), CC BY-SA 3.0, https://commons.wikimedia.org/w/index.php?curid=17191406

Chapter 10

Fig. 0, 1_Photographer: Liliane Wong Fig. 2_Photographer: Design Milk, Flickr Fig. 3_Unité d'habitation, Marseille, 1945, Schéma d'organisation des services communs, Plans FLC 27145, © Fondation Le Corbusier/ADAGP, Paris/Artists Rights Society (ARS), New York 2016 2016 Fig. 4_© OMA Fig. 5_Kolossos [Creative Commons Attribution-ShareAlike License 3.0], via Wikimedia Commons Fig. 6_Specialpaul [Creative Commons Attribution-ShareAlike License 4.0 International], via Wikimedia Commons Fig. 7_Diagram by Liliane Wong Fig. 8_Photographer: Clara Halston Fig. 9a_Courtesy KÖNIG GALERIE; photographer: By Semra Sevin Fig. 9b_Courtesy Tatiana Trouvé and KÖNIG GALERIE; photographer: Roman März Fig. 9c_Nathan Hylden and KÖNIG GALERIE; photographer: Roman März Fig. 10a_Massimiliano Calamelli, Flickr Fig. 10b_Carole Raddato from Frankfurt, Germany (The Engine Room, Centrale Montemartini, Rome) [CC BY-SA 2.0 (http://creativecommons.org/licenses/by-sa/2.0)], via Wikimedia Commons Fig. 11a_August Mau [Public Domain], via Wikimedia Commons Fig. 11b_Courtesy of rome101.com. Rome101 is a registered DBA of LiveSky, Inc. Fig. 12a_J. B. (Jean Baptiste?) Guibert—postcard of old engraving, scanned by Robert Schediwy, Public domain, https://commons.wikimedia.org/w/index.php?curid=11470312 Fig. 12b_Oakenchips (Own work) [CC BY-SA 4.0 (http://creativecommons.org/licenses/by-sa/4.0)], via Wikimedia Commons Fig. 13a_Von Times—Eigenes Werk, CC BY-SA 3.0, https://commons.wikimedia.org/w/index.php?curid=10286172 Fig. 13b_Public domain

Chapter 11

Fig. 0_Photographer: Wolfgang Rudorf Fig. 1_Photographer: Achim Hatzius © Alape Courtesy of Heine Lenz Zizka Fig. 2_Fletcherspears (Own work) [CC BY-SA 3.0 (http://creativecommons.org/licenses/by-sa/3.0) or GFDL (http://www.gnu.org/copyleft/fdl.html)], via Wikimedia Commons Fig. 3_Photographer: urbz, Flickr Fig. 4_Photographer: Kellan, Flickr Figs. 5a–b_Courtesy of Lee Boroson Fig. 6_Architect: Adam Kalkin/Industrial Zombie, architect; photographer: Peter Aaron/Otto Fig. 7_Courtesy of Caterina Tiazzoldi; photo by Luca Campigotto Figs. 8a–b_Courtesy of i29 interior architects Fig. 8c_Rijksdienst voor het Cultureel Erfgoed [CC BY-SA 3.0 nl (http://creativecommons.org/licenses/by-sa/3.0/nl/deed.en)], via Wikimedia Commons Fig. 9_Inga Knoelke—Inga Knoelke, CC BY 3.0, via Wikimedia Commons Fig. 10_Photographer: Heather Anne Campbell, Flickr Figs. 11a–b_Photographer: Clara Hernandez Lopez Fig. 12a_Joe Ravi, CC BY-SA 3.0, https://commons.wikimedia.org/w/index.php?curid=15260356 Fig. 12b_Photographer: Tom Mascardo 1, Flickr Figs. 13a–d_Courtesy of César Rueda Arquitecto; photography: José Hevia Figs. 14a–b_Courtesy of Claudio Greco Fig. 15a_Terrycohn (Own work) [CC BY-SA 4.0 (http://creativecommons.org/licenses/by-sa/4.0)], via Wikimedia Commons Fig. 15b_Jack Boucher, [Public domain], via Wikimedia Commons

Chapter 12

Fig. 0_Courtesy of Sui Park Fig. 1_Photographer: Cea [Attribution 2.0 Generic (CC BY 2.0)], via Flickr Fig. 2_Photographer: John Lord [Attribution 2.0 Generic (CC BY 2.0)], via Flickr Fig. 3_Courtesy of MassMOCA Fig. 4_Photographer: Mirko Tobias Schäfer, Flickr Fig. 5a_Maurizio OM Ongaro (Own work) [CC BY-SA 4.0 (http://creativecommons.org/licenses/by-sa/4.0)], via Wikimedia Commons Fig. 5b_By Pava (Milano)—Own work, CC BY-SA 3.0 it, https://commons.wikimedia.org/w/index.php?curid=33273341 Fig. 6a_Photographer: Jérôme Falcou, Flickr Fig. 6b_Photographer: Maurice, Flickr Fig. 7a_Wikiwal [Creative Commons Attribution-Share Alike 3.0 Unported license], via Wikimedia Commons Fig. 7b_Pixabay Fig. 7c_Guilhem Vellut [Attribution 2.0 Generic (CC BY 2.0)], via Flickr Fig. 8_NAParish [Attribution-ShareAlike 2.0 Generic (CC BY-SA 2.00], via Flickr Fig.9a_Photographer: ..colb.., Flickr Fig. 9b_ By Wiiii—Own work, CC BY-SA 3.0, https://commons.wikimedia.org/w/index.php?curid=5079090 Fig. 9c_Photographer: Forgemind Archimedia, Flickr Fig. 10_Photographer: Nathan Williams, Flickr Fig. 11_Photographer: Jason Chan, Flickr Figs. 12a–d_Courtesy of UN Studio, photograph by Christian Richters Fig. 13_Photographer: Dana Gordon, Flickr Fig. 14_Photographer: Digitalshorts Mark Bryant, Flickr

Chapter 13

Figs. 0, 1_Diagrams by Liliane Wong Fig. 2a_Photographer: Tony Bowden, Flickr Fig. 2b_E. de Rolland & D. Clouzet—Bibliothèque nationale de France, Public domain, https://commons.wikimedia.org/w/index.php?curid=23819604 Fig. 2c_Photographer: Anthony V, Flickr Fig. 3a_Specialpaul [Creative Commons Attribution-ShareAlike License 4.0 International], via Wikimedia Commons Fig. 3b_K.l.a.u.s. (at German Wikipedia, transferred from de.wikipedia to Wikimedia Commons, [CC BY-SA 2.0 de (http://creativecommons.org/licenses/by-sa/2.0/de/deed.en)], via Wikimedia Commons Fig. 4a_Hugh Manatee (from a c. 1905 postcard), [Public domain], via Wikimedia Commons Fig. 4b_[Public domain] Fig. 4c_Detroit Publishing Company (http://digitalgallery.nypl.org/nypldigital/id?74363), Public domain, https://commons.wikimedia.org/w/index.php?curid=10711060 Fig. 5a_Photographer: bobistraveling, Flickr Fig. 5b_Photographer: Richard Moross, Flickr Figs. 6a_Courtesy of © David Chipperfield Architects; photograph © Simon Menges Fig. 6b_Courtesy of © David Chipperfield Architects Fig. 7_Pi.1415926535 (Own work) [CC BY-SA 3.0 (http://creativecommons.org/licenses/by-sa/3.0) or GFDL (http://www.gnu.org/copyleft/fdl.html)], via Wikimedia Commons Fig. 8_Courtesy of Coop Himmelb(l)au; photographer © Duccio Malagamba Fig. 9_David van der Mark [Attribution-ShareAlike 2.0 Generic (CC BY-SA 2.0)], via Flickr Figs. 10a_Kamel15 (Own work) [GPL (http://www.gnu.org/licenses/gpl.html) or CC BY-SA 3.0 (http://creativecommons.org/licenses/by-sa/3.0)], via Wikimedia Commons Figs. 10b, d_Photograph by Carole Aizenstark from her article "Transcending Time: La Fabrique," *The Int|AR Journal*, Vol. 4 Fig. 10c_Diagram by Yue Zhang Fig. 11a_Photographer: Clara Halston Fig. 11b_Von Janericloebe (Own work), Public domain, https://commons.wikimedia.org/w/index.php?curid=8479427 Fig. 11c_Von Lenie Beutler (Own work), CC BY-SA 3.0, https://commons.wikimedia.org/w/index.php?curid=6126001 Fig. 11d_Public domain Fig. 11e_Public domain, https://commons.wikimedia.org/w/index.php?curid=312215 Figs. 11f–g_Diagrams by Yue Zhang Fig. 12a_Photographer: Rosa G, Flickr Figs. 12b–c, 13a_Photographer: Javier1949, Flickr Fig. 13b, c_Diagram by Liliane Wong; photographer: Liliane Wong Fig. 14_Courtesy of Roberto Collová Fig. 15a_Paolo Monti—Available in the BEIC digital library and uploaded in partnership with BEIC Foundation.The image comes from the Fondo Paolo Monti, owned by BEIC and located in the Civico Archivio Fotografico of Milan. CC BY-SA 4.0, https://commons.wikimedia.org/w/index.php?curid=48053746 Fig. 15b_Di I, Sailko, CC BY 2.5, https://commons.wikimedia.org/w/index.php?curid=3587438 Fig. 15c_CC BY 2.5, https://commons.wikimedia.org/w/index.php?curid=885777 Figs. 16a–c_ Courtesy of Markus Scherer Architekt; photographer:

Alessandra Chemollo Figs. 16d–f_Photographer: Klaus Civegna, Italy, Flickr Fig. 17a_Anonymous [Public domain], via Wikimedia Commons Fig. 17b_Pixabay Fig. 18a_HenkvD (Own work) [CC BY-SA 3.0 (http://creativecommons.org/licenses/by-sa/3.0)], via Wikimedia Commons Fig. 18b_Frank Van Laanen (Bunker 599) [CC BY 2.0 (http://creativecommons.org/licenses/by/2.0)], via Wikimedia Commons Fig. 18c_Diagram by Yue Zhang Fig. 19a_By Alexander Lütjen (originally posted to Flickr as Caixa Forum) [CC BY 2.0 (http://creativecommons.org/licenses/by/2.0)], via Wikimedia Commons Fig. 19b_Marco Pagni from Firenze, Italia (19) [CC BY 2.0 (http://creativecommons.org/licenses/by/2.0)], via Wikimedia Commons Fig. 20a_Photographer: Liliane Wong Fig. 20b–c_Courtesy of Roberto Collová Fig. 21_ Courtesy of © Archive Olgiati Fig. 22a–b_Courtesy of Koonshing Wong, photographer: Mariko Reed Fig.23a_Andreas Praefcke (Own work (own photograph)) [GFDL (http://www.gnu.org/copyleft/fdl.html) or CC BY 3.0 (http://creativecommons.org/licenses/by/3.0)], via Wikimedia Commons Fig. 23b_Photographer: Adam Smith, Flickr Fig. 24_ Courtesy of Allen Memorial Art Museum, photo by Ralph Lieberman Fig. 25_Photographer: Liliane Wong Figs. 26a,c_Courtesy of Adam Kalkins, architect; photo by Peter Aaron/Esto Fig. 22b_Courtesy of Adam Kalkins, architect Figs. 27a–c_Diagrams by Yue Zhang

Chapter 14

Fig. 0_Miguel Hermoso Cuesta (Own work) [CC BY-SA 4.0 (http://creativecommons.org/licenses/by-sa/4.0)], via Wikimedia Commons Fig. 1a_[Public domain], via Wikimedia Fig. 1b_Charles Herbert Moore, [Public domain], via Wikimedia Commons Fig. 2a_OyundariZorigtbaatar (Own work) [CC BY-SA 4.0 (http://creativecommons.org/licenses/by-sa/4.0)], via Wikimedia Commons Fig. 2b_Passivhaus Institut (copied to Commons from http://en.wikipedia.org, original source Passivhaus Institut, Germany – http://www.passiv.de, CC BY-SA 3.0, https://commons.wikimedia.org/w/index.php?curid=1256683 Fig. 3a_chensiyuan [Creative Commons Attribution-Share Alike 4.0 International, 3.0 Unported, 2.5 Generic, 2.0 Generic and 1.0 Generic license], via Wikimedia Commons Fig. 3b_Hanno Böck (Own work) [CC BY-SA 4.0 (http://creativecommons.org/licenses/by-sa/4.0)], via Wikimedia Commons Fig. 4a_ Charles Marville, [Public domain], via Wikimedia Commons Fig. 4b–c_Courtesy of © Édouard François Fig. 5_Photographer: 準建築人手札網站 Forgemind ArchiMedia, Flickr Fig. 6a_Gouwenaar (Own work), [Public domain], via Wikimedia Commons Fig. 6b_Photographer: Arjen Dijk, Flickr Fig. 7a_[Public Domain], via Wikimedia Commons Fig. 7b_RadioFan at English Wikipedia, CC BY 3.0, https://commons.wikimedia.org/w/index.php?curid=10561778 Fig. 8a_Zureks—Own work, CC BY-SA 3.0, https://commons.wikimedia.org/w/index.php?curid=4183500 Fig. 8b_[Public Domain], via Wikimedia Commons Fig. 9a_ By Ken Lund from Las Vegas, Nevada, USA—London Bridge, Lake Havasu City, Arizona, Uploaded by LongLiveRock, CC BY-SA 2.0, https://commons.wikimedia.org/w/index.php?curid=9696374 Ken Lund [Creative Commons Attribution-Share Alike 2.0 Generic license], via Wikimedia Commons Fig. 9b_Cornell University Library—Flickr: London Bridge from the A. D. White Architectural Photographs collection, Cornell University Library, Accession Number: 15/5/3090.01026., Public domain, https://commons.wikimedia.org/w/index.php?curid=15532300 Fig. 10_Fletcher6 (Own work), CC BY 3.0, https://commons.wikimedia.org/w/index.php?curid=32347419 Fig. 11_Di Manfredonia Apulia Caput (Own work), CC BY-SA 4.0, https://commons.wikimedia.org/w/index.php?curid=47477392 Fig. 12a_Bernard Gagnon [Creative Commons Attribution-Share Alike 3.0 Unported, 2.5 Generic, 2.0 Generic and 1.0 Generic license], via Wikimedia Commons Fig. 12b_Photographer: Juan Llanos, Flickr Fig. 13_Diagram by Liliane Wong

Chapter 15

Fig. 0_Adobe Fig. 1_Jeroen Bennink [Attribution 2.0 Generic (CC BY 2.0)]. via Flickr Fig. 2_Metro Centric [Creative Commons Attribution 2.0 Generic license], via Wikimedia Commons Fig. 3_David Kasparek [Attribution 2.0 Generic (CC BY 2.0)], via Flickr Fig. 4_Photographer: Matadero Madrid, Flickr Fig. 5_Georges Jansoone, [Public Domain], via Wikimedia Commons Fig. 6_Charles Le Brun [Public domain], via Wikimedia Commons Fig. 7_Paolo Monti [CC BY-SA 4.0 (http://creativecommons.org/licenses/by-sa/4.0)], via Wikimedia Commons Fig. 8_Photographer: Turboff, Flickr Fig. 9_Photographer: Liliane Wong